HANDBOOK OF INTERNATIONAL
DISASTER PSYCHOLOGY

**Recent Titles in
Contemporary Psychology**

HANDBOOK OF INTERNATIONAL DISASTER PSYCHOLOGY

Volume 2
Practices and Programs

Edited by Gilbert Reyes and Gerard A. Jacobs

Preface by Charles D. Spielberger

Foreword by Benedetto Saraceno

Praeger Perspectives

Contemporary Psychology
Chris E. Stout, Series Editor

Westport, Connecticut
London

Library of Congress Cataloging-in-Publication Data

Handbook of international disaster psychology / edited by Gilbert Reyes and Gerard A. Jacobs ; preface by Charles D. Spielberger ; foreword by Benedetto Saraceno.
      p. cm. — (Contemporary psychology, ISSN 1546–668X)
  Includes bibliographical references and index.
  ISBN 0-275-98315-3 ((set) : alk. paper) — ISBN 0-275-98316-1 ((vol. I) : alk. paper) — ISBN 0-275-98317-X ((vol. II) : alk. paper) — ISBN 0-275-98318-8 ((vol. III) : alk. paper) — ISBN 0-275-98319-6 ((vol. IV) : alk. paper) 1. Disaster victims—Mental health. 2. Disaster victims—Mental health services. 3. Disasters—Psychological aspects. 4. Disaster relief—Psychological aspects. 5. Humanitarian assistance—Psychological aspects. 6. Community psychology. I. Reyes, Gilbert. II. Jacobs, Gerard A. III. Contemporary psychology (Praeger Publishers)
  RC451.4.D57H36   2006
  362.2'2—dc22   2005018786

British Library Cataloguing in Publication Data is available.

Library of Congress Catalog Card Number: 2005018786
ISBN: 0-275-98315-3 (set)
     0-275-98316-1 (vol. 1)
     0-275-98317-X (vol. 2)
     0-275-98318-8 (vol. 3)
     0-275-98319-6 (vol. 4)

ISSN: 1546–668X

First published in 2006

Praeger Publishers, 88 Post Road West, Westport, CT 06881
An imprint of the Greenwood Publishing Group, Inc.
www.praeger.com

Printed in the United States of America

The paper used in this book complies with the Permanent Paper Standard issued by the National Information Standards Organization (Z39.48–1984).

10 9 8 7 6 5 4 3 2 1

DEDICATION

The *Handbook of International Disaster Psychology* would not have been possible without the compassion and commitment of the international humanitarian community. In a world where millions are killed or harmed each year, either by natural hazards or because of the intentional and accidental actions of humankind, legions of caring people rise to these occasions, determined to relieve the suffering and protect the welfare of people who are in the most dire of circumstances.

The recent history of humanitarian operations has seen a surge of violence directed against these most charitable and nonpartisan individuals who have sacrificed the safety of their homes and families, and who have risked their lives to comfort distant neighbors and to promote peace in the face of force.

Those of us living in zones of relative safety, passing our days and nights in homes and workplaces equipped with modern conveniences, and having plentiful access to clean water, should feel humbled by the courage, dedication, and resilience of those who journey unarmed to enact the values and embody the virtues of our better nature.

In light of these things, it is a small thing indeed to dedicate this book to the international humanitarian personnel who are its inspiration.

Gilbert Reyes

CONTENTS

viii　　　　　　　　　Contents

SET FOREWORD

As I write this, the media are filled with video footage and written accounts of survivors and relief workers in the aftermath of "The Tsunami." For many this is a word newly added to their vocabulary, along with words like "al Qaeda" or "anthrax" that were added a few years ago—formerly foreign and unknown, now sadly popular and common in use, as is "tsunami." But disasters—whether man-made or nature-born—share the common thread of victims in need. Historically the psychological and emotional impacts of disasters, regardless of genesis, on those impacted were largely left unconsidered. Thankfully, this has changed, and these books demonstrate another critical step in this evolving process and area of endeavor—a global consideration.

Too often, once psychological aspects of a phenomenon were considered, they were done so through a narrow lens of exclusively Western or Northern perspectives. Such work, while of definite merit, rigor, and additive benefit to knowledge, was limited in its generalizability. I very much enjoyed the turn of phrase that a reporter for the *Wall Street Journal* used in citing coeditor Gerard Jacobs: "Care for traumatic stress," he warns, "can't be delivered by Western experts parachuting into affected cultures without an appreciation of the cultures infused with strong Islamic, Hindu, and Buddhist beliefs." So true in so many additional ways, and yet so often unwittingly ignored—but thankfully changing.

At this point in time there is a growing appreciation, understanding, and grateful application of the adage that one size does not always fit all. Reyes and Jacobs have woven together a group of authors whose perspectives and work clearly demonstrate the differential aspects of dealing with the trauma of disasters from a global, diverse set of perspectives. Such is a major step forward, and I congratulate them.

For some reason still a mystery to me, it is very easy for most observers to consider post-disaster aid and relief efforts to exclusively include food, shelter, and medical attention. But what cameras cannot capture as well as food stations, vaccination lines, and pitched tent encampments are the psychological wounds that without intervention (when called for) can become scars at best, or risk the infection of apathy or stigma, and result in the deadly consequences of suicide, substance abuse, and other manifest ills. Perhaps this inability for many to "see" fosters a concomitant inability to understand. People can see grain being trucked in and food stations preparing and distributing it, but they cannot see those who cannot eat it for lack of will.

Still More to Do

Much of my work involves medication distribution and medical interventions in areas of need. And again, and thankfully, while there is still a massive amount to be done globally in the battle for treating HIV/AIDS and getting retrovirals distributed, it is equally important to distribute culturally based and relevant psychosocial support for those who need such care. Both are necessary to save their lives. Both.

It is said that there are often opportunities in crises. Perhaps we may see some as a result of the current worldwide focus on the region impacted by the tsunami. Many had never heard of or cared about Aceh prior to the disaster, but there had already been a 15-year-long "disaster" when the water hit that the world had ignored—an often brutal Indonesian military dominion that has resulted in deaths of over 10,000 in Aceh alone, resulting from guerrilla skirmishes with separatist rebels. Along with this loss of lives are comorbid human-rights abuse allegations of torture and rape at the hands of the troops. Now with Kofi Annan's pronouncement that "the UN is the lead in the coordination of the humanitarian effort," there is renewed hope that a side effect will have a kindling influence for the end of such political violence. Likewise, in Sri Lanka then U.S. Secretary of State Powell visited vis-à-vis relief efforts, and it is hoped that the tsunami will also be a catalyst for restarting the stalled peace talks between the government and the ethnic-based insurgency known as the Liberation Tigers of Tamil Eelam (ETTE), or Tamil Tigers.

Psychologically trained researchers and clinicians obviously have much to offer, as evidenced in this set of books. It is a positive evolution that such psychological professionals are now considered along with other colleagues when the proverbial yellow tape is strung in the aftermath of a catastrophe. It is also important to have like involvements in preparation—be it in conflict resolution, resilience training, or other related aspects.

Irony?

Perhaps it is the psychology of indifference or just irony, but last year the United Nations proclaimed that the world's "worst humanitarian disaster" was . . .? The tsunami? No, in fact they were referring to the mass killings in the Darfur region of Sudan by militias. This appears on few television screens or newspaper front pages, and thus is not on many people's minds or touching many people's hearts. Not that there is some morbid competition for compassion, response, and intervention between tsunami victims and the Sudanese, but it certainly is easier to offer relief to an area after a natural catastrophe than it is to intervene in an armed combat situation. The ghosts of Rwanda come to mind, however, and many mental health professionals are focusing efforts there a decade after the genocide, and it makes me wonder what the psychological aftermath will be in Sudan.

Most of the world has empathetically responded to those impacted by the tsunami—they have contributed, volunteered, prayed, and shed tears. And this is how it should be. But such is not so for Darfur today or Kigali a decade ago. Perhaps psychology and mental health professionals should add to their already overburdened to-do lists to work on how to move the world away from such indifference. I remain hopeful based on the work of those herein.

Chris E. Stout
Series Editor

FOREWORD

Every day millions of people in the world are affected by disasters. For many reasons, people in resource-poor countries tend to be hit especially hard by disasters. Data from Red Cross and Red Crescent societies suggest that resource-poor countries tend to be confronted with more conflict and more natural disasters compared to countries that are rich. Resource-poor countries tend to have weaker physical infrastructures that are less likely to withstand extreme conditions, such as earthquakes or cyclones. Also, resource-poor countries tend to have fewer financial resources to prepare for and respond to disaster. Most resource-poor countries often invest relative few resources in their health systems. Most resource -poor areas in the world hardly invest in mental health services and do not have well-functioning community-based mental health systems through which a post-disaster mental health response may be organized.

Disaster psychology is a complex field. Disaster psychology deals with psychological trauma (i.e., an extreme stressor that is likely to elicit a strong acute anxiety and/or dissociation reaction in most people) as a risk factor for mood and anxiety disorders and for nonpathological physical and emotional distress. Psychological trauma is an area that is generating rich research in the areas of anthropology and sociology, child protection and social work, epidemiology and health economics, history and philosophy, neuroscience and pharmacology, clinical and social psychology, psychiatry and psychotherapy, public health and health services research, political science and social policy, and alcohol and other substance abuse management. Thus, disaster psychology practitioners need to be able to think beyond their discipline. Disaster psychology deals not only with psychological trauma but also with enormous losses, which often tend to be forgotten. Affected persons may have lost family members, community support structures, employment and valued material possessions during the disaster. Like trauma, loss is a well-known risk factor for mood and anxiety disorders, for nonpathological distress as well as social problems. Thus, a disaster psychology practitioner needs to be not only an expert on psychological trauma but also an expert on loss and community change. Moreover, the practitioner needs to know how to work in and with communities in a culturally appropriate way. Also, the practitioner needs to know how to work in a collaborative and coordinated manner with others, because uncoordinated aid responses are not in the best interest of disaster survivors.

Concern for people's mental health after disasters is a relatively recent phenomenon. Disaster psychology is a young field; practitioners and researchers alike need to learn from one another. We all need to learn from one another on how to achieve meaningful objectives in a culturally appropriate and sustainable manner in order to reduce avoidable mental and social suffering without causing harm. This handbook provides a rich collection of writings by many of the world's experts on disasters. Reading these chapters will prepare both novice and experienced practitioners for a better response. This is an important book.

Benedetto Saraceno
Director
Department of Mental Health and Substance Abuse
World Health Organization

PREFACE

Catastrophic events causing great damage and destruction have been a part of human life since the beginning of world history. The earth-shaking, cataclysmic eruption of Mount Vesuvius in 79 AD, which wreaked terrible destruction and loss of life, and completely destroyed the Roman city of Pompeii, continues to be reflected in recent excavations. The devastation caused last year by four hurricanes in Florida during a period of less than six weeks and the great seawave produced by the tsunami in the Indian Ocean and Southeast Asia have received major recent attention. Hundreds of people in Florida are not yet back in their homes nearly a year after the fourth hurricane; victims who lost their lives in the tsunami disaster are still being identified and survivors are still searching for them months later.

Not so visible or readily recognized are the psychological effects of disasters for survivors, effects that can linger large and long in the minds of even those with no apparent physical injuries. Effects from the horrific and huge loss of life. Loss of home. Loss of identity. Loss of nearly all that was familiar. Sometimes, too, loss of dignity, faith, or even the will to live.

The development of theory, research, and professional practice by psychologists and other mental health specialists evaluating and helping the victims of such catastrophic events is relatively new, and much needed. This four-volume *Handbook of International Disaster Psychology* provides a solid foundation to facilitate understanding of the terrible effects of traumatic disasters. Vital information is also provided on assessment of disaster victims, and on interventions to help those who are directly affected to deal with their resulting emotional distress and physical injuries.

The general goals of these volumes are to provide information for furthering the assessment of the psychological impact of disasters, and to report procedures for developing, implementing, and evaluating the effectiveness of these programs. Many contributors to this set have been deeply involved in projects to reduce the suffering of disaster victims, and to help them adapt to life circumstances substantially and adversely altered. The editors here have remarkable experience in disaster psychology, reflected in the chapters that they have contributed. Professor Gilbert Reyes is a tireless activist and educator in the field and Professor Gerard Jacobs was recently appointed to coordinate the activities of the American Psychological Association in providing assistance for victims of the recent tsunami.

The chapters first focus on fundamental issues pertaining to international disasters. Significant political and philosophical issues are also examined, and the need for effective collaboration among culturally diverse groups providing assistance is emphasized. The critical importance of understanding the particular needs and interests of populations indigenous to a disaster site is also spotlighted, along with the necessity of assessing available resources. Several contributors show us community-based models for assessment and intervention, as opposed to Western-oriented clinical approaches. Clearly, providing effective, culturally appropriate psychosocial support requires a great deal of skill and flexibility in programs that are delivered under very difficult circumstances.

We also come to understand, with these volumes, programs and practices that have been carried out in diverse geographical and cultural settings in Europe, Latin America, and Africa. In most, the interventions have focused on small groups, along with individuals and families, as the basic targets of intervention. The critical impact of national disasters in parts of the world where poverty, disease, and civil strife have weakened the capacity for coping with adversity is especially difficult to navigate, due to a persistent sense of danger that interferes with the healing process. Yet excellent examples of interventions are described, demonstrating why organizations such as the International Red Cross and the Red Crescent are considered best suited for dealing with disasters.

Reading in these books of interventions with refugees and "special needs" populations, we see that cultural diversity compounds the difficulty of developing effective programs. A prevailing climate of hatred and violence in many refugee populations further impairs effectiveness. And special emphasis is given to interventions that address the psychosocial needs of women and children, and to crisis interventions with military and with emergency services personnel.

These four volumes on international disaster psychology will be of great interest to psychologists, mental health workers, and other professionals working with disaster victims and their families. Trauma researchers, those interested in topics such as post-traumatic stress disorder (PTSD) and related disorders, will also find a wealth of useful information here. Indeed, these books will also well serve all students, scholars, and general readers focused on understanding how the most horrific, trying, and torturous of events can tear at psychological health, and how we all might play a role in helping heal the wounds.

For the past 30 years, I have personally worked in collaborative cross-cultural research with colleagues from more than 50 countries, and in developing adaptations of our anxiety and anger measures. I have also enjoyed and greatly benefited from participation in international meetings and conferences. While international psychology has addressed a wide range of topics, including stress and emotions, which have been the major focus of my work, these volumes pioneer new directions in psychological research and professional practice. Tsunamis, earthquakes, and other worldwide disasters are frequently encountered in modern life. Effective clinical and community interventions are urgently needed to help people cope. These volumes provide both a solid foundation for the emerging field of international disaster psychology and important guidelines for future research.

Charles D. Spielberger, Ph.D., ABPP
Distinguished Research Professor
University of South Florida, Tampa
Past President, American Psychological Association

ACKNOWLEDGMENTS

It goes without saying that the writing and editing of such an extensive book as this takes a great deal of effort and patience on the part of all concerned. What is perhaps less evident is that it also takes a great deal of trust and respect. As first-time editors undertaking a project of this scope and complexity, we required the trust of our publisher that we could indeed complete what we started. In this regard, we were extremely fortunate to be working with Debbie Carvalko at Greenwood Publishing, who came at this project with such infectious enthusiasm and confidence that she inspired the same in us. She also gently but firmly guided us through the unfamiliar process of delivering an edited book in four volumes consisting of over 40 chapters by authors from around the world. Without her patience, persistence, and professionalism, it is doubtful that this project could have proceeded so successfully.

We also required a great deal of trust from our colleagues, the authors who toiled for months over these chapters, that their efforts would not be in vain and that our work as their editors would prove commensurate to their investment in us. Many of these humanitarians and scholars knew us personally, but several did not, and all had only our word that the project would be completed as promised. We thank them sincerely for their confidence in our ability to make worthy use of their contributions.

The editors also wish to acknowledge the work of Mary E. Long, Ric Monroe, Sandra Schatz, and Tina Waldron, graduate research assistants who helped us to organize and process an almost unmanageable amount of information. Particular gratitude is owed for the editorial assistance supplied by Sandra Schatz, who labored tirelessly and diligently over the final drafts to detect and correct any errors or omissions. The efforts of these assistants are greatly appreciated and are reflected in the quality of these volumes.

Overview of the International Disaster Psychology Volumes

Gilbert Reyes

The four volumes that constitute the *Handbook of International Disaster Psychology* are composed of chapters addressing most of the pressing issues being confronted in this relatively new and expanding area of research and practice. Each volume and the chapters it contains are designed to inform a diverse audience of readers about the activities that have been undertaken around the globe to improve the psychological and emotional well-being of people affected by disasters. Many of the authors are deeply involved in developing programs and projects designed to relieve the psychological suffering of people exposed to disasters. They are mostly citizens of the Western nations, though the editors have attempted to attract contributions from colleagues residing in Asia, Africa, and South America. The objectives pursued by these authors in their humanitarian roles include, among other things, the assessment of the psychosocial impacts of disasters, implementation of prevention and intervention programs, and the development of strategies for improving the effectiveness of their programs. This in turn requires a sophisticated appreciation of factors that exert influence on the success of these operations. The authors have drawn from their own experience and what they have learned from other sources to share the key ideas and practices with the greatest promise of succeeding under the least favorable conditions. Their dedication to serving the psychosocial needs of people coping with terrifying and debilitating circumstances is deserving of the highest respect and admiration. Each is a humanitarian in the truest sense.

Volume 1: Fundamentals and Overview

The first volume of the *Handbook of International Disaster Psychology* provides readers with an orientation to the field of international disaster psychology

(Reyes, 2006) and an overview of the fundamental issues that pertain across most disasters and humanitarian emergencies. Toward that aim, the contributors identify and discuss many of the political and philosophical issues and assumptions involved in the humanitarian "therapeutic" enterprise and the "psychosocial" lens that magnifies the existence and importance of trauma to suit Western expectations (Pupavac, 2006). These matters cannot be easily dismissed, disputed, or ignored and reflect a perception among some that an intentional or inadvertent cultural imperialism comparable to "White Man's Burden" is at work.

The recent blending of military operations with humanitarian relief services has further complicated these issues by blurring the boundaries between partisan use of force to coercively serve national interests and impartial initiatives compelled by empathy and compassion (Wessells, 2006). Sadly, at the same time that agents of humanitarianism are accused of having sacrificed their fundamental principles to political expediency (Rieff, 2002), the casualty rates among relief personnel have skyrocketed, leading even the most courageous of NGOs to withdraw in the face of mounting dangers (Burnett, 2004; Gall, 2004; Kelly, 2004). And while few question the benefits and necessity of providing the tradition "survival" supplies, the value of psychosocial support has been a more contentious issue than most and remains unresolved. As a matter of conscience and ethics, anyone involved in promoting services of questionable benefit under conditions of mortal danger must acknowledge and respond respectfully to these concerns (Beech, 2006).

In order for psychosocial programs to be implemented successfully, effective collaboration among culturally diverse groups of people must take place (Peddle, Hudnall Stamm, Hudnall, & Stamm, 2006). Perhaps the most distinct intercultural partnership is that which forms between the populations indigenous to the disaster-affected areas and the relief agencies that are foreign to those regions. International humanitarian agencies employ expatriate (ex-pat) staff from around the world, so there is also a great deal of cultural diversity among their personnel. However, it is an undeniable reality of the hierarchical structure of these agencies that most of the managerial staff are of European or North American origin, while middle- and lower-level personnel comprise a more diverse assembly representing the less wealthy nations. Providing culturally appropriate psychosocial support under these conditions requires considerable skill and flexibility at every level, since the people with the most useful cultural knowledge and insight are often not those who decide policies and practices. Development of approaches that could be applied in any event and context is perhaps a desirable goal, but an unlikely one given the diversity of situations, values, cultures, and customs. Nevertheless, there are similarities across events that allow for construction of flexibly structured templates based on tested principles of good psychosocial practices (Ager, 2006).

A basic necessity for any relief operation is to assess the needs and resources of the affected populations, and in this regard psychosocial programs are not substantively different. Supplies and services based entirely on typical assumptions are unlikely to accurately match the types, levels, and characteristics of what is truly required in a specific context. Moreover, this profile of needs and resources is a moving target and must be persistently assessed and modified to remain pertinent (Dodge, 2006a). Among the many options for efficiently matching needs and services and making them available and useful to those who are most likely to benefit, the preference has shifted strongly toward community-based models, both for assessments and for intervention designs. Consequently, psychosocial planners and implementing personnel are less concerned with "clinical" training and skills because of the growing importance of methods associated with community psychology (Dodge, 2006b). The roles of ex-pat personnel are also increasingly educational in nature, with direct human services often being reserved for local staff, who are more likely to have the requisite language skills and cultural knowledge to work effectively within the communities where needs are greatest.

Communities constantly gather information to inform their decisions and guide the actions of their members. Thus, the importance of public information in disaster management should never be ignored. The mass news and entertainment media, especially television and increasingly the Internet, provide a critical resource in disasters, and the effective use of these media may spell the difference between success and failure in some instances (Kuriansky, 2006). Inaccurate rumors can have destructive consequences, and urgent transmission of vital information can save lives. And given the education components of psychological support, the print and electronic media are crucial to the mission of disseminating information that can help to reduce distress and direct survivors toward resources that are most likely to meet their needs. Therefore, it is important to make effective use of these techniques and technologies, in the interest of public education and according to well-proven public health models (Cohen, 2006).

Volume 2: Practices and Programs

The second volume of the *Handbook of International Disaster Psychology* addresses various psychosocial programs and the practices they employ to provide services to a variety of populations under difficult circumstances. The contributors describe not only what they do and with whom, but also the underlying reasons for certain decisions and activities. The approaches employed in designing effective intervention programs vary according to the types of problems being targeted and the types of people being helped. Some interventions are designed to work with people one at a time, though most are conducted with small groups or across entire communities. For instance, faculty at Massey University in New Zealand have developed and refined a model for providing optimal psychosocial care to youth and families (Ronan, Finnis, & Johnston, 2006). Their approach identifies the family as the basic unit of intervention, but it also makes optimal use of community resources such as schools and the news media. Under very different conditions, however, adaptations to cultural and sociopolitical conditions such as those encountered in Southeast Asia may require very different and innovative approaches (Armstrong, Boyden, Galappatti, & Hart, 2006). As is clear in these two examples, the approaches to such interventions are also profoundly influenced by the operational assumptions made by the designers and practitioners involved.

Ongoing violent conflicts produce perhaps the most difficult situations in which to implement such services, but the psychosocial needs that became evident during the collapse of the former Yugoslavia were urgent and could not wait until more peaceful times (Kapor-Stanulovic, 2006). The fact that hostilities have not ceased creates a perpetual sense of danger and dread, making it almost impossible to promote hope and healing with any sincerity. Similar horrors have been experienced across the African continent, whether stretched out over decades in such places as Uganda (Agger, 2006), or compressed into genocidal rampages as in Rwanda (Neugebauer, 2006). Although there are many important differences between conditions of persistent violence and singular events such as the terrorist bombing of the U. S. embassy in Nairobi (Ndetei, Kasina, & Kathuku, 2006), the psychological impact on survivors and the principles of psychosocial support are mostly similar.

Natural disasters can also wreak tremendous havoc, and they often occur in parts of the world where poverty, disease, and civil strife have already weakened the local capacity for coping with adversity. Latin American countries provide an example of such conditions (Cohen, 2006), with a recent string of major earthquakes and deadly storms having killed tens of thousands and left many times that number homeless and destitute. The prime example can be found in the recent history of Venezuela. That country was overwhelmed in 1999 by flooding and mudslides that killed over 30,000 people (Blanco, Villalobos, & Carrillo, 2006) and has since experienced a military junta, rioting, a disputed election, and extreme economic hardships. Given these worsening conditions, the psychosocial interventions initially mobilized for the flood survivors taught lessons about the need for developing long-range plans to deal with a succession of crises.

Among the organizations best suited for developing such capacities are the International Federation of Red Cross and Red Crescent Societies (IFRC), which has played an important role in teaching its member societies how to develop and sustain a national program of psychological support. An exemplary application of the IFRC model took place recently in Cuba, which had invited the psychosocial training director of the Danish Red Cross to provide a "training-of-trainers" for local Red Cross staff and volunteers. Those receiving the training then became trainers of others until, in just one year's time, they had disseminated the information and skills to every corner of their country (Atherton & Sonniks, 2006). The Cuban Red Cross has sustained and implemented its psychological support activities with great success as Cuba has endured a series of hurricanes and other disasters. More recently, the IFRC has published a manual consisting of six modules that is used to train its national societies in community-based principles of psychological support (Simonsen & Reyes, 2003). Training-of-trainers workshops employing that manual were field tested in Eastern Europe, Southeast Asia, and the Middle East and have since been conducted in several other regions around the world.

Concurrently, a number of other humanitarian NGOs have developed their own training procedures and begun to proliferate them wherever such a need is identified. Additional sources of training exist across various academic and clinical institutions scattered around the globe. Some of these institutions take a general approach to disaster mental health, while others specialize in assisting with a particular problem or population. What works best in any given instance is still an open question requiring further examination and resolution. What is clear, however, is that people and institutions interested in learning about the psychosocial programs and practices employed with disaster survivors now have access to more information and training options than ever before.

Volume 3: Refugee Mental Health

The third volume of the *Handbook of International Disaster Psychology* addresses several key issues confronted by those who have been involved in mental health work with refugees. Among the most persistently troubling aspects of international affairs in the twentieth century was the sharp increase in forced international migrations, which created refugee crises on a massive scale. This was one of the earliest and most pressing issues facing the fledgling United Nations, and it led to the creation of the United Nations High Commissioner for Refugees (UNHCR) in 1951. Worldwide estimates from international relief organizations indicate that there are more than 10 million refugees and twice that number of internally displaced persons (IDPs) at this time. The psychosocial impact of the countless horrific events that characterize the refugee experience are sometimes temporary and manageable, but can also be enduring and disabling. Among survivors of war, the prevalence of psychological distress and mental disorders is often strikingly elevated, as studies of Vietnamese and Cambodian refugees demonstrated over two decades ago (Kinzie, 2006).

To accurately assess the mental health needs of displaced and transient populations is a difficult task under the best of circumstances, and to do so during the emergency phase is in some ways the most difficult option (Jacobs, Revel, Reyes, & Quevillon, 2006). However, if we are to respond with immediacy and accuracy to refugee mental health needs, such an option must be explored and developed. Furthermore, it is important to conduct research that clarifies not only the most prevalent psychopathologies seen among refugees following migration, but also the risk and protective factors that differentiate the most resilient outcomes from those requiring clinical intervention. Culturally diverse perspectives and assumptions compound the difficulty of such research, which is most often conducted in Western industrialized nations to which large populations of refugees have migrated. However, since most people displaced by forced migrations return to their regions of origin, it is important to conduct culturally sensitive research that is congruent with local customs, rather than erroneously imposing a Western psychiatric perspective (Bolton, 2006). Moreover, if we are to fully comprehend how psychosocial healing can best be supported across varying conditions and cultures, we must find ways to study the most important factors with simultaneous sensitivity and responsiveness to the needs of the survivors.

Programs serving the mental health needs of refugees are often located in the Western nations where they have settled. Europe, Australia, and North America are the most popular destinations for refugees, and nearly all of the published studies evaluating intervention programs originate from these regions. Sweden and other Scandinavian countries are among the most welcoming of refugees, and many excellent programs have been developed to help relieve postmigratory distress and improve the adjustment of forced migrants to cultural conditions that are entirely foreign to their experience (Ekblad, 2006). Australia has also experienced an influx of refugees fleeing persecution and violence, many of whom arrived from neighboring Asian nations. Innovative and culturally sensitive programs have been implemented in response to trauma and torture that can serve as models of blending individual and community intervention strategies into a more integral whole (Silove, 2006). The United States also receives large numbers of refugees and has become home to many who fled the wars and persecution across the Balkan republics following the disintegration of the former Yugoslavia. An abundance of intervention programs have been implemented in major American cities to assist refugees with psychosocial concerns, some of which have become particularly influential examples of innovation. Among those is a program in Chicago that employs family therapy and other techniques to apply a framework of intervening with groups composed of multiple families (Raina et al., 2006).

The work with refugees taking place in postmigration countries is often enhanced by experiences working with corresponding populations that remained in their country of origin. Several researchers and clinicians who work with postmigratory refugees in the West also invest great effort in working with former IDPs in the countries from which refugees have recently fled. The mental health infrastructures of such countries were often poorly developed and are typically overwhelmed and underfunded for meeting the needs of their postconflict population. International collaborations between mental health professionals from poorly resourced and highly resourced settings offer countless opportunities for improvement on both ends of such partnerships (Weine, Pavkovic, Agani, Ceric, & Jukic, 2006). Of particular merit is the movement to assign the same level of human rights, commitment to healing, and compassionate regard for mental illness as that which is felt toward those with physical ailments and injuries.

As wars and other levels of massive violence continue to erupt in repetitious cycles in many parts of the world, some patterns and principle are clear. Among those is that hatred and revenge have long memories and can reemerge after extended periods of apparent peace. One approach to breaking the cycle of violence has been to seek social justice through human rights instruments and international criminal tribunals. Another approach emphasizes rapprochement through community processes of communicative expression, such as the Truth and Reconciliation Commissions in South Africa, Peru, East Timor, Sierra Leone, and elsewhere. Unfortunately, the idealistic goals of such an undertaking often run headlong into the sheer force and brutality of the hatred they are created to alleviate. Moreover, for many who continue to endure an ever-present pain borne of atrocities that can never blend into an innocuous past, forgiveness seems like a form of betrayal that joins victims with perpetrators in a profane alliance belying all truth. Nevertheless, without forgiveness, complete psychosocial health cannot be achieved and the transmission of violence is more likely continue across generations as children enact themes of revenge in a perverse pursuit of honor and retribution (Borris, 2006).

Volume 4: Interventions with Special Needs Populations

The fourth volume of the *Handbook of International Disaster Psychology* addresses populations whose needs differ in some critical way from more general expectations. There are many reasons why this might occur, including that the "special" population is at elevated risk of harm or that key aspects of what they have endured differ from the experiences of most disaster survivors. Another reason may be that the group's needs are not well matched to the practices that are typically effective with people. Groups with "special needs" have been identified in regard to several variables, including developmental characteristics (e.g., children, the elderly), gender, types of traumatic experiences (e.g., torture, sexual assault), and occupational roles (e.g., relief workers, military personnel, journalists). Although several elements of good psychosocial practice reliably combine to form a strong core that can be applied across most populations and conditions, it is important to take special needs into account and not to expect any approach to be universally effective.

The manner in which different groups of people are treated in disasters and humanitarian crises usually reflects how they are treated under more normal circumstances. That is, if categories of people are less privileged in general, they are unlikely to receive better treatment in the worst of times. If anything, the social destabilization characteristic of most crises tends to amplify disparities in power and encourage opportunistic exploitation of the weak and vulnerable. Among the populations most often targeted for exploitation are women and children. Gender inequities are prevalent in most societies and, from a global perspective, the gains resulting from social justice movements such as feminism have been meager and fragile. Thus, while women have made remarkable progress on some issues in some nations, the worldwide economic and human rights advances for women have been shamefully slow and sporadic in their progress. Therefore, to understand the special needs of women in disasters, wars, and other crises, one must grasp the conditions and obstacles with which women are faced even in the best of times (Hudnall & Lindner, 2006).

Among the many ways in which women and girls are demeaned and exploited, one of the most humiliating and pernicious is widespread sexual violence (Reis & Vann, 2006). Sexual coercion and assault are all too commonplace in women's lives, and the protection of women and girls against such violations is pathetically inadequate. When war and social upheaval are entered into this equation, the levels of sexual depravity against women achieve sickening proportions. Tenuous social restrictions designed to at least postpone the exploitation of female children until they have reached sexual maturity are easily swept aside in times of lawlessness and war. Civilian women have historically suffered under the domination of conquering armies, who have subjected them to systematic rapes and sexual slavery. The history of these atrocities has been disputed and denied by governments unwilling to take responsibility for the heinous acts that transpire under cover of war.

Given that, there is perhaps some comfort to be taken behind international human rights protections when governments war against one another. No such restrictions exist for outlaw bands of militia and other paramilitary fighters that dominate many regions of conflict in today's world. Therefore, while the member states of the UN enact resolutions and other instruments, such as the Convention on the Rights of the Child, to protect children from harmful practices such as child labor, sexual exploitation, early marriage, and premature military service, these problems persist and worsen in the darkest corners of civilization. Wherever societies crumble into chaos and bitter conflict, children are exposed to countless hazards and may also be drawn into battle, either as fighters or as captive workers to support the troops (Boyden, de Berry, Feeny, & Hart, 2006).

While the prototypical child soldier is a young boy armed with a light machinegun, girls too are forcibly ensnared into service (McKay. 2006). In such instances, girls are used as porters, domestic servants, sexual slaves, and "wives." Whether they are boys or girls, once these children escape captivity or are otherwise returned to civilian lives, the process of reunion and reintegration is often one of stigma, rejection, and shame. Girls in particular may be viewed as damaged goods and never regain the status and opportunities that were once within reach.

The type and intensity of traumatic events can also create differential impact characteristics that translate into unique needs for certain kinds of survivors. For instance, the impact of torture on the mind can be uniquely complex and intractable, thus requiring exquisitely precise skills unlike those which suffice for other types of disaster and trauma interventions (Holtz, 1998). In response to this need, dozens of excellent facilities, such as the Rehabilitation and Research Centre for Torture Survivors in Copenhagen, have developed noteworthy expertise in helping people who have suffered terribly at the hands of others (Berliner & Mikkelsen, 2006).

A paradoxical aspect of disasters and humanitarian emergencies is that, while most people flee from these zones of mayhem and destruction, others rush into the breach to assist survivors and pursue altruistic ends. The impact of facing death and other gruesome consequences of disasters fall particularly hard upon humanitarian aid workers, emergency services personnel, members of the military, and other occupations who perform heroic services. International humanitarian organizations (Ehrenreich, 2006), civilian fire and police departments (De Soir, 2006), and other agencies have recently come to recognize the importance of responding to the psychosocial needs of their employees and volunteers. Managing occupational stress among their personnel challenges these organizations not only to add a psychosocial component to their existing employee health services, but also to modify their systems so that they are less likely to create the stress that must then be managed. It is at least ironic, if not hypocritical, that humanitarian organizations charged with the mission of relieving the suffering of any and every unfortunate soul whom they encounter often fail to treat their own staff and volunteers with comparable compassion and regard for their dignity and well-being.

As noted earlier, the role of the news media in providing reliable information about crises and relief operations has become a critically important component of marshaling resources and public opinion in helpful directions. In viewing the "media" as a mammoth multinational corporate operation involving cameras, satellites, and high technology, it is easy to overlook the fragile human elements. International correspondents and their coworkers, many of whom are poorly paid local citizens, sometimes cover these stories at great risk to their own lives. In recent events it has become clear that journalists reporting from war zones and humanitarian crises are being killed and injured at historically high rates, sometimes due to their own risky decisions, though often at the hands of military forces they had trusted to protect them. Perhaps in part because the status of war correspondents in the journalistic community is so high, they are expected to shake off the ill effects of their occupation without complaint and bask in the glory they have earned through daring deeds. But recent collaborative projects have been initiated between journalists and psychologists that examine the psychological effects of covering traumatic stories, assess the mental health needs of journalists exposed to trauma, and design proactive interventions to reduce the negative psychosocial impact on those who inform the public about these critically important events (Newman & Shapiro, 2006).

Appendix of NGO Profiles (Volume 4)

The international humanitarian relief community that developed over the past century was pioneered by a small number of organizations dedicated to serving victims of war, disease, famine, and other natural calamities. Paramount among these was the Red Cross movement, which began in Switzerland in 1863 and slowly spread throughout most of the world over the next several decades. The red cross on a white background came to be recognized as a symbol of neutrality and compassion in the face of conflict and brutality. Hospitals, ambulances, and personnel marked with the Red Cross emblem earned a status as noncombatants that allowed them to function in war zones and other dangerous places with few direct attacks upon their operations. This philosophy of mercy within a context of violence eventually led to the Geneva Conventions and other international accords designed to provide limited protection for civilians and military prisoners as an ever widening swath of war engulfed the world. As the Red Cross movement proliferated, national societies were founded in dozens of countries and a new emblem, the Red Crescent, was approved to accommodate societies in regions where Islam was the predominate faith.

The founding of the United Nations at the end of World War II fostered a period of growing humanitarian aid through both governmental agencies and nongovernmental organizations (NGOs). Several agencies within the UN system, such as the United Nations Children's Fund (UNICEF), the United Nations High Commissioner for Refugees (UNHCR), and the World Health Organization (WHO), developed programs and policies that saved millions of lives and improved the quality of life for untold numbers of the world's most vulnerable citizens. The scourges of war, disease, and disaster were never abolished, but a countervailing force of hope and compassion was established, and hundreds of NGOs have been founded to serve the needs of people who might otherwise perish or wither.

Perhaps the most recent of humanitarian relief activities is the formal provision of psychosocial support, though this is certainly an element of any compassionate care to the afflicted. The story of international disaster psychology cannot be fully told without repeated reference to the humanitarian NGOs that have developed and disseminated psychosocial support training and services with great dedication and determination. Moreover, volunteers who aspire to work in this field of endeavor will almost certainly work closely with several of these NGOs and will benefit from obtaining at least a cursory knowledge of their missions, philosophies, histories, and activities.

Therefore, the editors of the *Handbook of International Disaster Psychology* have included an appendix consisting of brief profiles that describe some of the prominent humanitarian organizations operating in the world today. The information contained in these profiles was gathered from public sources and may contain accidental inaccuracies. Given the rapidly evolving nature of the NGOs profiled, it is also quite likely that some of the information will soon become outdated. However, these profiles are substantially accurate, and the contact information given for each agency makes it possible for interested readers to obtain more current and detailed information.

References

Ager, A. (2006). Toward a consensus protocol for psychosocial response in complex emergencies. In G. Reyes & G. A. Jacobs (Eds.), *Handbook of international disaster psychology, Vol. 1. Fundamentals and overview.* Westport, CT: Praeger Publishers.

Agger, I. (2006). Approaches to psychosocial healing: Case examples from Lusophone Africa. In G. Reyes & G. A. Jacobs (Eds.), *Handbook of international disaster psychology, Vol. 2. Practices and programs.* Westport, CT: Praeger Publishers.

Armstrong, M., Boyden, J., Galappatti, A., & Hart, J. (2006). Participatory tools for monitoring and evaluating psychosocial work with children: Reflections on a pilot study in Eastern Sri Lanka. In G. Reyes & G. A. Jacobs (Eds.), *Handbook of international disaster psychology, Vol. 2. Practices and programs.* Westport, CT: Praeger Publishers.

Atherton, J., & Sonniks, M. (2006). Implementation of a training of trainers model for disseminating psychological support in the Cuban Red Cross. In G. Reyes & G. A. Jacobs (Eds.), *Handbook of international disaster psychology, Vol. 2. Practices and programs.* Westport, CT: Praeger Publishers.

Beech, D. R. (2006). Peace-building, culturally responsive means, and ethical practices in humanitarian psychosocial interventions. In G. Reyes & G. A. Jacobs (Eds.), *Handbook of international disaster psychology, Vol. 1. Fundamentals and overview.* Westport, CT: Praeger Publishers.

Berliner, P., & Mikkelsen, E. (2006). Serving the psychosocial needs of survivors of torture and organized violence. In G. Reyes & G. A. Jacobs (Eds.), *Handbook of international disaster psychology, Vol. 4. Interventions with special needs populations.* Westport, CT: Praeger Publishers.

Blanco, T., Villalobos, M., & Carrillo, C. (2006). The psychological support network of the Central University of Venezuela and the Venezuelan floods of 1999. In G. Reyes & G. A. Jacobs (Eds.), *Handbook of international disaster psychology, Vol. 2. Practices and programs.* Westport, CT: Praeger Publishers.

Bolton, P. (2006). Challenges in international disaster mental health research. In G. Reyes & G. A. Jacobs (Eds.), *Handbook of international disaster psychology, Vol. 3. Refugee mental health. Westport,* CT: Praeger Publishers.

Borris, E. (2006). The healing power of forgiveness and the resolution of protracted conflicts. In G. Reyes & G. A. Jacobs (Eds.), *Handbook of international disaster psychology, Vol. 3. Refugee mental health.* Westport, CT: Praeger Publishers.

Boyden, J., de Berry, J., Feeny, T., & Hart, J. (2006). Children affected by armed conflict in South Asia: A regional summary. In G. Reyes & G. A. Jacobs (Eds.), *Handbook of international disaster psychology, Vol. 4. Interventions with special needs populations.* Westport, CT: Praeger Publishers.

Burnett, J. S. (2004, August 4). In the line of fire. *The New York Times*, Late Edition–Final, p. A17, col. 1.

Cohen, R. (2006). Implementation of mental health programs for survivors of natural disasters in Latin America. In G. Reyes & G. A. Jacobs (Eds.), *Handbook of international disaster psychology, Vol. 2. Practices and programs*. Westport, CT: Praeger Publishers.

De Soir, E. (2006). Psychosocial crisis intervention with military and emergency services personnel. In G. Reyes & G. A. Jacobs (Eds.), *Handbook of international disaster psychology, Vol. 4. Interventions with special needs populations*. Westport, CT: Praeger Publishers.

Dodge, G. R. (2006a). Assessing the psychosocial needs of communities affected by disaster. In G. Reyes & G. A. Jacobs (Eds.), *Handbook of international disaster psychology, Vol. 1. Fundamentals and overview*. Westport, CT: Praeger Publishers.

———. (2006b). In defense of a community psychology model for international psychosocial intervention. In G. Reyes & G. A. Jacobs (Eds.), *Handbook of international disaster psychology, Vol. 1. Fundamentals and overview*. Westport, CT: Praeger Publishers.

Ehrenreich, J. (2006). Managing stress in humanitarian aid workers: The role of the humanitarian aid organization. In G. Reyes & G. A. Jacobs (Eds.), *Handbook of international disaster psychology, Vol. 4. Interventions with special needs populations*. Westport, CT: Praeger Publishers.

Ekblad, S. (2006). Serving the mental health needs of postmigratory adult refugees in Sweden: A transitional augmentation approach. In G. Reyes & G. A. Jacobs (Eds.), *Handbook of international disaster psychology, Vol. 3. Refugee mental health*. Westport, CT: Praeger Publishers.

Gall, C. (2004, June 3). Aid agency halts operations in Afghanistan. *The New York Times*, Late Edition–Final, p. A5, col. 3.

Holtz, T. H. (1998). Refugee trauma versus torture trauma: A retrospective controlled cohort study of Tibetan refugees. *Journal of Nervous & Mental Disease, 186,* 24–34.

Hudnall, A., & Lindner, E. (2006). Crisis and gender: Addressing the psychosocial needs of women in international disasters. In G. Reyes & G. A. Jacobs (Eds.), *Handbook of international disaster psychology, Vol. 4. Interventions with special needs populations*. Westport, CT: Praeger Publishers.

Jacobs, G. A., Revel, J. P., Reyes, G., & Quevillon, R. P. (2006). Development of the Rapid Assessment of Mental Health: An international collaboration. In G. Reyes & G. A. Jacobs (Eds.), *Handbook of international disaster psychology, Vol. 3. Refugee mental health*. Westport, CT: Praeger Publishers.

Kapor-Stanulovic, N. (2006). Implementing psychosocial programs in the Federal Republic of Yugoslavia: Was it really mission impossible? In G. Reyes & G. A. Jacobs (Eds.), *Handbook of international disaster psychology, Vol. 2. Practices and programs*. Westport, CT: Praeger Publishers.

Kelly, A. (2004, December 15). Caught in the crossfire. *The Guardian Weekly.* Retrieved March 4, 2005, from http://society.guardian.co.uk/societyguardian/story/0,,1373410,00.html

Kinzie, J. D. (2006). Personal reflections on treating traumatized refugees. In G. Reyes & G. A. Jacobs (Eds.), *Handbook of international disaster psychology, Vol. 3. Refugee mental health*. Westport, CT: Praeger Publishers.

Kuriansky, J. (2006). Working effectively with the mass media in disaster mental health. In G. Reyes & G. A. Jacobs (Eds.), *Handbook of international disaster psychology, Vol. 1. Fundamentals and overview*. Westport, CT: Praeger Publishers.

MacDonald, C. M. (2003). Evaluation of stress debriefing interventions with military populations. *Military Medicine, 168*, 961–968.

McKay, S. (2006). How do you mend broken hearts? Gender, war, and impacts on girls in fighting forces. In G. Reyes & G. A. Jacobs (Eds.), *Handbook of international disaster psychology, Vol. 4. Interventions with special needs populations*. Westport, CT: Praeger Publishers.

Ndetei, D., Kasina, R., & Kathuku, D. (2006). Psychosocial responses to the bombing of the American Embassy in Nairobi: Challenges, lessons, and opportunities. In G. Reyes & G. A. Jacobs (Eds.), *Handbook of international disaster psychology, Vol. 2. Practices and programs*. Westport, CT: Praeger Publishers.

Neugebauer, R. (2006). Psychosocial research and interventions after the Rwanda genocide. In G. Reyes & G. A. Jacobs (Eds.), *Handbook of international disaster psychology, Vol. 2. Practices and programs*. Westport, CT: Praeger Publishers.

Newman, E., & Shapiro, B. (2006). Helping journalists who cover humanitarian crises. In G. Reyes & G. A. Jacobs (Eds.), *Handbook of international disaster psychology, Vol. 4. Interventions with special needs populations*. Westport, CT: Praeger Publishers.

Peddle, N., Hudnall Stamm, B., Hudnall, A. C., & Stamm, H. E. (2006). Effective intercultural collaboration on psychosocial support programs. In G. Reyes & G. A. Jacobs (Eds.), *Handbook of international disaster psychology, Vol. 1. Fundamentals and overview*. Westport, CT: Praeger Publishers.

Pupavac, V. (2006). Humanitarian politics and the rise of international disaster psychology. In G. Reyes & G. A. Jacobs (Eds.), *Handbook of international disaster psychology, Vol. 1. Fundamentals and overview*. Westport, CT: Praeger Publishers.

Raina, D., Weine, S., Kulauzovic, Y., Feetham, S., Zhubi, M., Huseni, D., & Pavkovic, I. (2006). A framework for developing and implementing multiple-family groups for refugee families. In G. Reyes & G. A. Jacobs (Eds.), *Handbook of international disaster psychology, Vol. 3. Refugee mental health*. Westport, CT: Praeger Publishers.

Reis, C., & Vann. B. (2006). Sexual violence against women and children in the context of armed conflict. In G. Reyes & G. A. Jacobs (Eds.), *Handbook of international disaster psychology, Vol. 4. Interventions with special needs populations*. Westport, CT: Praeger Publishers.

Reyes, G. (2006). International disaster psychology: Purposes, principles, and practices. In G. Reyes & G. A. Jacobs (Eds.), *Handbook of international disaster psychology, Vol. 1. Fundamentals and overview*. Westport, CT: Praeger Publishers.

Rieff, D. (2002). *A bed for the night: Humanitarianism in crisis*. New York: Simon & Schuster.

Ronan, K. R., Finnis, K., & Johnston, D. M. (2006). Interventions with youth and families: A prevention and stepped care model. In G. Reyes & G. A. Jacobs (Eds.), *Handbook of international disaster psychology, Vol. 2. Practices and programs*. Westport, CT: Praeger Publishers.

Silove, D. (2006). The impact of mass psychological trauma on psychosocial adaptation among refugees. In G. Reyes & G. A. Jacobs (Eds.), *Handbook of international disaster psychology, Vol. 3. Refugee mental health*. Westport, CT: Praeger Publishers.

Weine, S., Pavkovic, I., Agani, F., Ceric, I., & Jukic, V. (2006). Mental health reform and assisting psychiatric leaders in postwar countries. In G. Reyes & G. A. Jacobs (Eds.), *Handbook of international disaster psychology, Vol. 3. Refugee mental health*. Westport, CT: Praeger Publishers.

Wessells, M. G. (2006). Negotiating the shrunken humanitarian space: Challenges and options. In G. Reyes & G. A. Jacobs (Eds.), *Handbook of international disaster psychology, Vol. 1. Fundamentals and overview*. Westport, CT: Praeger Publishers.

CHAPTER 1

PSYCHOLOGICAL FIRST AID: PRINCIPLES OF COMMUNITY-BASED PSYCHOSOCIAL SUPPORT

Gilbert Reyes

The emotional and psychological impact of disasters is not easily absorbed, and survivors may benefit from some immediate psychological support even under the best of conditions. However, it is no simple task to determine who should deliver what kind of support to whom and at what time. Disasters and wars are so dangerous and disruptive that it would be absurd to address people's psychological needs when their very lives are threatened. Moreover, even after the imminent threats have subsided, there continue to be imperative survival needs that must be given the utmost priority. Therefore, if immediate psychosocial support is to be supplied at all, it will most likely require an informal method of delivery that fits seamlessly with the provision of the most essential services (e.g., medical, nutritional, and sanitation) and must neither conflict with the priorities of the humanitarian operations or the cultural values of the beneficiaries.

News coverage of the Indian Ocean tsunami relief efforts have frequently described devastating psychological reactions (e.g., Associated Press, 2005), while the world's preeminent authority on health issues confirmed this viewpoint and declared the need for immediate widespread psychosocial assistance (World Health Organization, 2005). The advice given by some international mental health experts, however, has mostly been to hold back on providing professional intervention for trauma until the emergency period has subsided (Anderson, 2005). Nevertheless, there are well-respected and experienced mental health professionals who quickly traveled to the disaster-stricken region and offered their services (Kuriansky, 2005).

These polarized points of view typify an ongoing debate about whether trauma counselors and other psychosocial response personnel should provide their "services" immediately or wait a suitable time until survivors are less occupied with more pressing concerns.

Part of this debate is about priorities, with mental health support being characterized as something of a luxury or irrelevancy when people are struggling to meet basic survival needs (Satel, 2005). The alternative position argues that the time has come for recognizing that psychosocial functioning is as critically important to survival as many other things that are traditionally given higher priority (International Federation of Red Cross and Red Crescent Societies, 2001). With no scientific evidence to go on, both sides use uncorroborated anecdotes (e.g., horror stories), emotional appeals, and compelling analogies to argue that their perspective is unquestionably correct. Opponents are stamped with unflattering labels, such as "trauma tourists" or "ambulance chasers," which does little to advance the discussion toward rapprochement. One predictable effect of such antagonistic debates is an absence of reliable information on which to base well-reasoned decisions, thus prolonging the confusion, inefficiency, and inaction.

Issues such as the timing, objectives, and methods of intervention are amenable to negotiation and compromise, and the operative assumptions can be successfully modified in response to feedback from the field. Unfortunately, the politics of humanitarian relief are such that they leave little room for objective testing of policies and practices, since the results might prove embarrassing to those who forcefully formulated the prevailing arguments. Hopefully, a mature and cooperative international humanitarian community will eventually place the needs of its beneficiaries above the fruitless distractions of internecine bickering.

Beyond the argument over whether psychosocial support should even be an urgent priority in humanitarian responses to disaster, there are debates over the timing of such interventions, the mode of delivering that service, and the qualifications of those who would provide the support. Proponents assert that earlier intervention is better than waiting because the goal is to prevent harm, but opponents caution against intrusive counselors who might interfere with more urgent needs, interrupt "natural" healing processes that must take precedence over more artificial means, and ignorantly impose their own cultural mores where they are neither welcome nor helpful. Moreover, some have argued that psychological support is far from being a technical or clinical skill and can therefore be adequately delivered by people with little training or advanced education. The hypothetical benefits of having psychological support delivered by local community members include that these indigenous providers will be more plentiful than outside "experts," more culturally astute, and more likely to be available for the long-term needs of their neighbors. This particular prescription is increasingly popular and has been colorfully labeled as psychological first aid (Glass, Drayer, Cameron, & Woodward, 1954; Knudsen, Hogsted, & Berliner, 1997). The remainder of the present chapter will describe the essential principles and practices that make up psychological first aid.

Psychological First Aid (PFA)

The primary mission of the mental health disciplines has historically been directed toward abnormal psychological processes and the invention of methods for curing or managing mental illness. A secondary focus has been on assisting people whose psychological processes are within the normal range of functioning, but who are struggling to recover from the impact of extraordinarily stressful life events (Dohrenwend & Dohrenwend, 1974). Situational disturbances in psychological functioning have long been acknowledged, and prior to the advent of the mental health professions they were often attended to by relatives or by adherents of a religious order or a compassionate secular philosophy. Psychologists and others who studied the human response to stress (e.g., Selye, 1978) found that situational stressors could impair psychological functioning, though the impact was usually temporary. Under conditions of extreme or persistent stress, however, the effects can be more lasting, as is the case when post-traumatic stress disorder (PTSD) is diagnosed (American Psychiatric Association, 1994). The major approaches to intervention were modeled either on psychoanalytic techniques aimed at traumatic neuroses or on medical treatments for the alleviation of disease. These required highly skilled clinicians and were considered among the most difficult cases one might encounter (van der Kolk, Weisaeth, & van der Hart, 1996). Thus, expertise in trauma work became among the most admired of psychiatric specialties, and patients with traumatic disorders were considered beyond the abilities of all but the most gifted therapists.

Mental health clinicians involved with military personnel and other highly dangerous occupations long ago recognized that psychological reactions were impairing the effectiveness of operations conducted under extreme stress. Given that trained clinicians were in short supply near these danger zones, they looked for solutions that were analogous to the first aid training that was well distributed among corpsmen and medics. The concept of psychological first aid was promoted as a way of providing a calming and supportive influence for personnel who were wounded or stricken with fear under conditions where expert intervention was impossible or impractical. That is, just as these co-workers could provide temporary nonmedical aid to the injured until more sophisticated care became available, so too could they use simple psychological techniques to ease the mental anguish or panic of their comrades and possibly prevent the need for any formal psychiatric intervention (Blain, Hoch, & Ryan, 1944). Other authors, professions, and contexts of application eventually followed, and PFA was recommended for use not only in wartime, but in disasters and other crises affecting both adults (e.g., Glass et al., 1954; Thorne, 1952) and children (e.g., Pynoos & Nader, 1988).

It should also be noted that there are remarkable similarities between PFA and crisis intervention, which evolved concurrently and in response to similar phenomena (Lindemann, 1944). But unlike crisis intervention, which has consistently been understood as a set of techniques reserved for professionals, PFA has been inconsistently described as either a clinical intervention or as a set of simple activities for use by modestly qualified non-clinicians. This identity crisis among the advocates of PFA remains unresolved, though several major mental health and humanitarian organizations in the United States and elsewhere are presently moving forward to disseminate this approach as a means of relieving psychological distress during crises and preventing the development of enduring stress reactions.

The following descriptions of PFA are adapted from numerous public sources, one of which is a training manual on community-based psychological support published by the International Federation of Red Cross and Red Crescent Societies (IFRC), for which the present author served as a technical consultant and coauthor (Simonsen & Reyes, 2003). It must be noted that the present author takes complete responsibility for these descriptions.

Fundamental Principles of PFA

Protection

Disasters, wars, and other catastrophic events have the potential for deadly or injurious consequences and must be taken very seriously. The effects of extreme stress can impair the ability of survivors to exercise good judgment, resulting in circumstances that could lead to further losses or injuries. Therefore, the first and foremost principle of PFA is damage control. This is consistent with medical first aid, in which the primary objective is to stabilize the survivor's condition to prevent it from becoming worse. Accomplishing this objective may require the PFA provider to temporarily take a very directive stance so as to gain the survivor's attention and understanding of the need to get to a safer place. Despondent or uncooperative survivors can endanger themselves and place anyone who intervenes to protect them at risk of harm as well. Thus, it is imperative that PFA providers endeavor to protect survivors from further harm without engaging in foolhardy heroics, which have no place in humanitarian operations. Psychological first aid must wait until physical safety and security, both for survivors and for practitioners, have been established.

Social Support

Psychological first aid describes a strategy for helping people affected by disasters to cope with their immediate reactions to extreme stress without further avoidable harm. People are often able to endure great hardships without major assistance, but that does not mean they do not benefit from social support (Cohen & Wills, 1985) when it is given in a manner that does not worsen their existing stress. Psychologists have classified social support into three categories, based on what is provided to the person needing help (Schaefer, Coyne, & Lazarus, 1981). *Tangible* (or *material*) support means providing someone with money, supplies, housing, medical aid, or other things that carry some tangible or financial value. *Emotional* support is anything someone says or does that helps another person to bear up under the burden of stressful emotions that are commonly felt in times of crisis. This can be as simple as being a caring and attentive companion and does not require any great feats or insights. *Informational* support describes the simple act of sharing some valuable bit of knowledge that helps someone to solve a problem, helps gain access to resources, or somehow provides comfort. These acts of generosity and compassion are staples of human kindness and can be provided without need of mental health training.

People trained to provide PFA need to be well informed about the disaster operations and the resources available to survivors so that they are able to provide accurate and timely *informational* support. Practitioners of PFA also need the interpersonal skills that are crucial to being an effective provider of *emotional* support. These include providing a calming, comforting, and confident presence, listening at least as much as talking, and offering unreserved compassion without judging whether a person is deserving of such. Psychological first-aiders are seldom in a position to directly offer *material* support and may even be in need of such assistance themselves (e.g., local spontaneous volunteers). Nevertheless, humanitarian organizations and relief agencies may provide material items to PFA providers for dissemination, thus affording them an opportunity to blend all three types of social support into one well- integrated intervention.

Arousal Reduction

Disasters and other life-threatening events stimulate fear and other self-protective emotions that arouse the nervous system in preparation to survive an attack. This reaction, often called the fight/flight response, creates a state of physiological alarm. The resulting effects on people's thinking abilities and emotional functioning are both necessary in the short run and debilitating in the long run. If at all possible, the primary step is to ensure that neither the survivor nor the PFA provider is in any imminent danger, so that reduction of arousal can begin in earnest. Effective PFA critically depends on the ability to soothe and reduce this arousal so that the survivor is able both to function at a higher level and to rest or even sleep. Persistent or chronic activation of nervous system arousal severely depletes people's physical, mental, and emotional resources and must be recognized as a serious threat to health and survival.

In addition to immediate or looming threats to survival, loss or separation from loved ones also activates nervous system arousal. This was often noticed among survivors of the Indian Ocean tsunami, as parents who had lost their children and children separated from their parents displayed extreme anguish and frantically searched in hopes of reunion (Waldman, 2005). The obvious and optimal solution in such events is to assist people in finding their missing loved ones, and whenever possible this is an important function of psychological first aid. However, this is often impossible, and instead the PFA provider can seek to help the survivor to locate and unite with others who have been or will become part of their social support network. In any event, it is often helpful to simply support survivors as they hunt for their loved ones, while also encouraging them to rest and seek sustenance or medical attention while others continue the search.

Assisted Coping

Coping is anything that people do to improve their lives or avoid losses in the face of adversity. This requires having a goal or objective and a plan for achieving a desirable outcome. Under the catastrophic stress of a disaster, even people who normally cope quite well will find it hard to function in a deliberate and systematic fashion. Assisting people with the coping process is a part of PFA that requires practitioners to adopt a balanced stance between helping people and empowering them to help themselves. Survivors should always be treated with respect and encouragement for their resilience, competence, and dignity. Providers of PFA are in a position to provide only modest temporary assistance, so it is important not to foster dependency or undermine the confidence survivors have in their own coping abilities.

A systematic problem-solving approach to coping can be used by PFA practitioners to assist survivors with deliberating, planning, and decision making. The first step is to define the problem. It is important to keep the scope of this definition limited so that the problem is manageable in some realistic sense. The definition will help to make clear which of the three common ways of coping will be most effective. People tend to cope either by *confronting* a problem directly, *enduring* the problem, or managing their thoughts to decrease the *emotional* impact of the problem. Assisted coping is focused on helping the survivor to find the best available solution that doesn't make the situation worse in some way.

The next step is to formulate multiple solutions that are possible, acceptable, and practical. Solutions that sound too good or simple may have hidden costs that will make them unacceptable or impractical, while those that are comprehensive may also be too complicated and fragile to actually succeed. It is better to have a minor success than a major failure, so solutions should be fairly simple and only modestly ambitious. The third step is to formulate a plan of action with clear and practical steps that are within the reach of the survivor. It is often good to discuss the plan in a form that allows a rehearsal so that problems can be accurately anticipated and accounted for before they occur. If possible, the PFA practitioner should monitor the progress of the survivor in the course of enacting the plan and provide additional coping assistance until it is no longer needed.

Advocating

People in distress may feel intimidated or unable to gain access to assistance and resources from powerful entities such as government ministries and large organizations, and this perception is often accurate. Agencies have policies that structure their activities, and these can sometimes work to the disadvantage of people with legitimate needs. Practitioners of PFA may have access and influence within these agencies greater than that which is wielded by survivors. Therefore, PFA includes advocating for the needs of survivors who might otherwise not receive the services they need and deserve. This activity may also prove beneficial for the agencies involved since it helps them to accurately assess and respond to survivors' needs. Nevertheless, agencies are unlikely to appreciate aggressive advocates, especially if they appear not to respect the merits of these policies or attempt to manipulate the process in order to bypass the rules. Therefore, advocacy should be understood as a relational process with the advocate as an intermediary attempting to balance the interest of all parties.

Routing and Referral

Disaster survivors vary in their levels of impairment and in the types of problems with which they need assistance. It is necessary for the practitioner to quickly recognize when the limitations of PFA have been reached and know how to route the survivor to an appropriate service or resource (sometimes called *triage*). This requires the PFA provider to ascertain whether the survivor is merely disoriented and distressed or is severely traumatized or physically injured and in need of professional care. *Routing* means directing survivors toward a service or resource that they need more than PFA at the moment, whereas *referral* means arranging to transfer survivors to a more expert provider based on a decision that they need something more extensive than PFA. Therefore, it is an important qualification of PFA practitioners that they take steps to maintain accurate and timely information regarding available services and resources, and to be familiar with ways of arranging for successful routing and referral to take place.

Community Mobilization

The descriptions of PFA provided above may convey a sense that this work is conducted entirely like medical first aid in that one or more providers are working to help survivors on an individual basis. This is not ideally the case, for a basic principle of psychological first aid is that it must be implemented in a manner that involves the affected community in its own recovery process. Disasters such as the Indian Ocean tsunami illustrate quite clearly that the devastation is inflicted not only on individuals and families but rather on whole communities, and that the process of recovery involves every social class, ethnic group, religious faith, and sector of society. In recognition of the fact that the journey toward recovery is a long one for most and will require support of many kinds, PFA is meant to provide not only immediate short-term assistance, but also to empower the building of stronger and more durable capacities for psychological support in the affected communities. Possible outcomes might include examples such as the development of locally operated support groups, training programs in PFA, and public education campaigns to disseminate information about mental health needs and resources.

Working with communities requires skills in identifying and allying with key resource persons, such as community leaders with sufficient influence to help mobilize people toward achieving collectively desired objectives. Providers of PFA can help to initiate such a process, but they can neither motivate nor control it. Instead, if such an endeavor is to succeed, then communities must define their own needs and objectives and become powerfully committed to achieving them. This aspect is sometimes referred to as "buy-in," meaning that those involved feel fully invested in the success of their mission. Buy-in is necessary if the process is to weather the predictable ups and downs that are certain to follow. The combination of buy-in, effort, emotional investment, and increments of success provide the foundation for a sense of community ownership that will help to assure the sustainability of community psychosocial projects long after the relief effort has ended.

Cultural Sensitivity

Psychological trauma, disaster mental health, and psychological first aid are all concepts rooted in Western social movements and thus reflect values and ideals that should not be assumed to be universal. Nevertheless, people of goodwill have long proven helpful to each other and have done so by finding common ground upon which to build bridges spanning their differences. What must always be avoided for joint efforts to succeed is any sense of dominance or inferiority on the part of anyone involved in an intercultural partnership. Where two or more culturally distinct groups meet, there are usually people with experience in more than one culture who can assist with information that will ease the collaborative process by preventing misunderstandings. In the event of someone providing PFA to others from a culturally different group, it is considered helpful to have some functional familiarity with the customs and expectations of each other's cultures and societies. It is entirely unrealistic, however, to expect that PFA providers will always know these things in advance. Rather, it is more likely that culturally informed practices will evolve over time by trial and error. Thus, good will on both sides will be the key to smoothing over the rough spots that are almost certain to emerge.

An essential practice for ensuring a proper fit between generic PFA and any given cultural milieu is the enlistment of local people as translational agents. That is, the role of the expatriate PFA operative is mainly to facilitate the adaptation of the basic psychological support model by members of the cultural groups who intend to adopt it. Selected representatives of the local community, who are often bilingual or biculturally competent, work with expatriate trainers to master the basic ideas and activities that define PFA and tailor these to suit the realities of their situation and conditions. Such a process helps to overcome problems of language, customs, logistics, and sustainability. It may also reduce accusations of cultural imperialism, since it is difficult to argue that community members should be discouraged from seeking access to Western practices they consider to be meaningful and desirable.

Supervision

Even experienced providers of PFA will encounter situations that strain their individual abilities and resourcefulness. Those with much less experience may feel timid or anxious about approaching people and providing PFA and are likely to encounter conditions for which they feel unprepared. A good solution for all concerned is for more experienced and confident PFA practitioners to provide supervisory support to others who might draw benefits from their experience. Good supervisors do not adopt a stance of authority or superiority, but rather provide gentle and respectful support and advice. They must also convey to those they supervise a sense of being gladly available, flexible in their expectations, and that there is no need for concern that the supervisor will look down on them for requesting help. In this way trainees and novices are mentored into becoming highly competent and confident, so that they too may develop the skills for providing supervision to others.

Helping the Helper

The stresses and strains of working with distressed and devastated human beings take a toll on those who provide PFA. Humanitarian service activities tend to attract very sensitive and idealistic people as practitioners. These are people who can readily feel compassion and identify with the experience of people facing extreme adversity, and so they are well suited to this work in a special way. However, they may also be particularly vulnerable to the negative effects of intensive and extensive daily exposure to pain and hardship. Occupational hazards may include developing a sense of helplessness or hopelessness in the face of such adversity, difficulty managing one's involvement in the lives of others, intrusive or obsessive thoughts or mental images of what happened to people one has helped, or a loss of the ability to feel compassion any longer. Along with these, providers may experience a sense that the organization with which they are working is inefficient, ineffective, incompetent, or even corrupt. Such perceptions are likely to lead providers to feel as though their efforts are useless and wasted. This condition is called *burnout*, and is not at all uncommon among human service workers with high ideals and expectations.

Preventing occupational hazards is extremely important if psychosocial support activities are to both help disaster survivors and treat practitioners with humanity and compassion. In recent years most humanitarian organizations have come to recognize the need for staff and volunteers to practice compassionate self-care as a preventive measure against burnout and other hazards. In theory this means that PFA providers should not work long shifts; should exercise moderation if they indulge at all in using alcohol, coffee, and cigarettes; and should eat healthy foods and get plenty of sleep. Additional recommendations include finding time to be alone, maintaining supportive relationships with family and co-workers, observing one's faith (e.g., prayer), maintaining a sense of humor, seeking supervision if tension builds up, and not getting caught up in the internal squabbles that are common in most organizations.

Although these suggestions are quite idealistic and unlikely to be closely followed by many humanitarian workers, it is important that PFA providers observe as many self-preserving strategies as they are able to follow. It is difficult and draining to provide daily support to others while not following the very kinds of advice that one commonly dispenses, but the historically heroic and stoic culture of humanitarian relief work will not easily adopt a more humane and compassionate doctrine toward its own personnel. Nevertheless as a matter of principle, humanitarian organizations bear an obligation to care for their workers and volunteers with compassion and humanity comparable to that which they espouse for refugees and survivors of disasters.

Summary

International humanitarian relief organizations have recognized the need to provide psychological support for disaster survivors and refugees who have endured extremely stressful events (van Ommeren, Saxena, & Saraceno, 2005). An effective model for delivering such services must address several concerns, such as accurate assessment of needs, coordination with competing priorities, timing, targeting, training, qualifications, and quality control. Conventional Western mental health approaches, which rely on medical models of psychopathology; strictly controlled environments; clinical expertise; conversational therapies; and medications are poorly suited for adaptation to the needs of disaster field operations, particularly in the least-developed nations. A variety of creative approaches have emerged over the past decade for serving the psychosocial needs of populations affected by massively traumatic events, but no clearly defined and systematic model has gained widespread acceptance.

Although it is neither a new nor a strikingly original approach, psychological first aid (PFA) provides promising principles for providing psychological support to disaster survivors. This method relies on self-evident activities that are likely to reduce the extraordinary stress felt by survivors without the need of professionally trained mental health workers. Humanitarian organizations have already begun to develop ways of incorporating PFA principles into the overall package of relief services they are prepared to provide. While there is no scientific evidence to support PFA as an effective intervention for the prevention of mental health problems, there is also no obvious reason to believe that these practices are in any way harmful.

The principles of PFA require providers to protect survivors from further psychological harm while supporting them through the course of their recovery. The basic goals of PFA include reducing physiological arousal, assisting with coping, and advocating for those who are unable to gain adequate access to resources or services. Community-level interventions are viewed as being more efficient, appropriate, and sustainable when compared to individual methods. Persons affected by disasters are not seen as passive victims, but rather as active and resilient survivors who can ultimately take responsibility for their own recovery. These survivors are understood to be undergoing normal adaptive processes, rather than being mentally ill or traumatized. Practitioners of PFA are not necessarily mental health professionals, but instead may simply be competent local providers of culturally appropriate social support. More experienced practitioners can provide mentoring supervision for newer PFA providers, both helping to ensure adequate service quality and providing emotional and informational support to their less experienced co-workers. In the event that survivors require help that exceeds the competencies of a PFA practitioner, they should be routed to other services and possibly referred for professional mental health management. In recognition of the negative impact that cumulative occupational stress can have on PFA practitioners, the providers themselves are cautioned to take proper care of their own physical and psychological health, and humanitarian organizations are obligated to provide adequate support, leave, and supervision for their PFA staff and volunteers.

References

American Psychiatric Association. (1994). *Diagnostic and statistical manual of mental disorders* (4th ed.). Washington, DC: Author.

Anderson, N. B. (2005). The APA tsunami relief effort, part 2. *APA Monitor, 36* (4), 9.

Associated Press. (2005, Jan. 5). Psychiatrists worry tsunami will cause stress in some survivors for years. Retrieved June 30, 2005, from http://abcnews.go.com/Health/Tsunami/wireStory?id=385369

Blain, D., Hoch, P., & Ryan, U. G. (1944). A course in psychological first aid and prevention: A preliminary report. *American Journal of Psychiatry, 101*, 629–634.

Cohen, S., & Wills, T. A. (1985). Stress, social support, and the buffering hypothesis. *Psychological Bulletin, 98*, 310–357.

Dohrenwend, B. S., & Dohrenwend, B. P. (1974). *Stressful life events—their nature and effects.* New York: John Wiley & Sons.

Glass, A. J., Drayer, C. S., Cameron, D. C., & Woodward, W. D. (1954). Psychological first aid in community disasters. *Journal of the American Medical Association, 156*, 36–41.

International Federation of Red Cross and Red Crescent Societies (IFRC). (2001, April 6). International Federation stresses immediate psychological support for disaster victims [Press release]. Retrieved April 25, 2005, from http://www.ifrc.org/docs/news/pr01/2901.asp

Knudsen, L., Hogsted, R., & Berliner, P. (1997). *Psychological first aid and human support*. Copenhagen, Denmark: Danish Red Cross.

Kuriansky, J. (2005, February 21). Finding life in a living hell. *New York Daily News*. Retrieved May 2, 2005, from http://www.nydailynews.com/front/story/283039p-242333c.html

Lindemann, E. (1944). Symptomatology and management of acute grief. *American Journal of Psychiatry, 101*, 141–148

Pynoos, R. S., & Nader, K. (1988). Psychological first aid and treatment approach to children exposed to community violence: Research implications. *Journal of Traumatic Stress, 1*, 445–473.

Satel, S. (2005, January 14). The therapy reflex. *National Review Online*, retrieved April 25, 2005, from http://www.nationalreview.com/comment/satel200501140730.asp

Schaefer, C., Coyne, J. C., & Lazarus, R. S. (1981). The health-related functions of social support. *Journal of Behavioral Medicine, 4*, 381–406.

Selye, H. (1978). *The stress of life*. New York: McGraw-Hill.

Simonsen, L. F., & Reyes, G. (2003). *Community-based psychological support: A training manual*. Geneva, Switzerland: International Federation of Red Cross and Red Crescent Societies.

Thorne, F. C. (1952). Psychological first aid. *Journal of Clinical Psychology, 8*(2), 210–211.

van der Kolk, B. A., Weisaeth, L., & van der Hart, O. (1996). History of trauma in psychiatry. In B. A. van der Kolk, A. C. McFarlane, & L. Weisaeth (Eds.), *Traumatic stress*. New York: Guilford Press.

van Ommeren, M., Saxena, S., & Saraceno, B. (2005). Mental and social health during and after acute emergencies: Emerging consensus? *Bulletin of the World Health Organization, 83*, 71–76.

Waldman, A. (2005, March 6). Torn from moorings, villagers from Sri Lanka grasp for past. *The New York Times*. Retrieved March 6, 2005, from http://www.nytimes.com

World Health Organization (2005, January 19). WHO warns of widespread psychological trauma among tsunami victims [Press Release SEA/PR/1384]. Retrieved April 25, 2005, from http://w3.whosea.org/en/Section316/Section503/Section1861_8571.htm

CHAPTER 2

Interventions with Youth and Families: A Prevention and Stepped Care Model

Kevin R. Ronan, Kirsten Finnis, and David M. Johnston

Introduction

New Zealand is a country subject to the full range of natural hazards as well as technical and man-made hazards, including terrorism. Over the last 50 years, it has experienced a vast array of disasters, ranging from plane crashes, ship sinkings, and railway accidents to severe earthquakes, cyclones, and floods. Fortunately, most of New Zealand's disasters have resulted in little or no loss of life; yet many have nonetheless caused considerable devastation and disruption to families, communities, and entire regions.

Physical disruptions in the environment, however, may in turn lead to social and psychological disruption. For example, youth with asthmatic problems reported higher levels of problems with psychosocial functioning than youth who did not have asthma (Ronan, 1997). Youth are particularly susceptible to problems because of their higher dependence on factors external to themselves. In addition, one of the most prominent fears of childhood is a fear of a hazardous event (e.g., natural and other disasters). When a hazard does occur, for a child it may represent the realization of a major, and perhaps hidden, fear. Perhaps it is not surprising then that after a hazardous event, youth have been identified as the most prominent risk group for problematic and severe reactions (Norris et al., 2002).

Youth are often reliant on adults for physical and emotional support. Following a disaster, parents not only have to try and regain normalcy in their own lives but also have to look after their children. This can create additional stress. When support cannot be provided, any initial problems being experienced by a youth may then escalate. In addition to direct support and guidance, youth also take cues from those around them on how to behave and cope. Thus, if a child sees that a parent is stressed and upset, these features are much more likely to be seen in the child. We have also found this to be a reciprocal influence: Children also influence their parents through the child's own learning and adaptations (e.g., Ronan & Johnston, 2003). This relationship between a youth's social and emotional functioning and his or her parents' functioning seems like common sense, but it also has empirical support (e.g., Larson & Richards, 1994; Ronan, 1997, Ronan & Johnston, 1999). In fact, for youth parental distress and family factors are among the more prominent, if not the most prominent, factors predicting their own distress. In other words, "as parents go, so too their kids." Being in a family also represents another risk factor, particularly when features we discuss later are apparent. On the basis of a large accumulation of evidence to date, it is clear that many youth and families will need assistance following a major event.

So after a disaster, how do we go about providing psychological support to youth and families? As in most countries, New Zealand does not have the economy to support vast sums being spent on providing mental health care following every disaster or hazard event, nor does it have the manpower to supply it. Therefore, any resources that are available must be used wisely. Interventions have to be planned to help the most people, most effectively, using the least costs and personnel in the shortest practical time possible. Moreover, the interventions used should be chosen on the basis of reliable evidence of their relative effectiveness. Evidence-based interventions are those that (a) use elements identified in the research literature and (b) are systematically evaluated in more local contexts using outcome evaluation tools that are compatible with the resources available to the practitioner.

In terms of using evidence-based interventions, we advocate the use of interventions that have the following elements, in order of priority: (1) validated components like exposure, (2) factors identified in hazards and disaster literatures as those that target directly risk and protective factors (e.g., involving parents in youth-based interventions), (3) factors that have promise based on research in other areas (e.g., interventions for anxiety-disordered youth), and (4) those that have promise based on theory.

Multiple-Gating Stepped Care

To capitalize on available resources, an optimal way of providing support is through a multiple-gating stepped care (MGSC) approach (Ronan & Johnston, 2005). This approach enables health practitioners to "do more with less" (Davison, 2000). An MGSC model incorporates principles to guide decision makers in what procedures should be used for whom and when (Sobell & Sobell, 2000). This approach was found to use available resources efficiently to provide interventions that successfully reduced post-traumatic stress disorder (PTSD) symptoms and increased coping in school-aged youth (Ronan & Johnston, 1999).

The MGSC model of assessment and intervention itself is designed to make optimal use of the resources available to address the needs within a community affected by crises (e.g., Johnston & Ronan, 2000; Ronan & Johnston, 1999). The model consists of the following components: (a) multiple gating assessment, (b) sequenced interventions, and (c) an inherent self-correcting feature aimed at helping those not assisted at earlier gates. This self-correction is possible as a result of prescribed monitoring of intervention effectiveness and the provision of additional services if a less-than-desirable outcome results (Sobell & Sobell, 2000). We describe this model later in the chapter and make more concrete its value following a disaster to the practitioner on the ground. However, in line with a MGSC philosophy, we first describe a prevention-based model designed to provide youth and families with the necessary psychosocial resources to cope more effectively in the event of a hazard event.

Prevention-Based Interventions

Preventive Interventions

There are three forms of preventive interventions: primary, secondary, and tertiary. Primary prevention is defined as both the prevention of problems before they occur and the rapid reduction of their effects. Secondary prevention activities are concerned with early detection and intervention in the potential development or worsening of problems. Tertiary prevention focuses on treatment of fully developed problems to lessen their effects and to prevent further deterioration.

Primary Prevention Intervention

Primary prevention interventions are carried out before the occurrence of a hazard. Here they are intended to assist people in coping both physically and psychologically with the immediate and longer-term effect of a hazard to prevent problems and hasten recovery. Education-based interventions in schools and communities, such as curriculum-based school programs and public education campaigns provided by school and emergency agencies, are aimed at assisting and motivating people to prepare physically and emotionally for the effects of a range of hazards. The youth and family who respond to the interventions (i.e., become prepared) are more likely to be resilient when hazards happen.

Interventions should begin by emphasizing greater preparedness, including helping to strengthen existing coping abilities. Reducing physical danger (i.e., risk mitigation) and increasing physical preparedness (e.g., rehearsing household emergency plans) can have a beneficial psychological effect by reducing anxiety through increased perceptions of control and competence (Myers, 1989). Including education regarding psychological reactions and positive styles of coping makes youth and families aware of normal reactions and the strategies research has identified as useful during and after events. Positive coping strategies, such as problem-focused coping (e.g., figuring out a way to fix the problem), are related to lower incidence of PTSD symptoms in youth following a disaster (La Greca, Silverman, Vernberg, & Prinstein, 1996; Vernberg, La Greca, Silverman, & Prinstein, 1996). Children with more unrealistic risk perceptions who use more avoidance (e.g., withdrawal) and blame-related coping demonstrate increased upset both before (Ronan & Johnston, 2001) and following a disaster (La Greca et al., 1996; Ronan & Johnston, 1999). Such coping strategies may also be problematic for adults, and as previously stated, children's distress is related to parental reactions. Therefore, initiatives aimed at correcting risk perceptions and promoting preparedness not only need to be provided to children but must also influence and educate parents.

As a consequence, education programs at school should include parents in some fashion. Preliminary evidence supports interactive programs over those that are based solely at school (Ronan & Johnston, 2001, 2003). In fact, in terms of the "how to" of disaster education and intervention with youth, a main tenet to be taken from this chapter is that involving parents is crucially important. In the area of primary prevention, we have found that when schools send youth home with easy-to-do interactive homework aimed at increasing household and family preparedness, youth and parents both report significant benefit (e.g., increased family and household preparedness) compared to programs that do not have such a feature. As indicated in this section, another main tenet of our own work is to assist youth and families before a hazard's occurrence, particularly in areas more vulnerable to a hazard event. Space limitations preclude a more detailed discussion. The reader is referred to Ronan and Johnston (2005) for more comprehensive coverage of this topic.

Secondary Prevention Intervention

As defined earlier, secondary prevention, also known as early intervention, is intended to take place once the first signs of a problem begin to emerge. However, hazard events vary in duration, ranging from a few minutes (e.g., earthquakes and tornadoes) to hours, days, or weeks (e.g., hurricanes, floods, and volcanic eruptions). The period immediately following a brief-duration hazard event is often marked by high emotional and physical arousal, uncertainty, and fear (Vernberg & Vogel, 1993). Longer duration hazard events can see these symptoms arise throughout the event or later within the immediate post-effect period (e.g., Ronan & Johnston, 1999).

The 1995 Ruapehu eruption in the central North Island, New Zealand, affected many communities around the volcano. Photo: GNS

Timing of Early Intervention

Secondary prevention interventions are generally administered within a couple of weeks of a traumatic event but can be carried out afterwards. Derived from a fairly recent consensus-based meeting sponsored by the U.S. National Institute of Mental Health (NIMH), Table 2.1 shows the phases after impact, the goals one is trying to achieve during these times, the associated behavior and the timing of the key components of early intervention (NIMH, 2002).

Key Components of Early Intervention

In this section, we provide the basics of early intervention with youth and families based on NIMH as well as our own more specific focus on youth and families (see also NIMH, 2002; Ronan & Johnston, 2005). We provide more specifics on the "how to" in following sections. The first principle is to expect normal recovery for the majority. However, given that youth are a high-risk group, attention paid toward identifying those in greater need while supporting initial response is important to consider from the first day of impact.

To support and enhance response and recovery while identifying those of higher need, the following are recommended components of early intervention.

Table 2.1
Phases of Early Intervention

	Impact (0–48 hours)	Rescue (0–1 week)	Recovery (1–4 weeks)	Return to Life (2 weeks–2 years)
Goals	Survival, communication	Adjustment	Appraisal/ planning	Reintegration
Behavior	Fight/flight, freeze, surrender, etc.	Resilience vs. exhaustion	Grief, reappraisal, intrusive memories, narrative formation	Adjustment vs. phobias, PTSD, avoidance, depression, etc.
Role of care provider (mental health professional)	Basic needs Psychological first aid, monitoring effect on the environment Technical assistance, consultation, and training	Needs assessment Triage Outreach and information dissemination Fostering resilience and recovery	Monitor the recovery environment	Treatment

Basic Needs

The most important first step of a care provider or mental health professional following the impact of a hazard is to provide basic needs to those involved. These basic needs are:

- Establishment of safety, survival, and security through the provision of food, shelter, clothing, medical supplies, and mitigation of any ongoing threat
- Direction to services and support
- Facilitation of communication with family, friends, and community
- Emphasis on the importance of linking youth with their families

Psychological First Aid

Similar to physical first aid, the provision of psychological first aid is to (a) protect survivors from additional harm and (b) to attend to the most distressed and provide or mobilize tangible, informational, social, and emotional support. There are other aims specific to psychological first aid, including keeping families together as much as possible and facilitating reunions with family and friends. Providing accurate information and education can also help normalize initial reactions. For example, providing parents with information on realistic expectations for normal recovery and support around their instrumental role of parents in their child's coping and recovery is recommended. Resources and supports available in the community and elsewhere (e.g., Internet, media) that can assist short- and longer-term coping and resilience are commonly provided. Another aim is to reduce psychological arousal and differentiate between those who appear to be having normal reactions and those at increased risk for longer-term problems.

Environmental Monitoring

It is important to continually monitor the postdisaster environment during the impact stage. This includes observing and listening to those who seem most affected to detect additional stressors and ongoing threats. During this stage, identifying services that are or are not being provided and media coverage of the event are also useful. With respect to youth and families, enlisting the support of local schools in these monitoring efforts is also recommended.

Technical Assistance and Consultation and Training

The intention of providing assistance, consultation, and training is to increase the capacity of relevant organizations, caregivers, responders, and community leaders to provide what is needed to reestablish community structure, foster family recovery and resilience, and safeguard the community. Schools are among the key community resources for providing structure, services, and support to families. By placing a significant amount of the assistance and consultation resources into getting schools back into action as soon as possible, communities can begin to resume pre-impact levels of functioning faster. Consistent with the principles of psychological first aid, giving children a significant portion of their daily routine back also gives parents the opportunity to get their daily routine back. It tells the community the value of getting its routine back, both with respect to the work day and with private family time. Normalcy and routine lessen the stress on everyone. In addition, school settings can be used for intervention efforts after a disaster.

Needs Assessment

Needs assessment is conducted during the period immediately following a disaster. This process determines the current status of individuals, families, groups or populations, institutions, and systems, and whether their needs are being addressed, what the recovery environment offers, and what additional interventions are needed.

Triage

The goal of triage is to do the greatest good for the greatest number of victims. This includes screening for those at most risk of longer-term problems and directing them toward appropriate treatment and resources.

Outreach and Information Dissemination

Outreach is recommended because most survivors do not seek mental health services following a catastrophic event. In fact, those youth and families most in need may be least likely to seek help (Ronan & Johnston, 2005). People need to be informed about different services, coping, and recovery processes. Information and education can be disseminated in the following ways:

- Flyers and brochures
- The Internet
- Mass media interviews, press releases, and informative programs
- Established community structures such as church groups and supportive agencies
- Face-to-face interaction by mental health care providers and social service personnel who physically get among the people and talk to them personally

Fostering Resilience and Recovery

The overall goal of early intervention after a hazard event is to promote resilience and recovery in those affected while screening for those who might need more direct forms of assistance. The steps to achieving this goal are as follows (NIMH, 2002):

- Promote social networking, especially with natural social (family, friends, neighbors, workmates, and school students) and community-based supports, but do not force it.
- Provide education and information on
  - How stress is normally experienced by individuals, families, and the wider community.
  - Normal reactions to abnormal events; including re-experiencing, avoidance/numbing/dissociative, and hyperarousal tendencies (subthreshold PTSD and acute stress disorder [ASD] symptoms) versus the abnormal reactions (PTSD and ASD symptoms).
  - Useful coping skills, including activating familiar and previously effective coping styles.
  - Risk and protective factors, including parents' importance to their children, the role of returning to family routines, active coping, and seeking social and other forms of support.

○ Available services and where to seek help.
- Provide personnel with training in risk assessment and screening skills, and then conduct screening and assessment and identify those of high need.
- Provide a mechanism for identification and referral of those at risk by others close to the at-risk youth (parents, teachers). Those of highest need may not recognize or may deny their symptoms and therefore not seek the needed services. Those close to the person, who have recognized the symptoms of stress, need to be able to know where help can be located for them. This is especially applicable to youth, because many, particularly young children, will not fully understand what they are going through or will deny symptoms (Ronan & Johnston, 2005). Parents may also deny their own symptoms, which in turn makes it more difficult to recognize problems in their children.
- Offer intervention for those who require it in the way best suited to their needs (e.g., individual, family-based, group-based, school-based, community-based) with the aim of reducing problems, increasing skills, and improving functioning. The level of intervention should also be a function of their needs combined with the resources available.
- Repair the organizational fabric (e.g., by facilitating interagency coordination and educating and training the relevant organizations and personnel).

The key components of early intervention approaches fit within our MGSC philosophy. First, in expecting normal recovery, our first efforts are aimed at supporting community recovery in a variety of ways, as discussed in this section. One way to provide information concisely to many in the community is through the press. We provide in Figure 2.1 an example of a recent press release following some recent large-scale flooding.

Second, while supporting recovery, locating those vulnerable to longer-term effects is imperative. Once identified, provision of training, resources, and actual interventions is crucial to make vulnerable populations more resilient. The next section provides information on how to implement the sequence of a MGSC approach. Having provided some initial support to the community, assessment then is used to identify the level of need.

The First Gate: School-Based Screening

The first gate after the impact of a hazard event is to conduct a general screening to locate those youth who might be at risk in a given community. To fit with the MGSC philosophy, screenings need to be conducted in the most efficient way possible, and in the case of youth, this can most efficiently be done in schools.

[Name of Organization and Contact Details]

Press Release

TO: [insert name]

FROM: [insert name]

Anxiety and stress a natural reaction to flooding

People affected by flooding need to understand that the symptoms of stress they may be experiencing are to be expected. Some can adapt to them in the short term, and the symptoms are likely to reduce once the situation returns to normal. Common reactions include different thoughts, concentration difficulties, recurring dreams, feeling numb or disconnected, feeling on edge, angry, depressed, or even having a sense of hopelessness about the future. Parents might feel overprotective. Sleep may be a problem for some; others may isolate themselves from natural support systems or have increased conflict with those close to them.

Disaster psychology expert **[insert name]** explained, "Take the example of feeling numb. It is not a dissimilar process physically when we go out into very cold weather. The body tries to adapt to that cold weather in various ways—one of them is to get physically numb, particularly in exposed places of the body. Similarly, when very stressful events happen, a common reaction for some can be a numbing feeling—an attempt psychologically to adapt to the situation in the short term."

[insert name] says that people have such natural coping systems and, despite extreme stress and loss, most are able to adapt and heal with time. This is particularly so when certain factors are in place.

"The majority of people recover naturally. Interestingly, one thing that can help some is simply being reassured that they are likely to feel better over time. Part of helping along this natural process can come through trying to resume regular activities and routines to the extent possible, not to be shy in asking for support from and talking to families, friends, neighbors and other supports in the community, and of course to try to look after oneself and one's family, to sleep well, eat well, re-establish family routines."

Figure 2.1   Sample Press Release

[insert name] says this natural process means many people will not require direct assistance from health and counseling professionals. Citing the aftermath of September 11 in the United States, [insert name] says the number of people diagnosed with post-traumatic stress disorder was less than expected and that the majority (over two-thirds) who received an initial diagnosis of Post-Traumatic Stress Disorder after the disaster were diagnosis free 4 months later.

According to [insert name], "Feelings of stress, depression, numbness, of being disconnected are normal reactions to an abnormal event. In the first instance, survival is the most important issue of course—organizing shelter, family, food, livelihoods—but once physical needs have been better secured, people may start to think about or experience problems with their psychological well-being. I would also add that when people are able to take care of physical needs and feel supported by others in a community, common sense and research, suggest that these activities themselves often have a useful effect on how people are feeling. However, it should also be stressed that a range of feelings is normal in events like this, and some acceptance of those feelings in oneself and others as normal can quite often be helpful as well. By extension, although it can be difficult at times, patience can also help—patience with others and with oneself. In addition, not isolating oneself and maintaining connections with others, while not easy for some in these circumstances, can also be helpful."

He stresses however, the importance of seeking help for people who are struggling with stress and unhappiness in the aftermath, particularly if it begins to interfere with daily living in a significant way or things don't get better for a period of time once the external situation has returned to a more normal state. If people do seek assistance, approaches have been developed, some supported by sound research, that are aimed at assisting people cope with the stress of such an event.

[insert name] can be contacted: [insert contact details here].

For more information please contact [insert contact person and contact information here].

Figure 2.1 (continued)

Despite the self-corrective emphasis of the MGSC philosophy, the natural recovery process is not sufficient for everyone. As a consequence, observations by teachers using a screening-based assessment can help with recognizing problems and identifying which children are at greatest risk. This process may continue into a post-treatment phase (a second gate) and even lead to a 1-year follow-up assessment (third gate) for identifying those who may not have responded well to previous interventions (Chemtob, Nakashima, & Carlson, 2002).

There is also a need for people other than parents to be able to provide referral for children. Parents have been found to underestimate the stress their children experience after a traumatic event (Giaconia et al., 1995; Handford, Dickson Mayes, & Mattison, 1986) and might mistake trauma symptoms for behavior that is characteristic of that age (e.g., play-acting, withdrawal). They also may simply deny the presence of their symptoms all together (Almqvist & Brandell-Forsberg, 1997).

Successful school-based screenings are not always achieved. A citywide school-based screening program was attempted following the Oklahoma City Bombing. Although supported by the superintendent of schools, individual schools were left to decide whether or not screening would occur in their school. A number refused to have their schools participate on the basis of a perception that children at risk had already been identified (Gurwitch, Sitterle, Young, & Pfefferbaum, 2002). Data on mental health use and the prevalence of PTSD symptoms appear to have later cast doubt on whether youth in need were in fact adequately identified.

Many youth choose to suffer in silence or minimize their reactions, perhaps thinking that they will protect their parents, teachers, and other adults by doing so (Gurwitch et al., 2002). They might also minimize distress to protect themselves from negative social consequences, such as being teased by peers (Ronan & Johnston, 2005). Although ultimately inhibiting recovery, the latter reason may be somewhat beneficial in the short term. Johnson, Thompson, and Wilkinson (2002) found that children with emotional problems who express emotion appear to be at increased risk of being bullied.

Research findings indicate that various factors may make youth and families with mental health needs difficult to identify. For instance, adults who are most in need of services may not be willing to identify themselves or seek assistance, perhaps as it might be perceived as revealing a weakness of sorts (e.g., Sprang, 2000). Mistrust of helping professionals, lack of awareness of the extent of the problem, and avoidance-related coping may be other reasons for not seeking help by both adults and youth. Therefore, any early form of assistance should emphasize not only providing information about additional help but also features that might indicate a potential referral for assistance.

Oiling the Gate: Overcoming Obstacles

Obstacles must be identified and addressed when planning a school screening program. Essentially, the first screening and assessment gate in particular may require some "lubrication." Assessment will be more difficult to undertake when a community is not particularly keen on letting school personnel, psychologists, and other mental health professionals screen children or families for signs of trauma. Therefore, lubrication in the form of information that clarifies the benefits of screening and assessment is recommended.

Community leaders should be the first people to which this information is supplied, as they are key to the community (Gurwitch et al., 2002). These include political leaders and local government staff, nongovernment agency personnel, emergency managers, school and education board staff, and media outlets. Information supplied to these key people before a screening is likely to reach many members of the community. The public is more likely to trust information from one of these sources, or better yet, when it is supplied by multiple credible sources. Importantly, the public should receive consistent messages from these sources, thus earning confidence and increasing the odds of participation in constructive activities. We know from research before a disaster that the public is more ready to follow recommendations from multiple trusted sources that provide consistent and specific messages (e.g., Mileti, 1999; Ronan & Johnston, 2005).

The information should be provided to school and community leaders and then to the public, first through face-to-face meetings and later by press releases and interviews. Once important stakeholders buy in, the message to the school community should consistently emphasize the following in direct and user-friendly language:

1. Early assistance that includes screening is beneficial.
2. Screening fits into the recovery process; demonstrate this by describing the basics of the MGSC philosophy and supporting research.
3. Screening is straightforward and brief.
4. The program reflects well on a school community's ability to look after its own.
5. There is no evidence that participation in such programs is harmful.

Evidence for this latter point comes from a recent study demonstrating not only that victims of traumatic, intensely personal experiences overall tolerated an assessment experience with little problem but that some actually viewed it as an "interesting and valuable experience" (Griffin, Resick, Waldrop, & Mechanic, 2003).

Engaging the School Community, Training, and Procedures

Once a school community is receptive to assessment, they then have to be engaged in the screening program. As yet, there is no consensus on how best to screen youth and families (Gurwitch et al., 2002). Various guidelines have been proposed for the screening and treatment of trauma as well as for the effects of disaster and mass violence. A strategy designed specifically for identifying and screening youth and families has been derived from these guidelines and other recent research (Griffin et al., 2003; Norris et al., 2002).

Means of engaging the school will also depend on the role of the screening provider. School personnel (e.g., principals, school psychologists, and guidance counselors) obviously should be closely involved in school-based screenings. These screenings need not be limited to (a) youth self-assessment in the classroom environment but can also include (b) a screening or nomination instrument filled out by teachers and (c) a similar measure that can also be filled out by parents. Emergency management and other personnel may be conducting community-wide screenings. If so, they should be done in coordination with school-based efforts. Remember, the best screening questionnaires are easy to administer, easy to complete, and easy to interpret. Finally, screenings of any sort need to conform to current ethical guidelines (NIMH, 2002).

School-based screenings and subsequent interventions should be carried out soon after a hazard event, during the transition from the response to recovery phase, and after the dissemination of some early intervention–based information (as described earlier). However, before the screening and subsequent intervention program are implemented, a range of school and community professional and volunteer groups may benefit from training about aspects of mental health care services. Basic content of training should include (NIMH, 2002; Ronan & Johnston, 2005):

- Response structures and processes:
  - Response plans and agencies, organizational relationships, mental health response, what to expect, ethics of disaster mental health response
- Evidence-based interventions, content and skills:
  - Goals of intervention, psychological first aid, social support, referral to mental health services, and reliable interventions (e.g., cognitive-behavior therapy [CBT])
- Considerations in intervention:
  - Matching interventions to settings, survivors, and post-event phases
  - Identification of those at increased risk for mental health problems, including at-risk youth and families
  - Other risk and protective factors
  - Other areas such as cultural issues, mass media, and support worker stress

Preferably, training programs should already be devised for such times or, better yet, ahead of time (e.g., a disaster mental health response team). School screening and early interventions can then be provided more efficiently.

For initial screening in the school setting, questionnaires can be administered to both youth and parents. Independent of the students' self-assessments, teachers can nominate students they feel to be at risk. The questionnaires then need to be examined by the collaborating mental health care professional or trained personnel to identify the youth and families at risk.

Once youth and families have been identified as needing assistance, they then can be contacted to advise them of the help available. Following contact and agreement to participate further, some additional screening and assessment for more specific features (symptoms of distress, coping strategies, availability of social support) is recommended. The purpose of this is to assess more completely the extent of the problem, identify the presence of risk and protective factors, and obtain a baseline measurement for intervention progress. However, such efforts are resource dependent and may need to be scaled back depending on the amount of resources and the level of need. Given our MGSC and local science philosophy, although we value assessment and measurement of progress, we are mindful of the practicalities in early assessment. In other words, even a little assessment is better than no assessment whatsoever.

School children visiting the Taupo Volcano Observatory, New Zealand. Photo: GNS.

Early Education/Information Interventions

In keeping with the MGSC philosophy, the next step should be to provide a form of early intervention involving education and information that normalizes expected reactions, identifies risk and protective factors, and promotes natural recovery. It should be simple and suitable for wide dissemination. For youth, one logical way to provide this intervention is through the school or classroom. Classroom groups provide a naturally occurring cluster of youth, enabling interventions to be administered in a familiar setting without singling out individuals or drastically altering routines (Vernberg & Vogel, 1993). Classroom interventions should comprise discussions of the recent hazard events by students, teachers, scientists, emergency management personnel, and mental health professionals. More specifically, the discussions should:

- Encourage open communication
- Provide relevant information about the hazard event
- Decrease confusion through exploring and normalizing responses to the hazard event
- Increase awareness of the potential aftereffects of hazard events
- Encourage the preparation of personal coping and safety plans (Ronan & Johnston, 1999; Shen & Sink, 2002)

These discussions allow students to normalize and better understand how their feelings and experiences of the event compare with those of their peers. The aim is to help them become less distressed as they begin to understand that others are experiencing similar feelings and that what they are going through is normal. In our research and experience (e.g., Johnston & Ronan, 2000; Ronan & Johnston, 1999), having scientists or emergency managers properly explain the event can also be helpful (see also DeWolfe, 2000). Making youth more aware of the potential for negative aftereffects of hazards, while providing them with coping and support plans to combat the effects, is intended to empower them to feel more in control and less fearful. Measuring the effectiveness of the intervention may also help in identifying those people who do not respond as well as most.

For parents and families, handouts provided from school are a practical and efficient way of disseminating information (e.g., referring them to useful web sites). Although referral to web sites provided by other emergency service or mental health organizations may be adequate, it is preferable to produce a site designed for the specific hazard event. The information in fact sheets should be brief, simple to read, and contain basic information on physical and psychological recovery for various needs. It should provide contact details of relevant people or organizations for further help and support. For information disseminated via web sites, it should be recognized that not everyone uses the Internet or will have access to it following a hazard event. Therefore, it is useful to distribute these fact sheets to the media and to various central locations in the community (libraries, council chambers, schools, etc.).

Linking local mental health services with schools and other community organizations (e.g., emergency services, social services) can improve coordination and service delivery. It is essential that the personnel from the community who conduct the screenings and provide the earliest interventions have some training in evidence-based practice in this area. Evidence of the benefits of multidisciplinary collaboration for the schools and communities also make this a valuable option (Ronan et al., 2000).

Getting children to define and understand their local hazardscape is an essential first step to building preparedness for future hazard effects. This picture is a child's view of Mt. Rainier from an Orting school in Washington. The community is exposed to a high risk from lahars, and a successful school education program has been running for the past 10 years (see Pinsker, 2004; Johnston, Paton, Driedger, Houghton, & Ronan, 2001). Photo: D. Johnston.

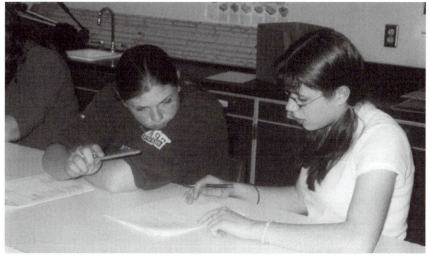

Children completing an assessment of hazard awareness in an Orting School (Johnston et al., 2001). Photo: D. Johnston.

Direct Early Interventions

Youth, parents, and families who have not been helped by educational and information-based interventions need to be offered and provided with more direct help. These interventions range from group-based and family-based interventions to individually based interventions if required. Mental health professionals are likely to be the most appropriate group to deliver these interventions because of the need for specialized skills. However, there is nothing to preclude other professionals from being trained by mental health providers (e.g., Ronan & Johnston, 1999).

Group Interventions

Among the few studies examining group interventions with youth following disasters, cognitive-behavior therapy (CBT) has emerged as the main form of intervention receiving the most favorable evaluations.

Cognitive-behavioral approaches to group interventions should:

1. Help youth to "master disaster," which includes restoring a sense of safety through discussions, education, normalizing (Ronan & Johnston, 1999); grieving losses and renewing attachments; adaptively expressing disaster emotions; and achieving closure about the disaster to move forward.
2. Encourage positive coping using a "coping modeling approach" (Ronan & Kendall, 1990).
3. Include anxiety management training techniques such as relaxation training, breathing training, and various forms of exposure (Goenjian et al., 1997; Ronan & Johnston, 1999; Ruggiero, Morris, & Scotti, 2001).
4. Cater to age groups. Younger children may need messages put more simply than older children and adolescents, whose interventions may more closely approximate those used with adults.

Family and Individual Interventions

Although the interventions used in the studies in the previous section did reduce trauma symptoms, postintervention assessment in at least one study (Chemtob, Nakashima, & Hamada, 2002) also found a number of youth who did not benefit and needed further or different treatment. From here, treatment should generally be taken to a more individual level, and for youth, this may necessarily include undertaking family-based interventions. Family-based interventions should incorporate those factors that are supported by evidence, including a CBT approach with added parent education or a family component (e.g., Ronan & Deane, 1998). This overall approach now has much empirical support over a range of anxiety disorders, including PTSD, and in research carried out in several countries (Ronan & Johnston, 2005). The key activities should include normalizing expectations, coping skills education, and information on parenting skills to assist parents in managing their own and their children's distress more effectively. More specifically, this might include information and discussions on how to seek support, manage anxiety, model effective coping, and support approach versus avoidant coping in their children.

With respect to individual interventions, it will come as no surprise to those who practice in this area that the term "individual therapy" is somewhat of a misnomer. In other words, even a more child-focused intervention more often than not includes a parent component, particularly for younger children. That is, given the crucial role of parents to children's functioning following a disaster, they need to be included in some form in any intervention with children and, in some cases, with adolescents. For individual and family-based interventions, we recommend CBT-based interventions (see Ronan & Johnston, 2005).

Summary

The MGSC model of assessment and intervention has the following steps:

1. Initial support for families, children, and the community through education should include provision of information on the normal recovery process and how to help this process along. Information on how to discern normal versus problematic functioning in oneself and others should also be provided.
2. Later, information that reinforces initial messages around normal recovery and risk and protective factors, and information to alert the community and schools to the value of early screening and how to accomplish it, should be provided.
3. Those in continuing need and provision of additional help through education and other forms of basic support should be identified, and measurement of the effectiveness of this effort made.
4. Those who do not respond to basic informational and educational interventions for referral to more appropriate settings should be identified.
5. Increasingly more intensive intervention and continuing screening (i.e., large and small groups followed by more intensive family- and individual-based interventions) should be provided.
6. A commitment to the ongoing evaluation of these attempts is vital. We use such evaluations routinely in our practice not only before and after an intervention but also in an ongoing way through the intervention itself. Even in very basic forms (e.g., through use of simple self-report and global measures), such assessment has a number of advantages: (a) continued monitoring for treatment response and the use of this monitoring to adjust services in the event of nonresponse, (b) as a type of fidelity assessment, and (c) related to this latter point, reassurance for those receiving help about the willingness of help providers

to assume accountability for measuring change and providing direct feedback on progress. This form of basic single-case evaluation represents our increasing emphasis on the value of local science to the everyday practitioner and to those children and families who deserve accountability for the services that they receive (Ronan & Johnston, 2005).

7. Figure 2.2 has a simple flowchart that outlines the basic steps. Of course, as we have indicated in this chapter, various steps in the figure may have some smaller steps (e.g., group interventions may first be school- or classroom-based; later or alternative groups for some might be smaller).

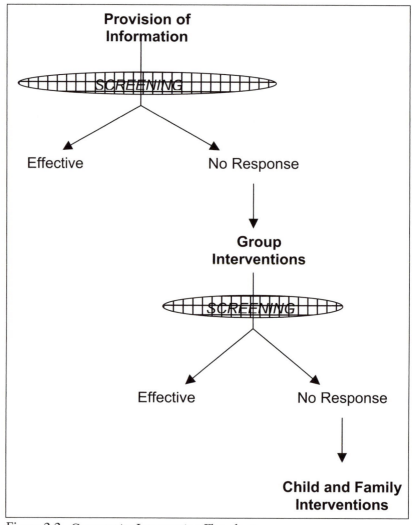

Figure 2.2   Community Intervention Flowchart

References

Almqvist, K., & Brandell-Forsberg, M. (1997). Refugee children in Sweden: Post-traumatic stress disorder in Iranian children exposed to organized violence. *Child Abuse and Neglect, 21*(4), 351–366.

Chemtob, C. M., Nakashima, J., & Carlson, J. G. (2002). Brief treatment for elementary school children with disaster-related Posttraumatic Stress Disorder: A field study. *Journal of Clinical Psychology, 58*(1), 99–112.

———, & Hamada, R. S. (2002). Psychosocial intervention for postdisaster trauma symptoms in elementary school children: A controlled community field study. *Archives of Pediatrics and Adolescent Medicine, 156*(3), 211–217.

Davison, G. C. (2000). Stepped care: Doing more with less? *Journal of Consulting and Clinical Psychology, 68*(4), 580–585.

DeWolfe, D. (2000). *Training manual for mental health and human service workers in major disasters* (DHHS Publication ADM 90–538). Washington, DC: Department of Health and Human Services.

Giaconia, R. M., Reinhertz, H. Z., Silverman, A. B., Pakiz, B., Frost, A. K., & Cohen, E. (1995). Traumas and posttraumatic stress disorder in a community population of older adolescents. *Journal of American Academy of Child and Adolescent Psychiatry, 34*, 1369–1380.

Goenjian, A. K., Karayan, I., Pynoos, R. S., Minassian, D., Najarian, L. M., Steinberg, A. M., et al. (1997). Outcome of psychotherapy among early adolescents after trauma. *American Journal of Psychiatry, 154*, 536–542.

Griffin, M. G., Resick, P. A., Waldrop, A. E., & Mechanic, M. B. (2003). Participation in trauma research: Is there evidence of harm? *Journal of Traumatic Stress, 16*, 221–227.

Gurwitch, R. H., Sitterle, K. A., Young, B. H., & Pfefferbaum, B. (2002). The aftermath of terrorism. In A. M. La Greca, W. K. Silverman, E. M. Vernberg & M. C. Roberts (Eds.), *Helping children cope with disasters and terrorism* (pp. 327–357). Washington, DC: American Psychological Association.

Handford, H. A., Dickson Mayes, S., & Mattison, R. E. (1986). Child and parent reaction to the Three Mile Island nuclear accident. *Journal of American Child Psychiatry, 25*, 346–356.

Johnson, H. R., Thompson, M. J., & Wilkinson, S. (2002). Vulnerability to bullying: Teacher-reported conduct and emotional problems, hyperactivity, peer relationship difficulties, and prosocial behavior in primary school children. *Educational Psychology, 22* (5), 553–556.

Johnston, D., Paton, D., Driedger, C., Houghton, B., & Ronan, K., 2001. Student perceptions of hazards at four schools near Mount Rainier, Washington, USA. *Journal of the American Society of Professional Emergency Planners, 8*, 41–51.

———, & Ronan, K. (2000). Risk education and intervention. In H. Sigurdsson, B. Houghton, S. R. McNutt, H. Rymer, & J. Stix (Eds.), *Encyclopedia of Volcanoes* (pp. 1229–1240). San Diego, CA: Academic Press.

La Greca, A. M., Silverman, W. K., Vernberg, E. M., & Prinstein, M. J. (1996). Symptoms of posttraumatic stress in children after Hurricane Andrew: A prospective study. *Journal of Consulting and Clinical Psychology, 64* (4), 712–723.

Larson, R. W., & Richards, M. H. (1994). Family emotions–Do young adolescents and their parents experience the same states? *Journal of Research on Adolescence, 4* (4), 567–583.

Mileti, D. (1999). Disasters by design. Washington, DC: Joseph Henry Press.

Myers, D. (1989). Mental health and disaster. Preventative approaches to intervention. In R. Gist & B. Lubin (Eds.), *Psychosocial aspects of disaster* (pp. 190–228). New York: Wiley.

National Institute of Mental Health (2002). *Mental health and mass violence: Evidence-based early psychological intervention for victims/survivors of mass violence–A workshop to reach consensus on best practices.* (NIH Publication 02-5138) Washington, DC: Government Printing Office.

Norris, F. H., Friedman, M. J., Watson, P. J., Byrne, C. M., Diaz, E., & Kaniasty, K. (2002). 60,000 disaster victims speak: Part I. An empirical review of the empirical literature, 1981–2001. *Psychiatry, 65* (3), 207–260.

Pinsker, L. M. (2004). Paths of destruction: the hidden threat at Mount Rainier. *Geotimes* (April): 18–23.

Ronan, K. (1997). The effects of a "benign" disaster: Symptoms of posttraumatic stress in children following a series of volcanic eruptions. *Australasian Journal of Disaster and Trauma Studies* (1). Retrieved September 30.2005, from http://www.massey.ac.nz/~trauma/issues/1997-1/ronan1.htm

———, & Deane, F. P. (1998). Anxiety disorders. In P. Graham (Ed.), *Cognitive behaviour therapy for children and families.* Cambridge: Cambridge University Press.

———, & Johnston, D. (1999). Behaviorally-based interventions for children following volcanic eruptions: An evaluation of effectiveness. *Disaster Prevention and Management, 8* (3), 169–176.

Ronan, K. R., & Johnston, D. (2001). Correlates of hazard education programs for youth. *Risk Analysis, 21*(6), 1055–1063.

———. (2003). Hazards education for youth: A quasi-experimental investigation. *Risk Analysis, 23*(5), 1009–1020.

———. (2005). *Promoting community resilience in disasters: The role for schools, youth, and families.* New York: Springer.

Ronan, K. R. & Kendall, P. C. (1990). Non-self-controlled adolescents: Applications of cognitive-behavioral therapy. In S. C. Feinstein & A. H. Esman (Eds.), *Adolescent psychiatry: Vol. 17. Developmental and clinical studies,* (pp. 479–505). Chicago: University of Chicago Press.

Ronan, K. R., Paton, D., Johnston, D. M., & Houghton, B. F. (2000). Managing societal uncertainty in volcanic hazards: A multidisciplinary approach. *Disaster Prevention and Research, 9,* 339–348.

Ruggiero, K. J., Morris, T. L., & Scotti, J. R. (2001). Treatment for children with posttraumatic stress disorder: Current status and future directions. *Clinical Psychology: Science and Practice, 8* (2), 210–227.

Shen, Y.-J., & Sink, C. A. (2002). Helping elementary-age children cope with disasters. *Professional School Counseling, 5* (5), 322–331.

Sobell, M. B., & Sobell, L. C. (2000). Stepped care as a heuristic approach to the treatment of alcohol problems. *Journal of Consulting and Clinical Psychology, 68* (4), 573–579.

Sprang, G. (2000). Coping strategies and traumatic stress symptomology following the Oklahoma City bombing. *Social Work and Social Sciences Review, 8,* 207–218.

Vernberg, E. M., La Greca, A. M., Silverman, W. K., & Prinstein, M. J. (1996). Prediction of posttraumatic stress symptoms in children after Hurricane Andrew. *Journal of Abnormal Psychology, 105* (2), 237–248.

———, & Vogel, J. M. (1993). Interventions with children after disasters. *Journal of Clinical Child Psychology, 22* (4), 485–498.

CHAPTER 3

IMPLEMENTING PSYCHOSOCIAL PROGRAMS IN THE FEDERAL REPUBLIC OF YUGOSLAVIA: WAS IT REALLY *MISSION IMPOSSIBLE*?

Nila Kapor-Stanulovic

Signs of strain between the republics of the former Socialist Federal Republic of Yugoslavia began in 1990 with the first incidents in Krajina (Republic of Croatia) in 1991, followed by the breaking of the federation when Slovenia and Croatia declared their independence. Fighting was brief in Slovenia but continued in Croatia until the United Nations ceasefire in January 1992. In Bosnia and Herzegovina, after a long period of tension, fighting intensified, and in April 1992, Bosnia and Herzegovina was recognized by the European Community as an independent state. Macedonia declared independence in 1992 and was later recognized as an independent state under the new name Former Yugoslav Republic of Macedonia.

The remaining two republics, Serbia and Montenegro, created a federation under the name the Federal Republic of Yugoslavia (FRY), declaring its rights to continuation of the status and rights of former Socialist Federal Republic of Yugoslavia (SFRJ). Fighting never spread to Serbia and to Montenegro, and war was never declared between FRY and other republics, now independent states, but the government of FRY and many individual and paramilitary groups took active part in the fighting outside the borders of FRY, in the regions that used to be part of former common country. The justification for their involvement was to help/protect the Serb minorities that lived in those regions.

By the end of 1992, almost 600,000 people fled from war-torn zones to Serbia and Montenegro. Thirty to 40 percent of the refugees were children, and the rest were largely women and elderly people. Ninety-seven percent of refugees at this point were accommodated with private host families. The remaining people were accommodated in collective accommodation centers. The hospitality of the local population was highly praised at the beginning. However, this "forced togetherness" placed a heavy strain on the host families. The local people, impoverished because of declining standards of living, could hardy manage to support the newcomers for a long period. On the other side, the newcomers were pressed by insecurity, uncertainty about the future, and concern about the remaining family members who had not fled—mostly men who had to engage in fighting back home. Thus, the psychological state of the entire population at the time was highly troublesome.

In August 1995, the FRY received additional influx of refugees from Krajina, Croatia. Around 200,000 refugees fled to FRY, including 50,000 children. Only a very small number of those refugees were accepted by the local families, as the economic decline of the country, because of war and sanctions, caused a sharp drop in the standards of living of the local population. Others found a shelter in collective centers. The life in collective shelters, in spite of governmental and international assistance, was degrading and hardly bearable. Children of marriages with mixed ethnicity or mixed religion had additional complications. It is estimated that in some parts of former Yugoslavia, such as Bosnia and Herzegovina and Vojvodina, about one-fifth to one-third of marriages were mixed. Thus, the displacement often involved the breakdown of the family unit.

Effect of War on Children

The psychological health and well-being of the children has been grossly endangered by both direct and indirect consequences of war. It had been estimated that around 30 percent of children refugees and 9 percent of domestic children were traumatized by direct war-related experiences. Those are, of course, only rough estimates, based on the results of a few small-scale projects; population-based screening never took place. However, in addition to direct war exposures, the psychological health of the children in FRY has been endangered in many other indirect ways during the 1990s. The dislocation of a large number of individuals caused a widespread breakdown of family units. It has been estimated that about 175,000 children lived in disrupted or dysfunctional families, are orphans, or are disabled or suffer from behavioral disorders (UNICEF, 1999).

Fighting in the neighboring regions and economic hardships caused increased rates of violence in the country. For the first time in the history of the region, Mafia activities flourished. The availability of small arms in the homes of their parents gave many teenagers the opportunity to engage in violent activities and breaking of the law. Violence on television became a strong and negative socializing agent for the children. Perhaps the most adverse factor in the development of young children in FRY was a sharp drop in the quality of parenting. Parents were stressed, frustrated at not being able any longer to provide for their offspring. Many adults decided to have two or more jobs, mainly in the grey economy, to enable them to earn a living wage and support their families. This led to their having no time for their children. Insecurity for the future troubled both the parents and the teenagers (Kapor-Stanulovic, 1999a, 1999b).

My Entry into the Task

At the time I was offered the post of a psychosocial program officer at a recently opened UNICEF office in Belgrade, my country and myself were in turmoil. The war was raging in the neighborhood—in the regions that used to be part of my own country—and there was a threat that the fighting might spread into the region where I lived at the time. I vividly remember how I felt—a pervasive feeling of helplessness and worry for the future. There was little I could do outside of my own narrow circle of private and family life, where I still felt I had some control of what was happening. To join UNICEF, I thought, was a welcome change and an opportunity to do something meaningful in the midst of a chaotic situation and resentful political system. I hoped this might be a task that would give me the opportunity to do some good and feel better again. A structure of an international organization, such as UNICEF, seemed to offer guarantees of a relatively easy entry into a new job.

On February 2 1993, I entered a newly opened UNICEF office in Belgrade. The second floor of what used to be an elegant private home in Belgrade was turned into a makeshift office, furnished with a few pieces of second-hand furniture, one telephone line, and one photocopier. No computer, no secretarial help. A handful of enthusiasts were busy delivering material assistance, medicines, food, and clothes to the refugees. I learned that UNICEF in FRY was running on an emergency program framework. In practice that meant literally "the emergency setting" and "emergency conditions for work." There was not a single manual or book and no time for needs assessment, for thinking it through, for writing project proposals, to consult, to formulate hypotheses, to rewrite the proposals, and so on.

The terms of references for my assignment were put on a piece of paper in a minute, a plan of operations for what would have to be called one day a new program of psychosocial rehabilitation in FRY was designed overnight, with little consultation with the area representative. The lack of structure in the situation seemed to me comforting—it gave me the feeling that I would have the freedom to create. Yet, at the same time, it was discomforting: The task was too challenging and highly responsible. Having had some framework and more detailed information would have helped me feel more steady on my feet.

I soon learned, to my astonishment, that I would be responsible for running the program that would serve approximately 250,000 child refugees and, to the extent needed, their parents (there were approximately 750,000 refugees in the country at that time). I knew very well myself that many of the local children also were in need of psychosocial assistance, as a result of the enormous changes in their country, caused by threats of all sorts to their security and even their survival. My first impulse was to run away from what I considered at that time a "mission impossible." Yet I stayed and managed to develop a program that a few years later would be evaluated as a successful psychosocial program for war-traumatized children.

Problems Encountered

Looking back at the time when I was asked to set in, design, run, and monitor and supervise UNICEF psychosocial operations in FRY, I can easily pinpoint a number of advantages but even more disadvantages for fulfilling this task successfully.

Advantages

All those concerned with children's well-being in the country in the early 1990s were greatly concerned. It was obvious that the children suffered. I received many calls from my colleagues and ex-students requesting instructions, mostly about what to do and how to handle child refugees, but also how to handle the local (nonrefugee)— children—their increased signs of distress, more frequent fears, panic attacks, nightmares, and growing behavioral problems. People were concerned, motivated to do "something," but how, and who was to make the first move, to organize, and to instruct were all mysteries.

I made one of the first moves in that direction by organizing, together with a group of colleagues, the first conference for over 600 local teachers and school psychologists, entitled "Children and War." However, the country needed much more than that. It was extremely important that UNICEF came in with funds and the goodwill to set in place a sound psychosocial program of operations. Without the organization's initiative, it would have taken much longer for the local professionals to get organized.

Disadvantages

The need for assisting the children affected by war came suddenly. The vast majority of the population of ex-Yugoslavia was taken by surprise with the political and socioeconomic changes that took place in early 1990s in the country. The professionals were totally unprepared for this kind of professional challenge. There were a large number of psychologists and psychiatrists in the country who were well trained but with no knowledge of trauma psychology, crisis intervention techniques, or the latest principles of community psychology. The psychological services at the time were conceptualized entirely on the medical model. Community-based services were nonexistent. Some professionals were acquainted with the basic principles of community-based approaches in providing service, but there were no practices. The medical and social services functioned on a rigid administrative structure that was centrally directed and state financed. No local initiative was possible. Volunteer work was nonexistent (even now, at the time of writing of this report in early 2004, volunteer activity is just in its beginning stages).

A sudden emergence of the needs of war-affected children and families was not planned for by the state budget, and therefore, there was no chance of getting any financial support from state resources. Anyhow, the country was getting poor. If any funds were available, those funds would have been directed to meeting the physical survival needs of the population. The feeling of deprivation prevailed among all the inhabitants. Deprivation of basic security, concerns about survival, fears of impoverishment, and for many the financial situation became grossly problematic. Unemployment rates rose and inflation reached levels never experienced before. In a country where until recently social and economic security were guaranteed for every single citizen, this represented a major decline in the quality of life. Sudden and high-speed deterioration in the standard of living made most of the population worried and concerned primarily about meeting mere survival needs. The psychological needs of the children in those circumstances were grossly neglected as the quality of parenting deteriorated as a result of the many concerns of the parents.

Although the physical health of the children has always been treated as a priority in the country, this was not the case with mental health. Mental health and the psychological well-being of the children have not been recognized as a separate issue from general health status of the children. As a consequence, talking about trauma and psychological assistance was always received with reserve. That, to me, was the major obstacle at that time for any person inside the country trying to initiate assistance to traumatized children.

The Barriers inside the Organization

UNICEF is known for its friendly atmosphere. I enjoyed being part of the organization. However, I encountered a few major obstacles in creating and running my program. My "fights" within UNICEF concerned three areas. My first fight concerned the major issue of who the target population is and should be. UNICEF policy at the time was that only those children who have been directly war traumatized could be eligible for receiving support. In the case of FRY, that meant the refugee children only.

The primary reason for UNICEF to donate funds for psychosocial programs to FRY was that FRY was flooded with refugees. These people were clearly severely distressed because of their experiences before their fleeing from their homes, in the regions where the fighting was raging; they were also distressed by their often-turbulent flight and, eventually, because they now had to live with the additional stresses that refugee status brings. There was no fighting in the territory of FRY—officially, "FRY was not in war" and no one declared war (the official statement of the government of FRY at that time). In reality, FRY was perceived as an initiator or supporter of the conflict in the neighboring regions. More specifically, FRY was perceived as the aggressor. Therefore, from an administrative point of view, the children from FRY were not eligible for the UNICEF-supported programs.

Although all those arguments were true and the policy that only refugees could be the target population for UNICEF psychosocial programs in FRY seemed logical, as they were indeed highly traumatized, I was not ready to accept this limitation for several reasons. For instance, the refugees were accommodated in the homes of local inhabitants to a large extent, and it was estimated that as many as 95 percent of all refugees lived in private homes. This made it highly difficult to imagine how to implement an effective program that would reach and include refugee children, scattered all around the country, with no proper identification of their whereabouts. The human and material resources needed to locate them would be great, and time would be an obstacle as well. Once they would be identified, we argued rightly, it would be unlikely that they would accept commuting to the premises where the program would be taking place to participate in something that the mentality of the people at that time did not consider important, such as psychosocial assistance.

One way out of this situation could have been that the refugee children be reached through the school system, as the vast majority of the refugees did attend the local schools. Initially, some attempts were made along those lines. This, however, proved to be more damaging for the refugee children than it was helpful. Namely, offering the programs for refugee children only meant that they were asked to join certain program activities that other children from the same school class would not. Regardless of whether participation in the program would have been perceived as a privilege or as a burden, those children would have felt treated as though they were different from the others. This would cause the resentment both from the refugees themselves and from the local children. In addition, this procedure would work against the proclaimed governmental policy that the refugee children should be helped to integrate into the local community as quickly as possible, with the prevailing aim that the refugee children not be treated as different in any way.

Yet another reason for my uneasiness about limiting the school-based psychosocial programs to the refugee children only was that the vast majority of the refugees felt uneasy being treated as "refugees." They felt that the term "refugee" was pejorative and was hurting them. Being of the same ethnic background and speaking the same language as the locals, they themselves wanted to be treated equally. They felt stigmatized by being called refugees and by being pushed into a separate category. There were a lot of efforts to replace the term "refugee" with more acceptable ones, such as "welcomers" or "our guests," and so on, but those attempts never succeeded.

In addition, whenever the refugee children and their parents understood that a program was aimed at providing psychosocial assistance, they would refuse their participation on the grounds that they did not need psychologists, they were not psychologically disturbed or insane, and so on. This reaction was a consequence of the fact that psychological help of any kind in the whole region has been (and still is) largely refused and is considered as something that implies psychopathology and illness on the side of those who seek or accept such a help.

The same arguments were formulated independently by psychosocial officers in other UNICEF offices in the ex-Yugoslavia newly independent states, such as Zagreb, Croatia, and Sarajevo, Bosnia and Herzegovina. Although not presented as joint statement and requests, because of technical difficulties in communications between the offices at that time, having the same requests come from those different offices made the pressure on the UNICEF administration stronger, and eventually we managed to get approval to serve both the refugees and the domicile population on equal terms.

Eventually, a school-based program for psychological assistance to war-affected children was offered to units of children (whether a school, a class, a group attending summer camps, etc.), that is, a mixture of local and refugees, but giving priority to these schools that served a larger percentage of refugee children. The most difficult argument to push through was that domicile children do indeed need psychosocial assistance and are therefore fully eligible on their own merits (i.e., level of suffering) for UNICEF psychosocial programs.

I felt that the psychological well-being of the local children was grossly endangered because they were directly affected by clear indications of the war raging in the neighborhood. Television programs were full of reports of atrocities. The world was exposed to pictures and stories depicting ethnic cleansing and concentration camps, stories of rape, forced pregnancies, and hunger, torture, and other forms of violence, touching Yugoslav people of both sexes and all ages and from all ethnic or religious backgrounds. Many children had fathers and other male relatives who participated in the fighting in the near vicinity. Those men would come home telling horror stories, and the women of the family were worried for their safety and lives. Many local children became orphans. Unofficial figures mention 600 children from just one province of FRY (Vojvodina, with 2 million inhabitants) who lost their fathers in the fighting in nearby regions. In addition, many male relatives came home as invalids. Children in the neighborhoods of those unfortunate soldiers learned quickly that it might happen to their fathers too. As a consequence, the family atmosphere was full of tension, and family life and dynamics changed for the worse. There was a forceful mobilization by the government at that time, and in addition, many young males from FRY volunteered to take part in the fighting in the countries that used to be part of FRY.

Yet another source of intense distress of the domicile children was the fact that the lives of everybody in the country were colored by a strong insecurity about the future—not a single parent could guarantee that the fighting would not spread into their homeland. Another reason for the distress of the local children was simply the fact that their parents became intensely worried about family survival. Standard of living dropped overnight, supplies became scarce, many parents lost their jobs, and many became involved in the "gray economy," which was illegal and energy consuming. Many others engaged in smuggling of goods and weapons over the border to make some money. Many parents took more than one job to make ends meet. All those parents became less caring, often depressed, often overworked, and less tolerant of their children. I knew very well that frustrated, depressed, and stressed parents cannot provide high-quality parenting.

Many children had to start making money by reselling smuggled goods. The streets were full of children selling smuggled items. For older children, there was a huge confusion about the "us" and "them." Those who were citizens of the same country became all of the sudden "them"—dangerous, evil enemies. Moral confusion was pervasive. Western mass media formed a strong campaign portraying "the Serbs" (a predominant ethnic group in the FRY) as being bad, conflict provoking, evil, and so on. These stereotypes made many youngsters (and not only youngsters) feel stigmatized—a crisis of identity for sensitive teenagers was a predominant feature at that age. In sum, domicile children have been stressed, traumatized, neglected, abused, and forced to labor, and I strongly felt that they also needed psychosocial assistance. After many discussions and debates I won the fight, and all the children living at the time in FRY became eligible for UNICEF programs.

My second "fight" was about the upper age limit of the children eligible for the assistance. UNICEF policy at that time (it has been changed since) was that this limit was 14 years of age. I was fully aware of the fact that older children—the adolescents—were in great need of help, often made even greater because many of them were fully aware of the effect of what had happened to them and their families and were also fully aware of the consequences for their future. In addition, many of them, having been old enough, had been treated by the "other" side in the conflict not as children but, rather, as grown-ups, meaning that they had been directly exposed to the atrocities. I won this battle by being allowed to implement the programs that would include teenagers on the grounds that they would soon become the parents. Naturally, parents have always been permitted into all UNICEF programs. Although cumbersome, this decision was a welcoming sign of flexibility and UNICEF readiness to accommodate the local requests. Finally, all the children from birth, preschool, elementary, and secondary school became eligible for the programs for psychosocial assistance.

The third "fight" was about the duration of financial support to each project. Namely, each project that I would prepare, together with my counterparts, was meant to be approved at that time in early 1990s for three months' duration only. Although I could understand the reasons for such a decision by the UNICEF management bodies, this policy was highly frustrating for me and my counterparts. We could be promised that the funds would be approved for continuation, but we could never know for sure that the next phase would be approved. This caused uncertainty and demotivated the counterparts.

Psychological intervention programs do need time—usually much longer than three months. They take time in the phase of project conceptualization and in the administrative arrangements phase. In addition, the implementation is never a "one-shot" intervention. Each intervention program requires time to be implemented if any reasonable effect is to be expected. Three months is a very short time for the preparation of the protocol, for sensitization of potential staff, for getting approvals from the local authorities (such as responsible ministries and school administrators), for training the staff who will be responsible for implementation in different settings, and for monitoring, supervision, and so on. This obstacle was never resolved, and we all had to learn to live with it.

What Helped?

What helped me the most was to become highly flexible and take an "open mind" stance, to be open for improvisations, for new twists in any situation, for new approaches in solving professional challenges, and for dealing with people. I also soon learned that emergency situations demand emergency responses. What I learned before had to be unlearned to allow for the acceptance of the principles of emergency psychology. What also helped was an immense professional satisfaction when I realized that I was able to help so many in so short a time—and that is what emergency psychology is all about.

Lessons Learned

Of many lessons learned I will mention just a few.

What to Do When a Large Number of People Need to Be Served

The main challenge in organizing and providing assistance to people affected by war (or any other type of disaster) is the large number of individuals in need of psychosocial assistance. That usually causes a disproportion between the number of professionals who can assist them and those who need assistance. To overcome that challenge, I found that the best approach is to attempt a so-called cascade system of training. A core group of professionals, carefully selected, undergoes training in techniques appropriate for providing psychosocial assistance and relief to the population. After having been trained, they are requested to spread their newly acquired knowledge to new groups of trainees. That is, each member of the first core group is to train another group of professionals. In that way, the skills required for the implementation of the assistance program spread through the region or the country quickly, increasing the number of providers and reaching even the most remote parts of the population.

Involve Nonprofessionals

An appropriate balance between professionals and nonprofessionals in each program of psychosocial assistance is welcomed. Nonprofessionals can be of help in at least two ways. Once being trained for provision of some simplified forms of assistance, nonprofessionals are capable of identifying those in need of more professional help and can refer them to specialists in the field.

How Much Is Research Needed?

I have often been confronted with proposals from local professionals to conduct in-depth research before implementing any intervention programs. Although I have been earning my bread and butter for years conducting academic studies, it is my deep conviction that research is not a priority in societies affected by an armed conflict. We do know that wars affect children in the most adverse way. What is needed is simple assessment and screening to identify those who are in real need of specialized services, but it is not justifiable to do research for the sake of research alone in times of emergencies. Research just for the sake of research should be avoided.

Physical versus Psychosocial Well-Being, or Both?

The psychosocial well-being of affected population deserves far more policy and program intervention than is often exercised. Too often, the only aim of policy makers and fund providers is material assistance. In any emergency, securing physical survival is clearly the first priority, but it should not be the only priority, as happens too often. This clearly results from lack of information about the detrimental effects of stressful experiences on the overall development of children.

I remember my many meetings with various decision makers in different parts of the world, frustrated in an attempt to get the idea through that the emotional well-being of individuals is as important as their physical health. This is especially true when the children are in question. Every effort should be made to convey to the policy makers and donors that traumatic experiences may forever influence how children perceive the world, how they think about themselves, and how they relate to others—that people should be protected from psychosocial harm resulting from the stress.

The Name of the Program Matters

On a number of occasions, I encountered dilemmas as to the nature of psychosocial assistance. I always insisted on naming the programs "psychosocial" rather than "psychological" or "counseling" or "recovery" What do I mean by psychosocial? The notion of psychosocial care gives greater recognition to the importance of the social milieu and social processes both at the causal as well as the intervention level. It also helps to alleviate the stigma attached to psychological care that is too often associated with psychopathological care. Psychosocial distress caused by armed conflicts and socioeconomic hardships is the result of seeking to respond to overwhelming threat, not a sickness to be cured or a mental dysfunction. The concept of distress, rather than disorder, is important to the individuals involved because it relieves them of the stigma of mental disorder and therefore facilitates assistance seeking. For service providers, it conveys the message that they are expected to adopt appropriate and novel crisis intervention strategies. Psychosocial assistance should be conceived as a process, a set of ongoing actions aimed at ensuring that children's normal growth and developmental needs are met and that the special needs created by traumatic experiences are filled to the extent possible. Psychosocial intervention is not and should never be a one-time intervention or an on-and-off process.

The concept of psychosocial assistance is difficult to communicate to the decision makers, donors, and humanitarian organizations. Psychosocial intervention is too often equated with medical assistance, a one-shot vaccination program, or a one-session physical checkup. At one point, we were asked, "Will a two-day training seminar be enough for you to train local people in war post-trauma interventions?" What this decision maker had in mind was the two days that were long enough to train locals in administering a vaccination program.

Circles of Vulnerability

In each disaster situation there will be differences in the extent of exposure to distress. Some children will be more exposed and more traumatized, but it is important to try to reach as many as possible. Thus, one should not search only for those who have been subjected to extremely severe traumatic experiences. They certainly need full attention, yet the focus should be much broader. In communities affected by many disasters or by armed conflicts accompanied by many hardships, what is needed is a broad-based concept of need and attention to be given to the individuals whose distress and needs are less obvious—"the silent majority," as I tend to call them.

Keep the Focus on Psychological Well-Being, Not on Distress

The medical model of disease is still the predominant model in many countries of the world. In the case of people distressed by armed conflict, there is the danger that, according to that model, those individuals could be perceived by the community as being sick, disturbed, and so on. PTSD symptoms are usually proclaimed as a sign of weakness, which is not an acceptable reaction to traumatic exposure. PTSD sufferers are stigmatized, which only worsens their problems and makes their recovery more difficult. What is needed is a switch from the concept of distress as a disease to a notion of distress and crisis as potential for development. Instead of focusing on symptoms and damages, it is recommended that focus be placed on coping and resilience.

Good programs should focus on coping strengths and psychosocial well-being, not simply distress and injury. Emphasis should be given to crisis as a potential opportunity for development. Programs are needed whose goal is not to treat symptoms of distress or label persons with distress. The goal should be to assist persons to assist themselves and those around them and not to become dependent (and therefore even more helpless) on outside help.

School-Based Intervention Programs

Children are the most vulnerable part of the population during wars (and other types of disasters), and they deserve special attention. Given the large number of children who are nowadays adversely affected by war stress and are traumatized by war-related adversities, the provision of assistance through the school system is a highly recommended approach. This is because, in each society, a large majority of the children attend schools and therefore can easily be reached by psychosocial intervention programs there. Teachers are already in close contact with their pupils, are closely involved in their lives, and are motivated to assist the children. Teachers and care providers are, in addition to parents, influential in maintaining the well-being and in meeting the urgent needs of the children affected by armed conflicts. My experience has shown me that teachers are receptive to and interested in understanding and improving the skills needed for dealing with the psychosocial difficulties of the children with whom they have contact. They often have little training in the psychosocial needs of children, however, and they should be warned that their need for control and authority has to give way to tolerance and understanding, so that they do not exacerbate the children's problems. Reaching children through their teachers and helping a child traumatized by war should be high on the priority list of all concerned. Enabling the school staff to implement recovery programs and provide relief to their pupils increases their feeling of professional competence and strengthens their self-esteem.

Involve Parents and the Family

Interventions should, above all, focus on enhancing family efforts to assist their children in times of crisis. Yet some families are unable to protect and provide for their children. In such cases, parents could and should receive assistance to deal with their own needs before they are fully able to meet the needs of their children. This is a much more appropriate approach than burdening the parents with "you should" and "you must." Such pressures and requests may only worsen their ability to function appropriately. Parents are already suffering when they are unable to protect and adequately provide for their children. In helping the parents to help the children, we achieve two goals: we empower the parents, and through this, we provide better parenting for the children.

Enhance Therapeutic Communication within the Family

That therapeutic communication with individuals in crisis is a must is a well-known fact. However, I observed that the parents themselves, when affected by adversities, often do not communicate in the most appropriate way. Sometimes this is a result of their lack of needed communication skills, and sometimes life was too harsh for them, and they may have stopped using the skills they had known before. Most often, in all the authoritarian societies there was a lack of communication providing for empathy, attentive listening, and permissiveness.

For both children and parents, discussion facilitates efforts to understand, plan, react, and emotionally process. High priority should be given to providing support that will help parents and care-providers to better understand and be able to meet the psychological needs of their children. Most important for children are the discussions that occur in the home. Suggestions concerning ways to stimulate constructive discussions with children about the difficulties and coping strategies can be of great help to the parents. Suggestions that enhance parental skills in listening to the children's responses can help both parents and their children.

In many communities, adults tend to avoid "difficult" subjects, such as death and dying, or tend to avoid sharing grief and mourning. Family members end up bearing their own worries and anxieties separately from each other. Children are especially affected by those practices. Discouraged by adults from initiating discussion about death and loss, they bear their own pain in isolation. Many times, I heard children saying that they never had a chance to tell anyone the pain they have been going through after the loss of a loved one. The boys were most powerfully inculcated with the culture of not having "permission" to share and mourn or work through the trauma experience. They are expected to be strong and brave—not to show emotions openly, and not to cry. Their recovery thus takes longer.

Special initiative has to be developed to encourage parents to stimulate and play with withdrawn and apathetic children. Effort should be made to provide emergency assistance to families in a way that enhances their self-sufficiency in managing the recovery of the children. Training in skills such as communication skills, decision making, principles of good parenting, and so on is much needed.

Support Recovery within Natural Settings

Not a single program aimed at children can achieve its goals by itself. The main part of recovery could, and in fact should, take place within the family.

The golden rule in establishing psychosocial programs for children is to give priority to helping families care for and protect their children.

Hatred Is the Problem

I found it much easier to address the needs of children whose distress was a result of causes beyond the control of human beings, such as victims of natural disasters, illness, and so on. Problems caused by armed conflicts raise moral and ethical dilemmas among both the providers of the services and their recipients. An additional problem is the intensified hatred that usually accompanies victims of armed conflicts, which clearly is not the answer. In addition, this hatred makes recovery and psychological resolution much more difficult, if not impossible. For the community, unresolved hatred may lead to victims becoming victimizers. That process has already happened too often in the countries of Eastern Europe and the former Soviet Union.

To go beyond hatred to a more positive stand and peaceful conflict resolution, to instill tolerance and focus on the positive rather than on revenge, is an immensely big and complicated task. For an emergency-type helper who is focused on emergency relief and is usually limited in time and deprived of the opportunity to continuously follow and monitor the implementation of a program, the issue of hatred and revenge that remains unresolved always causes bitterness and worry about the final outcome of the recovery.

Help the Helpers Too

Help to the helpers should be an integral part of every psychosocial program. A disaster situation is often perceived as a situation in which only those who have been exposed to the initial disaster event are to be helped. Rescue staff and all those assisting the victims are too often forgotten. It is necessary to set up programs to help them cope with the task and teach them to protect themselves from secondary traumatization. They should be assisted in exploring their own coping idiosyncrasies and using a variety of coping channels. Often the local resource persons have themselves been victims of traumatic experiences. The process of implementation of psychosocial assistance to a traumatized community should begin by giving the new staff opportunities to talk about and process their own experiences and needs.

My Most Dear Programs

To illustrate the diversity of challenges I met, let me briefly mention the programs that became special to me: the program for psychosocial assistance to Bosnian child invalids of war, the program for deinstitutionalization of the Caucasus children whose parents could not afford to feed them any longer and placed them in institutions, and the program for the recovery of 25 children who were polio victims from Kosovo. There was something in common in all three programs: permanent consequences, and seemingly little to be done to repair the harm that already had occurred, given our limited resources (both professional and material). All three regions (Bosnia, Georgia, Kosovo) lacked the material and human resources to appropriately assist those children at the time the programs had to be set in. I decided to use scarce time and resources to try to rebuild the self-esteem of those children, which had been so heavily shattered, to support coping strategies and provide anticipatory guidance for the future that realistically seemed to be burdened with the difficulties. This may seem a drop in the ocean of needs to be met, yet this was the most I was able to implement given an unimaginable variety of obstacles, from geographical distance to political and ethnical barriers, to continuing my involvement.

A Recurring Lesson

Living with the frustration of the limited opportunities to provide more help has always given rise to uneasy feelings, yet I learned to live with it. This is one of the lessons that I have to learn over and over again.

References

Kapor-Stanulovic, N. (1999a). Organizacija psihosocijalne pomoci [Organization of psychosocial help]. Belgrade: United Nations Children's Fund.

————. (1999b). Kako pomoci deci u krizi [How to help children in crisis]. Belgrade: UNICEF.

United Nations Children's Fund. (1999, March). Federal Republic of Yugoslavia: Progress report. Belgrade: UNICEF.

CHAPTER 4

Implementation of Mental Health Programs for Survivors of Natural Disasters in Latin America

Raquel E. Cohen

The population of Latin America is plagued by chronic, endemic, and tragic effects of poverty, guerrilla kidnapping, war, political upheavals, and man-made disasters. This chapter addresses the difficult challenges associated with the planning, organization, and implementation of mental health programs to assist survivors of natural disasters and other traumatic events in this region. It is designed to provide a model for the psychosocial response to traumatic events in places where survival is in constant peril. The approach reviewed in this chapter focuses on adapting the knowledge derived from worldwide disaster assistance programs to the Latin American region. The framework emphasizes conceptualizing the psychosocial effects of these events as one would any public health problem and builds on the guidelines and operational mechanisms of a "public mental health" model of mental health intervention (Lechat, 1990). It will not present the complex disorganization, fragmentation, and changes of the structures and social institutions affected by the disaster and the efforts of recovery and recon-struction. Although all these sudden changes and processes have a close relation to both the effects of trauma and the recovery of the individual, this chapter focuses only on the survivor's plight (Cohen, 2000).

Introduction

The boundary between chronic stress and the acute reactions following a disaster is often blurred. Although responses are confounded by multiple stresses, it is important to differentiate between the postdisaster situation and the decision-making necessary to assist the affected population because of the sudden increase in morbidity, mortality, and disjunction within a destroyed community. Although catastrophic disasters are random, occasional, and unpredictable, the long-term catastrophic effects on health and mental health remain for a very long time in underdeveloped countries.

The challenge becomes how to address the unique issues and consequences of natural disasters within the multiple characteristics of the countries in Latin America. What basic models can be developed that then could be adapted to the regional, social, traditional, and cultural systems of a country? Investigations and publications attest to the short- and long-term physiologic, psychological, and social sequelae that catastrophic events are likely to produce (Fuente, 1986; Lystad, 1985). The effects can be of short duration or go on to become chronic, depending on a variety of personal characteristics, including the degree of the community disorganization and the available resources for rehabilitation, emergency assistance, and reconstruction (Ahearn & Cohen, 1984; Myers, 1994; Quarantelli, 1999). These responses, which today are known and expected in the majority of the population, are considered normal for such abnormal situations (Flynn, 1999). Availability of social support systems and postdisaster events affecting the population's recovery and rehabilitation will influence the plans for psychosocial assistance to the survivors (Lindy & Grace, 1985). By using all the psycho-physiological and social knowledge accumulated in the last 30 years on how survivors are affected by catastrophic events, we can effectively organize our plans of assistance to individuals and communities (Cohen & Ahearn, 1990; Valero, 1996).

Profile of Catastrophic Disasters in Latin America

As one looks at the map of the Southern Hemisphere, starting at the U.S.–Mexico border and going through the region of Central America and South America, one could put a transparency overlay pinpointing the different types of disasters that affect each of the regions according to their geographic positions. Questions of where do hurricanes occur more often could be answered easily by plotting the events in Central America. Answers to the occurrence of earthquakes and volcanic eruptions could be pinpointed throughout the Andean Region in South America. The occurrence of inundations and landslides can be found in many countries where rivers transverse through deforested valleys and plains. Some countries like Uruguay and Brazil do not have a history of numerous catastrophic disasters, whereas others have repetitive multiple types of events. What follows are descriptions of selected disasters that had profound consequences for the people of Latin America.

1970   Callejon de Huaylas Earthquake, Peru: The worst natural disaster in that country struck a region of the Andes, killing 75,000 people—one-quarter of the valley's population.

Another 50,000 people were injured and 80 percent of the structures in the valley were demolished. The city of Yungay was buried under an avalanche as high as a 10-story building, killing nearly everyone. It would be four days before the first emergency resources arrived and two weeks before organized assistance was established (Infantes et al., 1970).

1972   Managua Earthquake, Nicaragua: Two days before Christmas, two consecutive earthquakes destroyed 70 percent of the capital of Nicaragua. The effect on all the government institutions that were housed in the city plus the extent of the damages affected thousands of citizens. Over 10,000 persons were killed, and thousands needed shelter. A group of U.S. volunteers organized a program for mental health and collaborated with local professionals to develop interventions assisting adults, children, and the elderly (Cohen, 1987). This initial mental health program heralded the increasing efforts of agencies like UNESCO, Pan American Health Organization, American Red Cross, Green Cross, and others that have increased their efforts through consultation, training programs, and budgets to assist the countries devastated by disasters.

1976   Guatemala Earthquake: This catastrophic event left 25,000 people dead, 75,000 severely injured, and more than 1 million homeless. Thousands in the capital of the country erected makeshift shelters from canvas, plastic covers, and bed sheets. They preferred these to their damaged homes as aftershocks continued throughout the day. The earthquake also affected Honduras and El Salvador, but with less damage (Bates, 1982).

1985   Mexico Earthquake: The strongest earthquake recorded in Mexico City devastated parts of the city, followed 36 hours later by a second earthquake. Damage, although limited to certain areas of the city, was severe. Loss of life was estimated into the thousands. The concentration of the damage in certain areas permitted the unaffected population to provide services and support to the survivors (Gavalya, 1987).

1985   Volcano Nevado de Ruiz Avalanche, Colombia: A volcanic eruption introduced lava, rocks, and chunks of ice into the main river that flowed down a canyon on the edge of the city of Armero. The force of this avalanche covered the city with millions of cubic feet of mud and stones and killed about 20,000 people. Homes, churches, hospitals, roads, and farms disappeared in a short time, leaving behind only vestiges of a city that had been a flourishing center of agriculture and cattle production. Rescue operations were impeded by torrential rain and the impossibility of bringing vehicles on the mud surface, where terrorized individuals held onto treetops or waited for help in mud up to their chins. Eventually a small fleet of helicopters plucked the survivors one by one, flying them to hospitals all over the country, where many of them had to have their legs amputated as a result of infection developed after their hours of waiting in the boiling muck (Cohen, 1987).

1986 and 2001   San Salvador Earthquakes, El Salvador: The first earthquake devastated several cities and left more than a thousand people dead or injured. The second temblor killed over 1,000 victims; 2,562 more were injured, and 46,000 were evacuated. Another earthquake occurred one month later in the central part of the country, adding to the death and injury totals. Over 660 aftershocks have occurred throughout El Salvador since the initial earthquake occurred. These strong "temblores" continued over the next six to eight months and tended to terrify the community. The mental health implications of continuous fear and anxiety arousal required continued support from the assisting agencies (Woersching & Snyder, 2004).

1998   Hurricane Mitch, Central America: This hurricane, which affected Nicaragua, Honduras, El Salvador, and Guatemala, was one of the most violent of the twentieth century. It entered Honduras with ferocious winds and torrential rains five days later as a tropical storm. Most rivers flooded everything in their path (towns, roads, bridges, houses) while killing humans and cattle. This event affected 1.5 million individuals, and the international assistance was correspondingly massive. Human losses were counted at 6,500 dead, 12,000 missing, and over 1 million individuals housed in shelters. The rapid humanitarian response included religious groups, nongovernmental organizations, and U.N. agencies (e.g., UNICEF, PAHO). The mental health programs varied, although an effort to coordinate all the volunteer teams was instituted by the Coordinating Government Committee established to deal with this area. The storms also produced disastrous consequences in Nicaragua and Guatemala, where the inundation of rivers produced the same type of damage but on a smaller scale than in Honduras (Prewitt & Saballos, 2000).

1999   Armenia Earthquake, Colombia: This earthquake destroyed
                several cities of an important coffee-growing region, affect-
                ing the economic health of the country. Over 200 individu-
                als were killed, and over 200,000 individuals lost their
                homes and jobs. Although efforts to develop mental health
                assistance programs were proposed, it took almost 18
                months to finally finance a team of multidisciplinary profes-
                sionals who were able to choose a sector of the destroyed
                region and apply a well-developed model of assistance
                (Restrepo, 2000).

1999   Tropical Storm and Landslides, Venezuela: For several
                weeks, torrential rain fell to record proportions and caused
                massive landslides and severe flooding throughout the
                country. Approximately 30,000 fatalities were recorded;
                7,000 more were missing, and 300,000 lost their homes and
                jobs. Several nongovernmental organizations and the fed-
                eral government initiated rescue operations assisted by the
                Venezuela Red Cross in collaboration with the American
                Red Cross. Training was provided for 50 coordinators from
                the local Red Cross and other professional who, in turn, dis-
                seminated the training and developed mental health pro-
                grams in the affected regions. The government used several
                of its military barracks to house the survivors and provided
                military psychologist teams to participate in the mental
                health component (Shriberg, 2000).

Why Public Mental Health Models for Latin America?

The region of Latin America already has many of the components necessary to organize a grassroots community mental health model of prevention
and mitigation within its traditional and cultural structures. Starting with
local benevolent organizations found in many villages, towns, and small
communities scattered throughout the Andes, river beds, and tropical valleys, many of them isolated from transportation networks for centuries until
the present time, their self-sufficiency modality has been transmitted from
generation to generation. Their government systems have generally relied
on native leaders to assist the officially elected mayors or religious representatives that have developed human links in their day-to-day needs.

This grassroots tradition can be used to build the foundation, first-level
system of an integrated health–mental health emergency program. The
organization of their health delivery system, ranging from simple "posts"
linked to primary health teams, to clinics, and to hospitals, lends the basis
for integrating emergency mental health following a disaster (Lima, 1987). It

can be accessed to build a system of preparedness for disaster response according to the natural dangers endemic in their region.

Organization Components of the Model

Additional components that could improve effectiveness immediately after a disaster and beyond include mental health principle education, guidelines for evaluating victims, communication technology linking providers and service units, and basic resources allocation. After the immediate postdisaster days, the regional governments would link their teams to the local groups (including teachers and clergy) in a "seamless system" of planned and organized approaches (Myers, 1994). A public health model would serve as a set of coordinated and integrated guiding directions to the expectations and objectives chosen by the region.

Few regions are currently capable of fully developing and organizing this integrated model, but they can start becoming aware of what resources are available. They can then identify the programs that are fragmented and have not been linked and integrated with the different organizations needed to develop the integrated program. Other communities may not have the component at the present, but they may build them during a period of time available according to their resources. It would be helpful for regions that have histories of disasters to have some preventive models to use as they obtain resources and experiences. For instance, in El Salvador there are accounts of seven earthquakes occurring between 1575 and 1854.

Use of Telecommunication to Enhance Disaster Programs

Today, with the capacity of the Internet and computer technology, the possibility of sharing knowledge across vast, distant regions is a reality. Using the methodology published and available on the Web worldwide, it is practical to consult, train, and problem-solve from the initial impact of a disaster to the final days of mental health programs months or years later, when all the experts, consultants, and agencies have left. A network of expert consultants could be identified and organized in advance to assist government officials when needed. They could provide technical advice for disaster policies, plans, and programs, which could assist in developing effective mental health interventions that adequately integrate language, tradition, culture, and other local resources.

Objectives of the Public Mental Health Model

The aim of a public health model is to promote the prevention and mitigation of negative effects on the health of populations. In disaster experiences, where little cross-cultural research has been published, much is known from experience. Knowledge can be increased from research publi-cations done in countries outside Latin America (Lima, Chavez, Samaniego, & Pai, 1992). This knowledge supports the belief that it is possible to strengthen the coping skills of individuals to deal with a disaster and to pre-pare them specifically to lessen its effect. A disaster-preventive public health model could be conceptualized to address "primary prevention" in all the activities structured to prepare and educate the population in countries of known risk in Latin America for the most often occurring disasters in their territory. Secondary prevention activities would describe the activities that would be instituted postdisaster to assist all citizens who have been trauma-tized and who could be helped using teams of local, native helpers and para-professionals supervised by mental health professionals available in that region. "Normal reactions to abnormal situations" would be differentiated from emerging signs and symptoms that could indicate pathological syn-dromes in need of further care from professionals (Lima et al., 1992). Ter-tiary prevention would consist of assistance to individuals with clear manifestation of chronic pathological signs and who would need specialized mental health intervention for a longer period of time (Logue, Hansen, & Struening, 1981).

Training, Planning, Organizing, and Delivering Postdisaster Mental Health Programs for Latin America

Governmental and nongovernmental emergency agencies should help to organize and coordinate disaster mental health programs at community and regional levels according to each country's Emergency Planning Legislation (Myers, 1994). Although most countries have national guidelines to deliver emergency services, few have elaborated their mental health component. Training and identifying individuals who assist survivors to respond effec-tively to the aftermath of disasters are a constant necessity in countries buf-feted by disasters. The workers may come from a variety of professional backgrounds and levels of education. Latin American countries must some-times wait hours or days before outside help is available, and so the first responders are typically community citizens who can respond immediately. Therefore, their knowledge of how to offer crisis assistance is paramount.

The mix and match within the groups assembled after a disaster will vary according to the region of the continent in which the disaster occurs and according to the human resources available. The initial response to an emer-gency, or "first disaster," will evolve as time goes by and the mental health assistance becomes organized, and training activities to address the specific needs of the survivors will change according to the characteristics of the "second disaster" (i.e., the challenges and frustrations that follow the disas-trous event). This period may present housing, bureaucratic, and interper-sonal difficulties, adding to the citizens' problems (Cohen, 1990).

Adequate preparation for disaster response includes training the workers of the mental health and human services agencies (Red Cross, nongovernmental organization, public, religious) that will deliver postdisaster counseling assistance including outreach activities, crisis intervention, and referral services. Training has to be adapted continually as survivors move through the different phases of the adaptive process. Continuous supervision and training is needed throughout the duration of the program as content keeps changing according to the postdisaster developmental phases. Curriculum content can be found through the Internet and computerized searches. A repository of disaster documents has been accumulated and can be obtained from the Regional Disaster Information Center, Apartado Postal 3745-1000, San Jose, Costa Rica. If videotapes are to be used for training exercises, it is important to use tapes depicting the same cultural groups as the survivors and the trainees.

Table 4.1 identifies a public health prevention program that organizes the type of assistance to fit the needs of survivors at each phase of postdisaster development. These transitional phases are used as a way to guide the appropriate intervention. Workers use this model worldwide and modify it to match local tradition, culture, religious customs, resources, and political environments.

The phases are relevant to the behavior and reactions of individuals who initially are threatened by a disaster, receive the impact of the disaster, and then begin the reconstruction, rehabilitation, and adaptive efforts of individual and community activities. Although preventive plans may be written in national mental health emergency programs, many communities only begin to mobilize mental health assistance several weeks after the impact, because of the lack of resources. Many of the programs that should be instituted rapidly when the threat is imminent could be developed in countries where disaster occurs frequently.

Threat Phase

Methods of raising public awareness in countries at elevated risk for disasters include consultation with emergency agencies, education of the public through the mass media, and shortwave radio programs including planned meetings, workshops, and conferences. The primary purpose is to educate people about ways of modifying the effects of a disaster by preparing to take care of themselves and their communities. To prepare and assist children and their family, school programs offer an excellent venue to transmit knowledge (Earls, Smith, Reich, & Jung, 1988). These messages should be crafted with sensitivity to the cultural beliefs and the ages of the children (Dana, 1993; Mileti, 1996).

Primary Prevention—Immediate Threat Phase

Modern technology has developed the capability to forecast many natural disasters with the use of weather satellites, radio signals, and television. Earth-

Table 4.1
Disaster Assistance Public Health Model

	Primary	Secondary	Tertiary
Threat Phase	• Collaboration with emergency agencies • Mental health program development • Community organizing • Consultation • Public education • Professional education		
Impact Phase	• Organize local help and link with survival efforts • Assist families during burials or shelter services • Children and elderly first aid assistance • Outreach	• Crisis intervention • Consultation to emergency and medical personnel	• Counseling •Collaboration with housing • Group therapy
Short Term	• School programs • Consultation • Education	• Counseling • Collaboration with housing • Group therapy	• Clinical care for all ages and conditions
Long Term	• Support programs	• Family guidance • Consult to community	• Care of chronic patients—physical/mental

quakes are the disasters that still surprise populations, but new building codes in some countries are mitigating the consequences of these tremors. When populations are forewarned of a threatening disaster and are given the probabilities of risk, the possibility of assisting them within the public health model exists. As shown in Table 4.1, there are multiple approaches that will maximize prevention and minimize damages. Communication, education, and coordination with emergency agencies prepare a community to act during the threat phase. It will be helpful to identify and develop a list of all the available resources that can be used during an emergency. Many of these activities, including integrated, documented plans with agencies and organizing a disaster response program for mental health, take time. There is a relation between the time expended in achieving these objectives and the effectiveness of response when the threatening catastrophe is approaching.

Impact Phase

Primary Prevention

The immediate effect of a disaster is to dramatically and catastrophically alter the situation. Individuals in the affected areas will immediately mobilize themselves and participate with the efforts of rescue, shelter, and safety for the citizens. During this phase, they will organize themselves in the most drastically affected areas and apply their knowledge of first emergency aid while waiting for resources from the outside. Following the news that a disaster has occurred, the mental health authorities of the region need to start organizing their programs of assistance and linking to community leaders to obtain data about the event.

After the first days, when the issues of survival, shelter, food, and water are the priorities, mental health issues present themselves as needing attention. These issues will continue for a longer period of time than expected by most communities (Green, Grace, Lindy, Gleser, Leonard, & Kramer, 1990). The following list presents a summary of the key issues that will need to be addressed when organizing and delivering a public health response to mitigate the mental health consequences of a disaster. If plans for preparation and training of mental health teams are identified during the threat phase, then the activities necessary to implement the program are ready to go during the impact phase. It is expected that the mental health teams are organized and trained and can be deployed to the geographic area of the disaster, where they will link with the organized, locally prepared groups and leaders. They need to be self-supporting in relation to shelter, food, transportation, and security. The following are activities that have been found helpful in assisting survivors of disasters in coordination with the local groups.

Outreach

These activities aim to provide emotional support during the acute period following a disaster and can be organized in shelters or congregated groups in devastated communities. Outreach assists survivors in expressing and understanding disaster-caused stress and grief reactions, aiding individuals to return to a state of equilibrium and function. Information is given to clarify that their reactions and behavior are normal and expected to result from the abnormal situation in which they suddenly find themselves (Cohen, 1982).

Assist Families during Burials

When death occurs following a disaster, families constitute a population at risk and in need of preventive mental health services (Kohn & Levav, 1990). The degree of loss, which may include loved ones, property, community, employment, and familiar surroundings, may be overwhelming. The effect of these multiple traumas in each individual is difficult to evaluate, but it is widely believed in clinical practice that the number of traumatic events has a relation with the difficulties in coping exhibited by the individual.

Prevention workers can also help in places where the dead are being kept (e.g., morgues) or near the common burial trenches where victims are sometimes buried as a result of fear of epidemics. Collaboration with a spiritual or religious representative is important in assisting survivors, especially when the body cannot be found or rescued.

Assisting Survivors in Shelters

Intervention procedures include the assessment of the survivors in shelters. The shelter mental health worker will have to evaluate the condition of the survivors and their ability to deal with problems and cope with the challenges of the crowded environment. A triage method to apportion resources needs to be developed, guided by the ratio of needs to the number of helpers. Interventions must be planned in terms of immediacy versus delay, depending on the emotional status of the survivor and the capacity of the workers in the shelter.

Intervention objectives for the survivors in a shelter include helping them achieve physical comfort and an increased capacity to organize their living area, as well as support to resolve problems with their surrounding survivors. The worker will mobilize available resources to help the survivors reorder their environment as the days (or weeks) go by, alleviate emotional frustrations that emerge at the slowness of the public assistance, and cope with the difficulty in waiting for the reconstruction phase with the promise of new homes.

One of the most difficult tasks for workers is supporting survivors who are dealing with the difficulties of living in shelters with minimal privacy, few comforts, lack of facilities for cooking or washing clothes, and fear of losing their meager possessions. Helping people to feel relatively comfortable in such a setting is an important goal. People of all ages reside in these spaces and each age group's needs may require different categories of resources, knowledge, and skill from the assigned worker. Therefore, programs to assist children have become a major component of the activities for workers in shelters. The objectives of these programs are to assist the children in recuperating and adapting to the trauma and a new living situation, as well as to support the parents in their efforts to deal with their own lives and exert their parental roles.

Secondary Prevention

Triage decisions during outreach activities identify the families that will need crisis intervention. This interactive process can be defined as "an active intervention technique that restores survivors' capacity to cope and handle stressful situations and provides structural assistance for restoring and reorganizing their unfamiliar world" (Cohen, 2000). Collaboration, education, and consultation with medical emergency personnel dealing with wounded survivors will assist in the recovery toward a healthy outcome (Cohen, 1987).

Emergency personnel and mental health workers will need well-trained and constant support as long as the program of assistance lasts. Techniques such as debriefing, defusing, and critical incident assistance have been found to have merit in preventing the signs of burnout in disaster personnel (Hartsough, 1985; Kenardy et al., 1996; Mitchell, 1986). Different investigators who have raised questions over their effectiveness have reviewed this preventive measure (Barron, 1999).

Tertiary Prevention

A percentage of the population will be struggling not only with the effect of the disaster but also with a myriad of health and mental health problems that preceded the disaster. The need for referral or long-term professional services may be needed. Both mental health services and physical chronic illnesses can be found in this population (Shalev, Bonne, & Eth, 1996; Ursano, Fullerton, & Norwood, 1995).

Short-Term Phase

Primary Prevention

The program objectives for consultation, education, and assistance change during the weeks and months following the disaster. The acute phase is over, and now a new, postdisaster phase, which can last months, emerges with different problems facing the survivors. Mental health disaster workers can be trained to identify the new problems, assist with their expertise, and help the local teams. Mitigation of further deterioration of the capacity of survivors can be achieved during this phase if preventive measures are taken. One important program that emerges is the school program for children, parents, teachers, and administrators. Since these individuals are congregated in schools, the opportunity to assist them as a nuclear population appears very effective if they are educated about preventive mental health approaches (Green et al., 1991). Women, as heads of households, are an important group in underdeveloped countries. Workers can assist them in their function as caregivers and help them obtain resources to reconstruct their lives.

Secondary Prevention

Counseling Survivors

This process of assistance can help individuals who need it or ask for it following a disaster. The more information is shared with a community, the more they will become aware that there are methods to ameliorate their problems. Training personnel to have the capacity to counsel is one of the most active approaches in public health programs. University psychology and public communication departments could be very helpful in this phase.

Another group that will need guidance is that of the survivors who have lost their homes and are frustrated by the lengthy rebuilding schedule of the country. Housing is a perennial problem in many communities of Latin America, and after a disaster it becomes a source of deep emotional impact. It can lead to aggressive and unusual group behavior, including violent protests against the authorities. Group therapy programs can be organized and provided by communal leaders that incorporate traditional and religious customs. These programs can be incorporated into the usual gathering rhythms of the community. This phase is beset by multiple problems, however, emerging from political agendas, diminishing international help and resources, increasing frustration, and disappointments resulting from broken promises. It will be helpful if emergency agencies are prepared for expected reactions that survivors may present some of these behaviors. They can make efforts to ameliorate its effects by anticipating this phase and by preparing supportive and assisting programs. The public media can play an important role to support healthy messages to the community but will need the help from experts to guide them.

Tertiary Prevention

As cases with diagnosable pathology increase, referrals to professionals need to be instituted. In general, these professionals can be itinerant through the distant areas or housed in nearby health centers. Professional capacity is needed to deal with postdisaster emotional disorders: severe acute stress, posttraumatic stress disorder, depression, and anxiety syndromes that increase in severity during this phase. Other problems like increased alcoholism and drug abuse will need specialized programs to deal with the increased numbers of patients.

Long-Term Phase

Primary Prevention

A program of support services needs to be extended to the traumatized individuals for longer periods of time than generally is expected (Bland, O'Leary, Farinaro, Jossa, & Trevisan, 1996). When agencies are aware that a percentage of individuals at risk are unable to fend for themselves for a variety of reasons, their services can include assistance with finding shelter, employment, and health resources. This part of the preventive program is difficult for certain countries in Latin America because of the lack of resources. In general, international assistance is necessary for extended periods of time but is difficult to obtain. Many of the residual, chronic cases found in countries where no prevention programs have been developed remain homeless and poverty stricken, adding to the unproductive strata of society. Efforts to mitigate the effects of a disaster may lower the number of these individuals. Traditional, local approaches should be instituted to ameliorate the long-term effects of the trauma.

Secondary Prevention

Family assistance, either in groups or individually, should be provided to families that are still manifesting signs of struggling with problems left by the aftermath of the disaster. Support for these families could be sought in the traditional or religious modality of their communities. Education remains a method of strengthening the capacity of helping groups, months or years later.

Tertiary Prevention

Most cases that are remaining months and years later present a variety of difficult problems, including mental or physical ailments. Although their numbers are small in relation to the total population that has returned to functioning in their community, it is a difficult population segment to ameliorate. In general, this group joins the chronic, unemployed citizens of their community. Linking them to welfare, religious, or volunteer support systems remains the only solution in regions where there is a lack of chronic care.

Summary

This chapter has presented an overview of the occurrence of natural disasters in Latin America and their effects on individuals and communities. The morbidity and mortality produced by the recurring disasters affecting the Latin American region indicates a need to develop programs that can service hundreds of affected individuals. The organization and deployment of service modalities that integrate health and mental health developed throughout the region lends itself to a rapid emergency response. A public health model is suggested to mitigate the effects of the catastrophic trauma. The procedures known to help individuals through the threat, impact, and short and long phases are identified. The historical knowledge accumulated, the different types of disasters, and the awareness of human reactions to catastrophic events are well known. The methodology and services documented to be useful in the last 30 years worldwide support the approach to implement a public health modality to assist the traumatized populations in the Latin American region.

Conclusion

The historical knowledge accumulated during catastrophic experiences—and the realization that disasters are unique but that the effects on individuals follow a similar sequence of coping patterns allows for the accumulation of knowledge that can be adapted to different regions of the world. The morbidity and mortality produced by the recurring disasters affecting the Latin American region indicates a need to develop assistance programs that can service hundreds of traumatized individuals. The organization and deployment of service modalities that integrate health and mental health services, a model used in many countries in the region, lends itself to a rapid emergency response if they include psychosocial approaches. The use of primary health centers supports a public health approach to assist postdisaster effects on traumatized survivors. By offering education, consultation, and crisis intervention through the threat, impact, and short and long postdisaster phases, the possibility of mitigating the effects of the trauma can be achieved.

Although preventive plans may be written in national mental health emergency programs, many communities only begin to mobilize mental health assistance several weeks after the impact, because of the lack of resources. Many of the programs that should be instituted rapidly when the threat is imminent could be developed in countries where disaster occurs with frequency. These activities should be operationalized and institutionalized within governmental systems in such a way that they do not change every time a new government takes the leadership of the country, but remain stable throughout the years.

References

Ahearn, F. L., Jr., & Cohen, R. E. (1984). Disasters and mental health: An annotated bibliography. DHHS Publication ADM 84-1311. Rockville, MD: Center for Mental Health Services.

Barron, R. A. (1999). Psychological trauma and relief workers. In J. Leaning, S. M. Briggs, & L. C. Chen (Eds.), *Humanitarian crises: The medical and public health response* (pp. 143–175). Cambridge, MA: Harvard University Press.

Bates, F. L. (1982). *Recovery, change, and development. A longitudinal study of the 1976 Guatemalan earthquake* (Vol. 1). Athens: University of Georgia Press.

Bland, S. H., O'Leary, E. S., Farinaro, E., Jossa, F., & Trevisan, M. (1996). Long term psychological effects of natural disasters. *Psychosomatic Medicine, 58*, 18–24.

Cohen, R. E. (1982). Intervention with disaster victims. In M. Killie and H. S. Shulberg (Eds.), *The modern practise of community mental health* (pp. 397–441). San Francisco: Jossey-Bass.

———. (1987). The Armero tragedy: Lessons for mental health professionals. *Hospital and Community Psychiatry, 38*, 1316–1321.

———. (1990). Post-disaster mobilization and crisis counseling: Guidelines and techniques for developing crisis-oriented services for disaster victims. In A. R. Roberts (Ed.), *Crisis intervention handbook* (pp. 279–299). Belmont, CA: Wadsworth.

———. (2000). Mental health services in disasters: Manual for humanitarian workers, Document 12855; Instructor's guide, Document 12856. Retrieved February 17, 2005, from http://cidbimena.desastres.hn/staticpages/index.php?page=20040611081925224.

———, & Ahearn, F. L. (1990). *Manual de la atencion de la salud mental para victimas de desastres.* Mexico: Harla.

Dana, R. H. (1993). Multicultural assessment perspectives for professional psychology. Needham Heights, MA: Allyn & Bacon.

Earls, F., Smith, E., Reich, W., & Jung, K. (1988). Investigating psychopathological consequences of a disaster in children: A pilot study incorporating a structured diagnostic interview. *Journal of the American Academy of Child and Adolescent Psychiatry, 27,* 90–95.

Flynn, B. (1999). Disaster mental health: The U.S. experience and beyond. In J. Leaning, S. Briggs, & L. Chen (Eds.), *Humanitarian crises: The medical and public health response.* Cambridge, MA: Harvard University Press.

Fuente, R. (1986). Las consecuencias del desastre en la salud mental. *Revista Salud Mental, 9* (3), 3–8.

Gavalya, A. (1987). Reactions to the 1985 Mexican Earthquake: Case vignettes. *Hospital and Community Psychiatry, 38,* 1327–1330.

Green, B. L., Korol, M., Grace, M., Vary, M. G., Leonard, A. G., Gleser, G. C., et al. (1991). Children and disaster: Age, gender, and parental effects on PTSD symptoms. *Journal of the American Academy of Child & Adolescent Psychiatry, 30,* 945–951.

———, Grace, M. C., Lindy, J. D., Gleser, G. D., Leonard, A. C., & Kramer, T. L.. (1990). Buffalo Creek survivors in the second decade: Comparison with unexposed and nonlitigant groups. *Journal of Applied Social Psychology, 20,* 1033–1050.

Hartsough, D. M. (1985). Stress and mental health interventions in three major disasters. In D. M. Hartsough & D. G. Myers (Eds.), Disaster work and mental health: Prevention and control of stress among workers. DHHS Publication ADM 85-1422 (pp. 1–44). Rockville, MD: National Institute of Mental Health.

Infantes, V., Veliz, J., Morales, J., Pardo-Figueroa, I., & Jeri, F. R. (1970). Psychopathological observations in the earthquake area (Ancash, 1970). *Revista de Neuropsiquiatria, 33,* 171–188.

Kenardy, J. A., Webster, R. A., Lewin, T. J., Carr, V. J., Hazell, P. L., & Carter, G. L. (1996). Stress debriefing and patterns of recovery following a natural disaster. *Journal of Traumatic Stress, 9,* 33–49.

Kohn, R., & Levav, I. (1990). Bereavement in disaster: An overview of the research. *International Journal of Mental Health, 19* (2), 61–76.

Lechat, M. (1990). The public health dimensions of disasters. *International Journal of Mental Health, 19,* 70–79.

Lima, B. (1987). *Manual patra el trabajador de atencion primaria en salud mental para victimas de desastres.* Quito: Ministerio de Salud Publica.

Lima, B. R., Chavez, H., Samaniego, N., & Pai, S. (1992). Trastornos Psiquiatricos en Victimas de Desastres en el Ecuador. [Psychiatric disorders among victims of disasters in Ecuador]. *Boletin de la Oficina Sanitaria Panamericana, 113* (1), 28–34.

Logue, J., Hansen, H., & Struening, E. (1981). Some indications of the long-term health effects of a natural disaster. *Public Health Reports,* 96, 67–69.

Lystad, M. (1985). *Innovations in mental health services to disaster victims.* Rockville, MD: National Institute of Mental Health.

Mileti, D. (1996). Psicolojia social de las alertas publicas efectivas de desastres. *Desastres y Sociedad, 4* (6), 104–116.

Mitchell, J. S. (1986). Crisis worker stress and burnout. In J. S. Mitchell and H. L. P. Resnik (Eds.), *Emergency response to crisis.* London: Prentiss-Hall International.

Myers, D. G. (1994). *Disaster response and recovery: A handbook for mental health professionals.* DHHS Publication SMA 94-3010. Rockville, MD: National Institute of Mental Health.

Prewitt, J. O., & Saballos, M. (2000). Salud psicosocial en un desastre complejo: El effecto del huracan Mitch en Nicaragua. Guatemala City: Kelly Litografia.

Quarantelli, E. L. (1999). *Disaster related social behavior: Summary of 50 years of research findings* Preliminary paper. Newark, DE: University of Delaware, Disaster Research Center.

Restrepo, H. E. (2000). Earthquake in Colombia: the tragedy of the coffee growing region. Health impact and lessons for the health sector. *Journal of Epidemiology and Community Health, 54,* 761–765.

Shalev, A. Y., Bonne, O., & Eth, S. (1996). Treatment of post-traumatic stress disorder: a review. *Psychosomatic Medicine, 58,* 165–182.

Shriberg, J. (2000). Program of psychosocial support for the Venezuela Red Cross. Washington, DC: American Red Cross.

Ursano, R. J., Fullerton, C. S., & Norwood, A. E. (1995). Psychiatric dimensions of disaster: Patient care, community consultation, and preventive medicine. *Harvard Review of Psychiatry, 3,* 196–209.

Valero, S. (1996). *Intervencion psicolojica en emergencias y desastres.* Lima: Ministerio de Salud.

Woersching, J. C., & Snyder, A. E. (2004). Earthquakes in El Salvador: A descriptive study of health concerns in a rural community and the clinical implications: Part III–Mental health and psychosocial effects. *Disaster Management and Response, 2,* 40–45.

CHAPTER 5

THE PSYCHOLOGICAL SUPPORT NETWORK OF THE CENTRAL UNIVERSITY OF VENEZUELA AND THE VENEZUELAN FLOODS OF 1999

Tamara Blanco, Martin Villalobos, and Claudia Carrillo

Introduction

The devastating flood of December 1999 in the Venezuelan state of Vargas, was undoubtedly the worst disaster that country has experienced in at least a hundred years, as measured by the magnitude of the disaster, the loss of human life, the environmental impact, and the economic losses. Despite the fact that there was no contingency plan in place at the time of the disaster, the civilian response was impressive. A few hours after the floods and mudslides had taken their most gruesome toll and the rescue efforts began, Venezuelan psychologists swung into action and began providing psychological support to the survivors as well as to members of the rescue teams. The Psychology Department of Universidad Central de Venezuela, including its faculty, its graduate and undergraduate programs, and its Psychology Institute, created a Psychological Support Network (PSN). In spite of a lack of experience, the need to improvise, and the initial disorganization that characterized the work, the PSN coordinated the work of 260 professionals (psychologists, psychiatrists, and psychoanalysts) and 400 psychology students from Universidad Central de Venezuela and Universidad Católica Andrés Bello, during the initial stage of response and in the four weeks that followed.

After only 48 hours, our first task groups were operative and working in concert with Defensa Civil (a governmental department that coordinates emergency response strategies). With the approval of the Ministry of Health and Social Development, we responded to the most urgent needs, including the provision of support to the people that had been rescued and transferred to Simón Bolívar International Airport in Maiquetia, as well as to those who had been transferred to shelters in the nearby Venezuelan capital of Caracas.

From this initial response, the PSN's tasks continued expanding to address the need for psychological support in 24 shelters and to establish a crisis hotline (800-PSICO; Pérez, 2000) with the support of Defensa Civil, the Panamerican Health Office, and Venezuela's telephone company. In addition, the Family Reunification Program, with support from the United Kingdom's Save the Children, was developed. Two mobile teams were also established and went into Vargas on special tasks in joint actions—one with Defensa Civil and the other with the Ministry of Education, Culture, and Sports.

It is also important to acknowledge that the PSN received valuable support and cooperation from the Unified Commando of the National Armed Forces, the Unique Social Fund, Venezuelan Oil Company, the Students Center's Federation, the psychiatry clinic El Cedral, and the food company Parmalat. This support enabled the PSN to become one of the most positive organizing experiences of our civil society, and one that was able to successfully join forces with private enterprises, governmental agencies, and international entities.

In spite of the fact that our first-stage response to the emergency was both satisfactory and appropriate, there were neither enough human nor economical resources, nor were there adequate and necessary programs and plans to sustain this effort during the following weeks and months. Thus, three weeks after the disaster, while academic activities in the university were returning to normal, the survivors of the flood were being transferred from their temporary shelters to military bases or fields, or in some cases to housing facilities far from the affected area. The PSN's immediate goals had been achieved. To continue operating under new conditions and to pursue new goals would have required new resources and instruments. Without them, the PSN drew its work to a close and ceased functioning.

Martin Villalobos is a clinical psychologist and was one of the four founders and coordinators of the PSN that operated in Universidad Central de Venezuela in response to the Vargas floods. As a senior professor, he teaches and coordinates both the undergraduate and postgraduate studies in clinical psychology. He also conducts triage in the student Psychology Welfare Service and in the Neurology Service of the Universidad Central de Venezuela's Hospital. Long after the initial response to the natural disaster, Villalobos continued his participation by coordinating efforts to reactivate the PSN to provide psychological relief to the population affected by political confrontations in 2002. In 2003, he coordinated the psychosocial support provided to an Andean village that survived floods.

Tamara Blanco is a clinical psychologist who, at the time of the floods, was a student of Universidad Central de Venezuela's Clinical Psychology Specialization. Since 1999, she has been teaching applied psychology courses in several private Venezuelan universities and was the psychologist of one of the schools that provided psychosocial assistance to the victims of the Vargas floods. In 2002, Blanco participated in the reactivation of the PSN and efforts made to provide relief for different groups affected by political confrontations in 2002. In 2003, she led the psychosocial support team that provided relief to children, teachers, and the general population of an Andean village that survived floods.

On the basis of the feedback we received from the survivors of the flood and the public entities involved, we believe that the improvised response of the PSN achieved positive results. Nevertheless, it is also important to address the fact that many mistakes were made and that many insufficiencies in our operation became evident. Today, four years after the flood, we need to reflect broadly on what was done at the time, what is being done now, and what is yet to be done.

It is also necessary to compare this Venezuelan experience with those of other countries in the provision of psychological support to the survivors of disasters—we hope our mistakes and the lessons we learned may be useful to other countries when faced with overwhelming natural disasters.

The Central Event

Vargas is a very thin strip of territory that lies between the mountains of the national park El Avila and the beaches of the Caribbean. For people in nearby Caracas, Vargas is a natural recreation spot with many public and private beaches, hotels, and restaurants. It has a population of about 320,000 people, but it is important to keep in mind that the population fluctuates and may increase fivefold on weekends and holidays. Maiquetía, in the central region of the state, is home to the Simón Bolívar International Airport—the largest and most important airport in the country. This is also where Puerto de La Guaira is located, the second largest seaport in the country. The state's economic activity is centered on the airport and the seaport, as well as the domestic and international tourist industry, but the state also has high rates of unemployment, marginality, child malnutrition, drug abuse, delinquency, insufficient sanitary services, and a serious lack of municipal planning and development. All of this leaves Vargas in a perpetual state of vulnerability.

By the end of November 1999, the western portion of the country had already been seriously affected by the aftermath of Hurricane Lenny, which destroyed or damaged thousands of houses. Plantations were also lost, and there were landslides along several roads. So the rains of December 1999, which had been unusually heavy and frequent, fell on ground that was already saturated. By December 12, Vargas had received two weeks of continuous rain, and the civil defense authorities (Defensa Civil) sent out an alert concerning this situation. By the next day, some areas had collapsed, and the land had begun to give way. Several people were left homeless, and many other homes had been affected.

At this point, it would have been possible to anticipate that something very serious could occur, particularly if history had been remembered. In 1798, it rained continuously for more than 60 hours, causing several rivers and creeks to overflow their banks, and in 1951 it again rained torrentially for 72 hours, also causing a major river to overflow its banks. When we look back on what happened between 14 and 16 December 1999 in Vargas, we discover that in three days it had rained almost twice the annual average. All of these continuous and intense rains soaked the land and caused more than 55 rivers and creeks to overflow their banks. It is estimated that more than 15 million cubic meters of mud, sand, and rock descended from the Avila Mountains into the surrounding towns and villages. These mudslides took away the topsoil, made beaches disappear, modified the coastline, damaged hospitals and health centers, made the water systems collapse, affected 80 percent of the roads, and paralyzed the airport, the seaport, and all recreational and economic activities.

Organization of the Psychological Support Network

One of the fundamental roles in an organized response to a natural disaster is that of the media. Faced with the lack of an official source that would efficiently organize and disseminate vital information, television and radio stations provided news about what was happening and what was needed, as well as information about lost or missing people. That attitude on behalf of the media was one of the key elements used to create the network. When the news of what had happened was transmitted, in coordination with those responsible for the Psychological Support Program of Defensa Civil, a telephone conference was conducted among Universidad Central's Psychology faculty professors. An initial meeting was held in the faculty's auditorium, followed by smaller meetings in several classrooms in the psychology department.

The psychologists in attendance were briefed on the situation in Vargas to help them understand the extent and nature of the problem. They were told about the rescue operations being carried out, which shelters were functioning, and of the desperate need for psychological support at the Simón Bolívar International Airport, where all rescued people were initially transferred. It is believed that 240,000 people were injured (72 percent of the population where the floods occurred), 8,000 homes destroyed, and 30 percent of the schools and academic centers damaged. The death toll is uncertain, but is estimated to be between 20,000 and 50,000 people.

Central Coordination and Its Support Teams

Once the psychologists had been summoned and attended the initial meeting, the next organizational task was to establish central coordination and send out the first psychological support teams to the airport and shelters. This structuring was basically spontaneous and tended to acknowledge the leadership of those who from the beginning had taken on the coordination of the network. The coordination of the PSN rested on four people: the director of the school of psychology, the director of the institute of psychology, a psychologist who is not part of the faculty, and the coordinator of the specialization in clinical psychology. Though the composition of the group was well balanced, that was really not a criterion in the formation of the group. In fact, being there and being willing to take on the responsibility were the determining criteria.

One of the Coordinating Commission's central tasks was to form a team that would provide communication support. To meet this need, several students formed teams that maintained communication 24 hours a day between the university, the different authorities, and the various work teams that were being sent out. The telephone center in the school of psychology provided access to the mobile phones of the coordinators and the students that were in the communications team. All issues related to logistics and financial aspect were handled by other teams under the orientation of the director of the school of psychology, who coordinated with the university's authorities, public and private organizations and managed all expenses of the network.

Finally, though the army took on all responsibility for external surveillance of the shelters, it was important to address internal security as well, and so security measures were put in place. Basic tasks included organizing families to coordinate their own precautions, intervening with persuasive measures when there were differences among the families, or intervening between families and military authorities. In some cases, it was necessary to call the military for assistance in establishing order and maintaining security in some shelters that had no protection. In other cases, we sent teams of psychologists to mediate and intervene. Security was also needed in the transportation and dispensing of psychopharmacological medications, as well as in providing security for the Central Commission team's 24-hour operations.

Psychological Support at the Airport

The most critical situation existed at the airport in Maiquetía, which had been transformed into a huge receiving center, shelter, and transfer center. An initial psychosocial team was scheduled to go to the airport right after receiving their briefing information. They received a crash course in crisis counseling and were required to have with them a basic survival kit. The volunteers stated they were ready for immediate transfer to the airport, in spite of the critical conditions in which they would have to work. However, the number of people willing to go was greater than our capacity to transport them, and late that afternoon the first 36 PSN workers were transported to Maiquetía airport.

It was very difficult and complicated work under the circumstances that existed at the airport. Sanitary services soon collapsed, and it became particularly difficult to maintain order. While rescue work continued, people at the airport were being counted and transferred to the shelters. Our plan was to relieve the first team with a second team after a certain interval, but when communication was cut, the first team was left to work continuously for 72 hours before we could send in a relief team. This work continued around the clock, day after day, while people were still being rescued, processed, and transferred. Soon afterward, the airport was closed for maintenance.

After the initial response measures described previously, Villalobos, as one of the coordinators of the PSN, organized a work plan (see Villalobos & Blanco, 2002), with teams to provide the needed psychological support. Teams were structured according to the age groups they would focus on (children, adults, and elderly) and were composed of members from various subdisciplines (e.g., school, social, clinical, and organizational psychologists). None of the volunteers had experience in organizing emergency responses, nor in preparing an organizational proposal, so organizational achievements and errors occurred as the tasks were performed. It was in this manner during the first few days following the disaster that the central coordination and support teams of the PSN were organized into a functioning emergency working group.

Psychological Support in the Shelters

During December 1999, Tamara Blanco had the opportunity to work as a volunteer psychologist in a victim shelter that was organized in the Technical Institute Jesús Obrero (ITJO). She was already working there as the school's psychologist and was additionally appointed as coordinator of the psychology team for providing psychosocial support to the victims. The combination of theses roles allowed her to be in contact with almost all the people that passed through that center, either as victims or volunteers. The following logistical details, as well as a physical description of the center, may help clarify how the support effort evolved through several stages at that center:

- Preparation and reception of the victims at the shelter
- First phase of assistance (Evaluation)
- Second phase of assistance (Adapting)
- Decision making (preparing for Christmas and farewell)
- Farewell, grief support, and closure

Preparation of the Shelter and
Reception of the Victims

Operations were set up in the two buildings called the Education Center. The first measure taken was to turn the classrooms into dormitories on the first floors by removing desks and installing mattresses to accommodate the affected people. This was done by the volunteers under the coordination of the Jesuits, who ran the school. Different areas like the gym and classrooms were transformed into geriatric wards, an infirmary, and storage for clothes, food, and other goods. This transformation took place in only one day, and that same night 160 people arrived at the ITJO shelter directly from the airport. Once their data were registered, they took showers, donned their donated clothing, and were fed a special holiday dinner. Dormitory assignments were made with respect for the unity of family and neighborhood groups.

First Phase of Assistance (Assessment)

The first day at the center, the scene was both shocking and very organized. Volunteers had arranged games for the children, and the first impression was that those who needed psychosocial assistance were mostly the adults. On the first "round," the psychologists were greeted with a range of reactions, including tears, disdain, and gratefulness. They met regularly with other volunteers, medical personnel, Jesuits, and military personnel, all of whom started making "referrals" of victims with priority needs. The task of helping so many people who had survived such terribly traumatic experiences felt overwhelming, and so a great deal of backing from coworkers was necessary. Blanco drafted basic procedural guidelines for supporting survivors, as well as some minimal self-care measures for preserving staff well-being. That same afternoon, a meeting organized by the PSN was held, in which materials and impressions were shared among the groups of professionals and psychology students. Compared to the other centers and shelters, ITJO wasn't considered big enough to warrant sending other psychologists in addition to those already in place. Therefore, the existing psychosocial team contacted four other psychologists and organized teams who then rotated on a 12-hour basis across the first four days.

Second Phase of Assistance (Adapting)

In working directly with the survivors, pain and grief needed to be validated, and problems were listened to and discussed, for which there were few ready solutions. It became difficult not to worry about what would happen to these people and wonder what could possibly be said that would actually help or relieve them. The work being done was a drastic change from the psychoanalytical setting, as we stayed in the same environment and mingled with our residents, who became more like confidantes than patients.

By the third day, Blanco felt emotionally weary, especially because most of the volunteers also turned to her to share experiences, seek advice, or release their exhaustion. Also, although they were doing a great job each day, very few psychologists were willing to cover night shifts, so she had gotten little sleep. Rather than wearing herself out, it made better sense for Blanco to focus on the coordination and support of other psychologists and volunteers. In this regard, she contacted the PSN coordinators about the need for more attention and support at her facility, resulting in a group of 16 volunteer psychologists being assigned to rotate for the 14 days that the shelter functioned.

The first organized measures taken regarding the psychosocial support were

1. Assessment and response to the psychosocial support needs initially observed:

    a. Directly affected victims: Population characteristics were assessed to detect any special needs that different groups of people might have.

    b. Volunteers group: The people from the home community had spontaneously organized themselves, aided by the Jesuits from the nearby parish. We met the different groups and outlined ways in which we could offer them psychosocial support, including receiving referrals of people in need of special assistance or offering guidance and support.

    c. Medical personnel: The coordinators and support members (interns, nurses, paramedics, and volunteers) were contacted to meet the psychosocial support team and to specify each team's aims and limitations.

    d. Psychosocial support group: Psychologists, other mental health professionals, and interns were contacted by phone to create lists of volunteers and their telephone numbers, as well as schedules and shifts. Minimal guidelines were established on how to proceed and intervene or to make referrals, and minimal standards were set related to self-care, support, and cordiality among the staff.

    e. Volunteers (in general): Meetings were set both general and among coordinators. These meetings served two purposes: to ease tension and to clarify decision making.

2. Support strategies applied:

    a. Offer support to the adults: At first, a space was transformed into an "office" to provide private consultation for people who were in crisis, or who simply wanted to talk about their discomfort. However, after observing that most of the people who had been affected did not want to be separated from their families, we exchanged the conventional "psychotherapeutic" approach or one more similar to counseling. Just having the volunteers walking around the grounds while chatting with victims turned out to be very effective for most people, who on an almost daily basis held "consultations" with the resident psychologists.

    b. Provide support for the children: Volunteers naturally tended to fawn over the children, swamping them with attention, toys, gifts, and special entertaining activities, thanks to the generous donations of their neighbors. We thought it would also be important to give these children certain structure by scheduling activities in the morning and afternoon. This, in turn, gave parents time to rest, talk, and become organized, as well as allowing the volunteers to rotate. After the children started explaining their experiences to the volunteers, we learned to include drawing activities that could then be used by psychologists to entice the children into expressing themselves in their own way and elaborating on their experiences.

   c. Give special attention to the elderly: Visits to the elderly, many of whom could not leave their ward, were made at least twice a day. We would accompany those who could still venture outside on walks around the grounds. An escort could also help to avoid further complications when people had psychotic symptoms, physical impairments, or cognitive impairments. We were also very alert to the depressive symptoms that are common among this age group.

   d. Psychosocial support for medical personnel: This mainly consisted of listening, offering supportive words, and an occasional touch of humor, as well as giving them an opportunity to feel relieved and accompanied.

On average we dealt with some 120 to 160 people, and as new survivors kept arriving, some particular challenges are worth mentioning here. For one, each day people left the shelter with relatives or friends who came to pick them up. Thus, with people coming and going, the task of keeping track of the affected people became one of our weaker points. Also, our volunteers began to bicker over small things like their shifts. As psychologists, we decided to intervene and enforce the measures listed in Table 5.1.

Table 5.1
Measures Taken to Support the Volunteers at ITJO

- Intervene to remind them about self-care: On several occasions we gave psychosocial support to the volunteers who were becoming either irritable or rather too fond of the survivors (e.g., not wanting to go home and rest). We later concluded that, more than being enthusiastic, they were showing signs of emotional and physical weariness.
- Conciliate and promote problem solving: After some days, the various support teams (e.g., military, health, volunteers) began arguing over any imaginable issue. We responded by smoothing over differences, sometimes reminding them of their duties, or by cracking jokes to relieve tension. Many times, just refocusing the situation by admiring their patience and hard work or by changing the subject to distract their attention relieved the tension.
- Conduct regular meetings to organize and assess our work. We also took advantage of these moments to relieve tension, resolve conflict, and promote a supportive and assertive working environment.

Despite the awful scenes of devastation being aired, we decided to allow radios and televisions to be watched, because lists of survivors were also broadcast. The first few days, the people we worked with were pretty similar in their reactions, which were typical of acute stress reactions observed in other disasters. That is, they reported feeling anxious or desperate, cried easily, had frequent nightmares, and felt remorse for not having saved loved ones who died. The kind of psychosocial intervention we provided was tailored to the symptoms we met on our rounds.

Once the survivors had recovered physically, they began requesting participation in the daily cleaning chores. So on the third day, each dormitory was assigned cleaning implements, and each family took care of their own laundry. Also, some residents started seeking temporary jobs nearby, visiting relatives, or searching other centers looking for survivors. Gradually, the dynamics that were typical in each family before the disaster began to emerge. Naturally, not all families were proactive initially, but most of them seemed to catch on to the enthusiasm and independence of others. This may have been related to the similarity of socioeconomic backgrounds between the volunteers and the survivors, allowing the help provided to be perceived as a matter of solidarity rather than as a handout.

Decision Making (Preparing for Christmas and Farewell)

Just before Christmas, the government informed the survivors that they would soon be moved from the shelters to new homes. This filled them with hope but also with concern about which state of the country to which they would have to move. The families began to hold meetings among themselves, trying to decide where it would be best to go. Having grown close to each other, we also began planning ways to enjoy the Christmas holiday under such difficult conditions and decided to hold a mass and to prepare a simple dinner for all concerned. On December 23, we began to hear parents telling their children, "I have no money for your presents," and "The river swept everything away, including your gifts." Because we hoped to organize contributions, we asked the kids to write letters to Santa (here we call him Baby Jesus). Reading them was heartrending, as some asked for just a toy, and others for a new home, jobs for their parents, or finding some lost relative. We actually got letters not only for Santa but also for the president, asking him to help their families. We fortunately received donations that quickly turned my car into an authentic Santa's sleigh full of presents and candies. Most kids were thrilled with their gifts, but others were disappointed. The mass created an intense reaction full of tears and gratitude, and we all agreed it was a very different Christmas.

On December 25, we had no formal activities, so most rested and played with their brand-new toys. On December 26, deliberations about where to go began, and we decided to draft lists of possible destinations, but the military in charge did not take them into account, so several Jesuits and one psychologist went to the military base to negotiate for the survivors. Logistics and time were not in our favor, however, which worried the survivors, who demanded concrete and straight answers that did not depend on us voluntary workers. We called a meeting to address these concerns, as the government had not offered definite destinations but had decreed that all shelters had to be evicted because classes would soon begin and epidemics were rising. In our particular case, we all found this last reason difficult to understand, because we had pretty good sanitary conditions, but other places were collapsing. Another fear was that not moving into the government's centers and system could probably leave the families without the possibility of being considered for new houses.

We decided to turn in a list on December 28 with two possible destinations listed for each family. Much to our surprise, that same afternoon buses arrived to take them away. Mixed feelings arose, ranging from relief and hope about their going to their new homes to anxiety and grief for leaving the shelter and facing another separation. Packing went quickly as we prepared some food and clothes for them to take along. The psychology team prepared a simple card with an encouraging message and acknowledgment for each family. Parting scenes were touching as, amid laughter and tears, telephone numbers were exchanged, promises exchanged to meet again (which were later kept), and invitations extended to visit their new homes.

Farewell, Grief, and Closure

Once the last of the residents departed, all of us volunteers divided into cleaning and packing teams, and as we had a surplus of donations, we thought it best to pass those on to other centers still in operation. With a festive and merry Caribbean zest, we all started singing and dancing while we worked, and some suggested we have a closing party. Amid pirouettes and buckets, many looked at their watches and wondered how far along their route the survivors could be. The school was left spotless, as if no shelter had ever been there. The Jesuits offered their house, and the closing festivity was organized. It was the last time all the volunteers got together, and even the Jesuits danced and celebrated. We commemorated and celebrated our efforts, the people we met and their bravery, but above all, we celebrated their coveting of life.

In case of ITJO shelter, the following characteristics seemed to have contributed to the effectiveness of the work that was done:

- Including the affected people in several of the functional tasks of the shelters: This not only promoted their progressive activities but also reduced the victim–role perspective.
- Prior existence of a community network: Many people who volunteered previously knew each other and showed a customary interest for supportive tasks and community efforts.

- The center was in a lower-middle-class neighborhood: Unlike other examples, this center was not in an upper-class area, nor in a stadium or other massive area. This minimized sociocultural differences between the volunteers and the people affected by the floods, and thus there was a very sincere atmosphere of solidarity and genuine support among equals. This may have contributed to the proactive participation of the affected people to quickly start taking care of themselves. In other centers, the affected people were reported as dependent, even lazy, and not willing to care for themselves, even after two weeks (having been waited on by higher-class volunteers).
- Spontaneous organization under natural or well-deserved leadership: Both the volunteers and the Jesuits were respected, somewhat because of being religious or community leaders, but also in response to the fairness and humbleness with which they led the shelter.
- Feelings among the volunteers of pride and of being part of the center: Most of the youngsters that worked as volunteers are in some way related to the sponsoring institution, having studied there or being neighbors for years. To this one must add the natural energy and enthusiasm that only a very young group of workers can put into the endless hours of work.
- High problem-solving skills, as well as the capacity and flexibility to cope with changes: This was partly a result of the official support we received, but it also came about by improvising effective alternatives through personal contacts.

Part of what we learned through this experience would be to:

- Have brief orientation meetings with volunteers to clearly define their tasks, responsibilities, and limitations, as well as measures for maintaining self-care and congeniality among the staff.
- From the beginning, hold formal meetings to exchange information and to relieve stress and discomfort among the volunteers and coordinators.
- Organize a registry of the volunteers to plan ahead about who might be available, as well as being able to rotate them more efficiently and prevent or reduce burnout reactions.

Recommendations forwarded by the group that gave psychological support in the shelter at the Universidad Central de Venezuela (Sánchez, Wiesenfeld, Gómez, Goncalves, & Ramdjan, 2000) stressed the importance of:

- Considering affected people (victims) as proactive beings, with the right to have opinions and participate in the process of the support they receive.
- Working with an emerging organizational model that is able to be flexible and encompass changes.
- Clearly defining the role of "coordination" in relation to the roles of each participating team.
- To reduce uncertainty, clearly identifying each area within the shelter, who resides where, which staff are assigned to which areas, and where visitors are allowed to congregate.

- Reorient the curriculum in undergraduate studies to prepare future psychologists to cope with these events.

The coordinators of the psychosocial support group that worked in Teo Capriles (Azuaje, 2000) emphasize the importance of measures such as:

- Census all the buildings that may serve as shelters, specifying their access routes, nearby organizations, and assistance centers.
- Prepare a basic assistance plan for each available center.

The Red Cross and the Aftermath

After many survivors were reassigned to new houses or went back to rebuild their ruins, they continued to require psychosocial services. Two recently graduated clinical psychologists (Delys Navas and Claudia Carrillo), having received training from the American and Mexican Red Cross teams, joined the Venezuelans' Red Cross psychosocial support team to provide psychosocial support to surviving communities in Vargas. They gave assistance in shelters, aided families living with other families, and trained teachers and other volunteers. Dr. Rachel Cohen's training on reducing the effects of traumatic events and viewing "victims" as "survivors" were cornerstones of the intervention and proved instrumental to the team's development.

The interventions objectives were to:

1. Provide psychological support to individuals and groups, referring when necessary.
2. Develop recreational, social, and cultural activities adjusted to the communities' needs.
3. Enable the process of adaptation to new geographic areas, jobs, and communities for displaced survivors.
4. Educate the population through the media about preventive measures and normal psychological and physical reactions to disasters.

At first, the population's needs were assessed to respond to each community's needs. The team's original intention was to establish a permanent prevention, intervention, and education program. Carrillo and Navas, with prior training in crisis intervention and brief psychotherapy, added community intervention to their tasks and assessed needs and strong points at the community level. In each community, the program adapted to their specific needs and demands, but it basically covered the following scheme.

A first session was dedicated to rescuing the collective memory of the community by expressing feelings and reactions amid ruins. This not only was a matter of symbolic relevance or emotional release but also was about strengthening social bonds and the collective sense of belonging. Children were encouraged to express their feelings and relate their experiences through their drawings. A later encounter addressed grief, mourning, and biding farewell to departed ones for the adults, whereas the children participated in theatrical activities. In the third and fourth sessions, adults acknowledged their communal strengths and joined in creative efforts on a collage representing the community in which they would like to live, whereas children participated in cooperative games.

As time passed, the communities demanded different types of intervention, requesting help with problems like grief, rape, juvenile delinquency, and drug abuse. Thus, it became difficult to address problems that actually were consequential of the catastrophe and did not exist previously. It also became clear that the disaster had been another crisis in the chain of critical events these people faced on a daily basis. Therefore, the program had to be very flexible, adjusting on a regular basis mostly on the basis of trial and error. Not all volunteers were psychologists, but as all wanted to help, they received training and were allowed to participate. Resources were scarce and the infrastructure inadequate, and because each program responded to different communities and needs, it became difficult to set comparable standards and sustain this program for long.

Judgment and Evaluation: Five Years Later

Five years after the floods, we can look back and say that the balance of the activities developed by the PSN and the different entities that supported it was quite positive, especially considering the extemporization circumstances it begun operating under and our inexperience in facing disaster response. A creative management of the human resources, particularly student volunteers and professors, allowed us to establish several work groups, giving flexible and quick responses to the different needs that arose. This way, very heterogeneous work teams composed of professionals from all of the diverse psychological subdisciplines (clinic, social, school, and counseling, among others) and different theoretical orientations (behavioral, psychoanalytic, cognitive, and others), were able to work together. The intense motivation of the volunteers of the PSN was linked to the success of this relief effort, which is congruent with remarks made by Banchs (2000), who suggests that physical or psychological proximity transforms the support provided to the victims into something of high priority.

The fundamental contribution of the PSN came in the form of helping to organize services and activities for the affected population (e.g., transfers from the airport to the shelters, activities in the shelters, recreational activities for children, and contacts with governmental and nongovernmental organizations). These organizational activities helped the affected populations to regain their sense of security and proved useful in helping them regain control of their daily activities, little by little. The nature of these activities also minimized the importance of theoretical and subdisciplinary differences among the psychologists, thus preventing their differences in providing support from adding to the problems faced at the shelters.

However, this achievement does not diminish the effect of not having had a systematic and appropriate training in crisis intervention techniques and disaster management principles and practices. Specific training of that sort would have made the teams more unified and effective in their work. Regrettably, today most of us still lack this type of training. As became evident through the activities of the PSN, psychological assistance in disaster situations is a necessary part of humanitarian relief. Thus, it is of paramount importance to train psychologists and other health-related professionals to adequately play important roles in disaster situations, as well as being able to acknowledge their personal and professional capacities and limitations. It is relevant to stress that there is an important willingness on behalf of highly trained professionals to provide assistance in disaster situations. Venezuela faces extreme social problems, not the least of which are severe poverty and large groups of people inhabiting geologically high-risk areas. These and other risk factors increase the vulnerability of the population in the event of disasters and aggravate psychosocial problems.

This leads us to outline the necessity of having the widest possible training in disaster management. It should not be directed only to the professors and university students that are members of our network but, also, to diverse sectors of the population, such as search and rescue personnel, primary school teachers, health professionals in general, and especially those in the mental health field (Lacasella, Cronick, & Vargas, 2000). Aiming in this direction, and as a research effort, it has since been possible to configure a training program directed to primary school teachers, concerning the first level of psychological assistance in disaster situations. This program has already been validated, and one hopes it will be disseminated thoroughly (Carrillo, 2003).

Through our work, we discovered that we did not offer sufficient psychological support to our volunteers in terms of training, clinical support, and rotating shifts. This was a result of our spontaneous response and the crisis nature of the situation, which forced us to improvise and do the best we could. It is worth mentioning that this improvisational character has been one of the factors that has prevented the PRN from stabilizing its operations. As of today, the network has only been able to have intermittent operations, being reactivated only occasionally and for very different types of crises, ranging from natural disasters to political unrest. This reliance on improvisational remedies has to do with three conditions: lack of a national plan for mental health in the event of disasters or emergencies; a practically nonexistent culture of prevention, and therefore no previous planning for adverse events; and the success of our intermittent initiatives, making it appear like a stable framework is already established.

Accomplishments

1. A program office was established in each state of the country, with custom-suited activities according to each region's needs.
2. Because of limited financial and material resources, to avoid duplicating efforts, and to be better able to follow up, smaller community groups were preferred over shelters or massive facilities.

3. We worked hand in hand with international delegates from several cooperating agencies while respecting local criteria. This was a point of honor that eased relationships, allowed us to activate help rapidly, and guaranteed that local human resources took over their own disaster relief work.
4. Brief training in psychological first aid was provided to teams that required it.
5. Activities and materials were constantly revised with updates based on similar experiences worldwide, but with proper adaptation for our reality.
6. We were part of Red Cross's activities, which was a strength because it fostered respect and trust amid a disaster situation. Survivors supported Red Cross's actions even more than those of the local governments.

Limitations

1. We did not continue with the training.
2. Turning psychosocial support into a massive program promoted quantity more than quality.
3. Monitoring and success criteria should be standardized but not rigid.
4. Cutting the program short meant not having continuity and leaving behind plenty to be done.
5. Insufficient direction and inadequate coordination affected the project's sustainability.
6. Institutional endorsement was inadequate because mental health is not considered a major priority.

What We Could Have Done Differently

1. For the first three months, work was voluntary. Later, when it did pay, resources were so limited that most of the team members left to find better-paying jobs. This personnel rotation also affected scheduling the activities.
2. Publishing much of the information to be conveyed could be a good way of reaching more people, and farther away, than we could otherwise affect.
3. Maintaining an office and operations space and resources would enable monitoring and follow-up of programs, activities, and individual cases.
4. Including psychosocial support as a standard Red Cross service.

Recommendations

In this area it is difficult to establish a formula for psychosocial support, as each disaster has its own characteristics. We need to think and reflect on these variables:

1. Not all psychologists work well in prevention, intervention, and so on, so we should consider our abilities when choosing which type of work to engage in.
2. Assessing what kind of attention and support local authorities can provide will help to ensure the best possible alliances.
3. Psychosocial response, in all its predictable phases, should be designed before being needed.
4. Data-registering strategies should be improved.
5. International delegates should seek the support of local psychologists.
6. Schools are prevention spaces, as well as intervention and reconstruction spaces.

Conclusion

The PSN was a valuable program for organizing health professionals, specifically psychologists, to provide support and counseling to the survivors of the flood in Vargas during the first three weeks that followed the disaster preceding Christmas 1999. In spite of having formally ceased its functioning, some components have developed new programs, although unfortunately without all of the coordination and coherence required for efficient and effective operations. We now need to establish an organization that includes high-level disaster psychology training for health professionals, development of response plans in anticipation of future disasters, and education to prepare the general public for the prevention of disasters or mitigation of their effects. In this way, we hope to create a consciousness of and preparedness toward natural disasters and other emergencies in our country.

Psychosocial support is a small but important part of a global disaster response, and all disaster services require our support to improve services provided to survivors. For the psychologists on the psychosocial support team, what was most appreciated was being respected and having the freedom to act under local criteria. All the same, the work developed in Vargas, as well as that done nationwide, was the result of international delegates promoting the importance of this program in a country with no prior similar experience. An activity of promising merit is the designing of manuals and other educational materials accessible to all kinds of populations. In May 2004, we participated in the International Network for Emergency Education's regional consultation on minimal standards on emergency education in the Caribbean and Latin American region. The intention of this chapter is to share experiences and doubts, with no intention of passing judgment on local or international humanitarian help assisting local emergency support.

References

Azuaje, L. (2000). Mitigar el impacto: Los albergues. El caso "Teo Capriles." *Revista Avepso*, 23, 133–160.

Banchs, M. A. (2000). Encuentro con lo desconocido: Ideas para el trabajo con personas afectadas por desastres naturales. *Revista Avepso*, 23, 251–269.

Carrillo, C. (2003). *Diseño, aplicación y evaluación de un programa de capacitación dirigido a docentes de educación basica I y II etapa, en atención psicolóica a niños ante situaciones de desastre* [trabajo especial de grado]. Caracas: Universidad Central de Venezuela.

Lacasella, R., Cronick, K., & Vargas, C. (2000). Evaluación de la situación de los psicólogos en la emergencia nacional de diciembre 1999. *Revista Avepso*, 23, 319–338.

Pérez, K. (2000). Línea 800-Psico. Apoyo Psicológico a través de la línea telefónica. *Revista Avepso*, 23, 161–165.

Sánchez, E., Wiesenfeld, E., Gómez, I., Goncalves, M., & Ramdjan, N. (2000). Desastres naturales y la contribución de la psicología social: El caso del 15 de diciembre de 1999 en Venezuela. El Albergue de la UCV. *Revista Avepso*, 23, 125–131.

Villalobos, M., & Blanco, T. (2002, August). *The Psychological Support Network*. Paper presented at the annual University of South Dakota: Disaster Mental Health Institute Conference on Innovations in Disaster Mental Health, Rapid City, SD.

CHAPTER 6

IMPLEMENTATION OF A TRAINING OF TRAINERS MODEL FOR DISSEMINATING PSYCHOLOGICAL SUPPORT IN THE CUBAN RED CROSS

Joan Swaby Atherton and Mette Sonniks

This chapter outlines a case study of the Cuban Red Cross (CRC) and their experience from developing a psychological support program within their overall plan for disaster relief work. With approximately 11 million inhabitants, Cuba is situated in the center of the Caribbean Sea. There are branches of the CRC in all 14 provinces of the country, as well as local chapters in many of the 169 municipalities. Over the last two decades, Cuba has been hit by 20 tropical storms, 18 cyclones, 16 hurricanes, 24 floods, and 10 tornadoes. Victims often have emotional reactions in the aftermath of these disasters, and some kind of psychological support is important to help them cope with their feelings and the losses they may have suffered. It has also become clear to the CRC that witnessing deaths, injuries, homelessness, and destruction has effects on our volunteers and relief workers that should not be ignored. Therefore, it is equally important to recognize and respond to the psychological needs of our workers.

The CRC is a member of the International Federation of Red Cross and Red Crescent Societies (IFRC), which launched a psychological support program (PSP) in 1995. The PSP was developed and operated by the Federation Reference Centre for Psychological Support, a small operational and technical facility hosted by the Danish Red Cross. The Danish Red Cross developed a manual for psychological first aid and implemented this PSP as part of their response services in the national department. The manual was translated into English, and within a short time, there was an increasing demand for it in other Red Cross and Red Crescent national societies. By 1999, about 45 national societies were involved in developing a PSP.

The program itself grew rapidly. National societies would initiate contact with the Reference Centre to obtain help in setting up a PSP, which follows a community-based approach. This approach is most important, because there is a wide difference in how to approach psychological support and psychological reactions within different cultures and countries. All national societies that contacted the Reference Centre were asked to answer the following questions:

- What is your target population?
- What are their needs?
- What resources do we have or do we need to meet these needs?
- On what and whom do we rely in meeting these needs?
- What should be the first step in implementing the program?
- What steps would be followed?
- What model should be adopted?

These ideas must always be discussed, as there is no perfect recipe for any given context. When a national society begins to develop a PSP, they need to know for whom, with whom, and how; therefore, a plan or method is always needed. Thus, when the CRC contacted the Reference Centre in 1999 to request support in developing their PSP, the first task for them was to discuss and decide answers to the above questions. This was the beginning of a very interesting and positive process, as the collaboration on the PSP became a model of successful project development within the Cuban Red Cross.

The model proposed in this chapter is the one that was used in CRC, but it can readily be adapted to other contexts. It is therefore important to think about adjustments in methodology and actions that may be necessary for other countries and for each unique situation. The model builds on a community-based approach toward developing resources, in terms of both financing and human resources. The Reference Centre began helping to initiate contact with educational institutions, health care organizations, and other systems in Cuba to facilitate getting in touch with relevant professionals.

Defining the Target Population

It is well known that people are affected by disasters, not only in terms of basic needs, but also in terms of emotional reactions. The specific situations vary from one country to another, so target populations may never be the same across different contexts. Countries may be affected by wars, racial or ethnic conflicts, pandemics such as HIV/AIDS, cumulative stress resulting from poverty, or displaced populations and large numbers of refugees. For the CRC, the initiating incidents were natural disasters, but as the program has developed, it has been adapted to many other circumstances.

The PSP is based on the fundamental Red Cross and Red Crescent principle of humanity, which recognizes the need to respond to all human suffering. This imperative is not limited to the results of natural and man-made disasters. It also includes daily stressful life events that may vary from serious illnesses to drug abuse, domestic violence, painful divorce, or the sudden death of relatives. Taking all this into account, the CRC selected the following target population:

- Victims of natural or man-made disasters
- Refugees and asylum seekers
- Haitian immigrants
- HIV-positive persons
- Volunteers and relief workers
- Firefighters and rescue workers
- Blind and disabled people; the elderly
- People in the community

Victims of Natural or Man-made Disasters

Each year Cuba is whipped by hurricanes, tropical storms, tornadoes, floods caused by heavy rains, and encroachment of the sea. These natural phenomena cause thousands of families to live in shelters with their children. In addition, traffic accidents have become the fourth leading cause of death in Cuba.

Refugees and Asylum Seekers

Thousands refugees and asylum seekers are cared for in Cuba, and more than 500 Haitian immigrants arrive on our shores every year. Many of these people live in a Red Cross camp in Guantánamo for months, waiting to be returned to Haiti.

Persons Infected with HIV

In Cuba, people with HIV/AIDS are cared for by a program in which the Public Health Ministry and other institutions are integrated to provide them with medical and psychosocial attention. Red Cross volunteers are part of this program.

Volunteers and Relief Workers

The CRC relies on more than 22,000 volunteers across all of its programs. The PSP aimed to train all Red Cross volunteers in psychological first aid, because in one way or another they are all exposed to stressful situations—especially those who work in disasters, including firefighters, police, and others. After defining the target population and their psychological needs, we assessed our options to determine who we could count on to meet those needs. The next step was recruiting volunteers to work on the program. The recruitment focused mainly on psychologists, but it also targeted medical doctors, nurses, and social workers. Assistance with training the volunteers and working out and implementing the program was requested from the Reference Centre. There was no background information or previous experience to build on. The Reference Centre assessed our needs, and Mette Sonniks agreed to come to Havana to conduct a workshop that would train approximately 25 volunteers selected from all the provinces in Cuba. Once trained in both PSP and the skills of conducting the training, these newly qualified trainers would return to their provinces and begin training other trainers, who would then replicate the process. In this manner, the PSP information would rapidly be disseminated to every corner of the country.

Before the arrival of the Reference Centre director, terms of reference outlining the tasks, expectations, and roles of all concerned were negotiated between the PSP trainer (Sonniks) and the CRC representative (Swaby). It was agreed that the PSP trainer would dedicate two weeks to the training, with the first week dedicated to meetings among the principals to adapt the fundamentally Danish model of PSP to the cultural context of Cuba. This included visits by the PSP trainer to various locations to familiarize herself with CRC operations and personnel. (This is an important step that should not be missed because it acclimates and informs the lead trainer in ways that are necessary to the success of the training mission.) The remainder of the first week was then dedicated to setting up the workshop location and materials, as well as consultation and team-building between the "external" lead trainer and the "internal" personnel of the CRC. Finally, because the external trainer was not conversant in Spanish, an expert interpreter was assigned to facilitate communication.

Developing the PSP through a Workshop

The CRC took several points into account before the development of the workshop. It is very important that discussions are held before preparations are completed for a trainers' workshop. First, a developmental objective had to be defined. That meant that the reasons for wanting a PSP had to be made clear, and the necessary resources and capacity for the development and maintenance of the program had to be allocated. Next, an immediate objective had to be identified, which meant clarifying what to expect from the program and specifying the activities within which that objective was to be implemented. That stage of the discussion then led to choosing a desirable outcome to aim for in terms of how many people to involve, what tasks they should learn to perform, and within what timeframe. An important aspect of this process was to identify which of the existing Red Cross and Red Crescent activities and programs would be used to implement the PSP and which specific activities that implementation would require from the involved personnel.

Resources are always a vital concern, and so the process needed to include clarification of the input (i.e., resources) expected from the Red Cross and Red Crescent national society and from the Reference Centre. It was particularly important to clarify the resources that would be dedicated for the development of the PSP by the national society, and what level of priority the management would give it. To make sure that the PSP would have sustainable training resources for continuous training of the target groups, it was also critical to take stock of existing educational resources and consider how to further develop that capacity within the national society. It was also important to identify participants, their profiles, and the tasks they must carry out after attending the PSP course. That process needed to be very specific in regard to recruiting people for the workshop, as well as carrying out the PSP once the phase of implementing it began. Furthermore, it was very important for the decision makers (politicians) to acknowledge the importance of the PSP component in each of the distinct Red Cross and Red Crescent programs.

Immediate Objectives

It is important to have discussions, as well as to decide the immediate (and long-term) objectives. In this process, the discussion in Cuba was as follows:

- How far have we come, and what have we achieved during the cooperation phase?
- How many courses should be provided?
- What is the participants' capacity?
- What tasks do the participants have, and what are they supposed to be able to cover?
- Have we established the level of knowledge and skills?

Outcome

When deciding on the immediate objectives, it is necessary to make a time frame for the implementation and to set goals for achievements. After the discussion process described above, the actual Training of Trainers workshop was developed. A five-day workshop, partly presentations and partly group workshops, was held. Because most presentations were in English, there was an interpreter working within the workshop for the full five days. To adjust the presentations to Cuban ways and the Spanish language, the bigger part of the workshop was held in the group discussions/group workshops.

The Workshop Agenda

Format

The participants and trainers convened each morning for informal conversations over coffee and other refreshments. Formal presentations of information on PSP were made before the entire group each morning and afternoon. The remaining time after these meetings was spent in small-group discussions. The makeup of these groups was determined by their service areas, so that those who worked in neighboring provinces could build relationships that would benefit them at later stages of training and response. This appeared to be an effective model. The members of these groups reported that they could readily see ways to cooperate on further training, and that they would also be available to support each other in a crisis. Plenary sessions involving the entire congregation were held following the small group meetings, allowing representatives of those groups to share the key results of their discussions with everyone. The benefits of those plenary sessions included the identification of patterns of similar thinking across the groups and the sharing of uncommon insights or concerns from one group to another.

Day One: Crisis in General, Viewpoints on Life, and Psychology

This was a very important part of beginning the development of the PSP. Because the program and manual are derived from Danish culture, it was important to adjust them to the culture of Cuba and incorporate into them how people in Cuba generally cope with crisis and disasters. Therefore, we began by discussing our viewpoints and attitudes toward life and values. There are three basic premises of the PSP that should be discussed:

- Behavior—including emotions—is learned
- Cognitions are simply another form of behavior
- Behavior can be changed through teaching and learning

The training groups were directed to discuss their own belief systems and their own coping strategies.

The workshop then continued with an overview of the emotional reactions to crisis, including grief and post-traumatic stress disorder (PTSD). How people tend to cope with traumatic stress was discussed as a foundation for understanding the goals and techniques of crisis intervention, which begins with supportive and caring actions and leads to increased comfort and better problem solving. Other interventions discussed included connecting people with resources they might otherwise not obtain and referring people experiencing the worst reactions toward higher levels of care. Great emphasis was placed on working with groups of people in a crisis. The participants produced a number of case descriptions for discussion and used role-playing exercises to practice their skills. These exercises were followed by a full-group discussion, in which the participants presented their viewpoints.

Day Two: Disaster Relief, Helper and Victim Roles, and Psychological First Aid

The image of victims, even if they are held to be blameless and deserving of compassion, has negative connotations of weakness and inferiority. In contrast, the image of helpers is a much more positive or even heroic one. The participants held small-group discussions concentrating on their own personal experiences of being either a helper or a victim. From these conversations, they were able to understand better how others might feel in those roles, and they were sensitized to the need for dignity and humility. The full group then gathered to discuss the potential pitfalls of disaster relief work, even when trying to provide psychological support.

The workshop then shifted to examining the psychological aspects of disasters. The lead trainer described how these reactions unfold in a sequence of predictable stages as the major sources of stress change across time. In the next step, the types of psychosocial services to be provided were considered in terms of how they fit into each of the stages of disaster response. Once these basic principles were mastered, the participants were then able to retire to their small groups and discuss how those principles applied to several recent case examples from CRC relief work. The day ended with a full-group presentation of results from the small-group discussions.

Day Three: How to Structure an Educational Program for the Training of Trainers

Having taught many basic concepts and practices over the first two days, the workshop turned to discussion of the methods needed to define and identify target groups for a training program. The most essential element of developing an effective PSP is good communication skills. Participants discussed the basic theory of communication and performed exercises to illustrate different levels of communication. Both verbal and nonverbal forms of communication were discussed in terms of how they might affect the process of assessing psychological needs and providing support. Supportive communication techniques known as *active listening* were described and then practiced through role-playing within case scenarios.

Day Four: Supervision and Helping the Helper

The presentations focused on other methods of providing psychological support, such as helping people to achieve aims that would alleviate stress and improve their situations. Particular emphasis was placed on how to recognize stress and signs of burnout among staff and volunteers, and on how to respond by providing support on a peer-to-peer level. It was also important to talk about how the supervisory relationship can increase or decrease stress, with an emphasis on supportive supervision that helps to maintain the mental health and effectiveness of the staff and volunteers.

A popular design for crisis intervention, known as either Critical Incident Stress Management or Critical Incident Stress Debriefing, was described and discussed. This approach provides a model for on-scene support services with three types of intervention (demobilization, defusing, and debriefing) for various situations and populations. Although it was designed for use with groups of emergency response personnel immediately following a critical incident, it evolved into being used with all types of survivors whenever they were encountered. Not long after this workshop was conducted, psychological debriefing fell out of favor with many mental health authorities and was dropped from the PSP training curriculum.

The fourth day ended with a discussion of strategies for effective and efficient program development.

Day Five: A Day of Practice and Evaluation

The final day of the PSP workshop was devoted to drawing on various case constructions and the participants' own experiences to practice the skills learned in the preceding days. Participants were assigned the task of designing a framework for their own PSP, which they then presented to the entire assembly. The final period of the day consisted of an evaluation of the entire seminar.

Implementing the Program: The Process and Experience

After the seminar we undertook the task of creating a structure and elaborating an action plan to facilitate implementation of the program throughout the country. The creation of a structure is necessary to organize the program, but the structure itself can vary according to conditions and the situation in each country. In Cuba, we found it necessary to consider the:

- Geographical characteristics of the country
- Economic aspects
- Population
- Cultural, religious, political, and socioeconomic issues
- Factors related to psychosocial needs
- Mental health policies and resources

There are many techniques and formats that can be useful at this stage, but the aim will be to move from conceptualizing goals and objectives to clearly defining actions, as well as roles and responsibilities for accomplishing those actions. A good action plan will start from general or broad activities and become more and more specific as the program grows. After assessing these indicators in Cuba, we adopted a structure that could facilitate the gradual implementation of the program throughout all of the provinces, starting at the national level of organization.

The Cuban Model

National Team

This team is made up of three psychologists, two medical doctors, and two social workers, all previously trained in the national workshop. This national team has the following tasks:

- Elaborate and articulate the design elements and personnel of the training programs
- Guide the implementation of PSP nationwide, providing technical and methodological advice on how to recruit volunteers and develop the program
- Organize and develop workshops in all the provinces to train the instructors
- Establish cooperation with the organizations and state agencies related to the program, such as the Ministry of Public Health, the Ministry of Education, the social welfare organization, the Federation of Cuban Women, the Union of Cuban Psychologists, the Organization of Blind and Disabled People, Civil Defense, firefighters, police, and so on.
- Organize psychological first aid (PFA) courses addressed to members of these organizations.
- Sign agreements with the organizations in which the psychologists and doctors work, so that they will be released from their normal obligations when needed by the Red Cross.

Three regional groups were set up to facilitate the work, representing the western provinces, the central provinces, and the eastern provinces.

Because of the country's geographical conditions, natural phenomena vary from region to region. In the west, there are often floods and encroachments of the sea; in the center, tornadoes are more frequent; and the east is a seismic area. Disaster preparedness programs should take these regional characteristics into account. This approach allows the CRC to deal with specific problems in a more direct way, and to hold meetings and conduct studies on common issues without heavy investments being required. The National Team held meetings with all three regional groups, and in six months all of the provinces had at least one copy of the draft of a working strategic plan for implementing the PSP and the training programs. The drafts were for study and analysis, in order to introduce new ideas and adapt to specific regional characteristics. Within three months, the drafts were discussed in a national meeting with all of the changes suggested by the regional groups.

Provincial Teams

The next step was to set up provincial teams made up of psychologists, nurses, medical doctors, and social workers. The members of the provincial teams are headed by a psychologist trained in the national workshop to be a trainer, and who is entrusted with the task of organizing training on the provincial and municipal levels. The number of team members varied according to the conditions and situations in the respective provinces. The tasks of the provincial teams were to:

- Organize a provincial emergency team to be activated in the event of a disaster. Each member of the provincial team is responsible for two or three municipalities.
- Recruit at least one volunteer from each municipality in the province to be trained as trainers, and guide them in the implementation of the program.

- Organize assistance for refugees, Haitian immigrants, HIV-positive persons, the elderly, and blind and disabled people.
- Establish cooperation with state agencies and organizations related to the program on the municipal level, and organize PFA courses for workers in those organizations.

Municipal Teams

The next step was to set up municipal teams made up of psychologists, school teachers, community leaders, and social workers on the municipal level, who were previously trained in the provincial workshops. The municipal teams are responsible for recruiting and training the greatest number of volunteers and for mobilizing the volunteers in case of a disaster.

The tasks of the municipal teams include:

- Organizing a local emergency team
- Recruiting volunteers to work on the program
- Organizing assistance for HIV-positive persons, the elderly, the blind and disabled, Haitian immigrants, and refugees
- Organizing community groups jointly with the Community Health Center to assist people with stressful events in daily life
- Developing PFA courses for volunteers, relief workers, disaster intervention groups, and the community

Emergency Teams

In addition to PSP teams, emergency teams made up of the members of special teams in disaster intervention groups were also formed. These teams are activated only in the event of a disaster. At the national and provincial levels, the PSP teams are usually headed by psychologists employed by the Red Cross. This team psychologist and the leader of the disaster intervention group are jointly responsible for organizing the emergency teams. In addition to those leaders, the teams include psychologists, medical doctors, social workers, and teachers selected from the PSP teams. Most of them are Red Cross volunteers and work in the emergency team in their free time. Both the PSP and emergency teams have a common leader.

The CRC now has a national emergency team as well as a team in each province. The number of people on each team varies according to the conditions and resources in the provinces. Of the 169 municipalities, there are now emergency teams in 74 of them.

Although the PSP teams are permanently activated and working on all programs with vulnerable groups, the emergency teams are activated only in the event of a disaster.

How Emergency Teams Are Activated in the Event of a Disaster

All of the teams in Cuba can be activated in the event of a disaster. According to the agreement between the CRC and the Public Health Ministry, psychologists, doctors, and nurses working as volunteers on this program will be released from their normal obligations when needed by the Red Cross in the event of a major disaster, or for training courses or other important events. The Red Cross officers and ambulance personnel at the three levels are permanently activated, with at least some of them being available at any hour.

These teams have a mobilization plan that consists of the names, addresses, and telephone numbers of the members of the PSP teams and disaster intervention groups. On receiving an alarm, the ambulance officer phones the head of each group immediately, and that person then activates the whole group. A telephone tree is used so that each member of the group has the responsibility to phone two or three other members, which allows the whole group to be activated within 20 to 25 minutes. The first step after the alarm and telephone calls is to get enough information about the scope of the event to assess the needs at the scene of the disaster. If the resources of the municipal emergency team prove insufficient, the provincial or national emergency team organizes additional help.

Training Programs: The Actual Outcome of the Initial Workshop

Our first training in psychological support was the national workshop conducted by Mette Sonniks in 2000. After this workshop we had the tools to develop our own training programs, taking our own cultural framework into consideration. With a number of duly trained instructors, we could now formulate a training strategy that took the country's peculiarities into account. We established four main training levels, according to the target population. At the first level, the target groups are the trainers, who receive a forty-hour program. These trainers are basically psychologists, medical doctors, nurses, and social workers recruited as volunteers at the provincial and municipal levels. At the second level, the target groups are special teams made up of social workers, volunteers working with HIV patients, and other Red Cross programs. They are trained in a twenty-hour program. At the third level, the target groups are relief workers, Red Cross volunteers and staff, firefighters, and members of organizations related to the program. They are trained in an eight-hour program. At the fourth level, the target groups are the people in the community, and they are trained in a two-hour unit.

Forty-Hour Program

The aim of the forty-hour program is to train the instructors in PFA and other human support, and how to develop the training programs at the other three levels. These instructors are basically psychologists, medical doctors, nurses, and social workers recruited as volunteers at the provincial and municipal levels. They receive full training with all of the activities included because they will be responsible for acting as facilitators in addressing the needs of the community through the mobilization of resources.

This program, as well as all the rest of the programs, was planned and developed by the national team and was discussed and approved in regional meetings by the provincial teams' instructors. These regional meetings were held in three provinces, grouping the provincial teams with the established regional organizations mentioned earlier. The two first days were for discussion and approval of the programs, and the third day was to practice the teaching methodology and techniques. These trainers are entrusted with the task of developing the twenty- and eight-hour course programs nationwide.

Twenty-Hour Course Program

The aim of this program is to train the members of special teams in the assessment process, to train all volunteers working in special Red Cross programs in PFA, and to provide human support to people in stressful situations. For the team managers, one of the objectives is to emphasize the assessment process. The aim is not to go into details about filling out the forms and which questions to ask, but rather to show them how psychological support should be part of the general assessment.

Eight-Hour Course Program

The eight-hour course is a psychological first aid course. The purpose is to encourage the participants to take action in case of critical life situations. It includes basic psychological first aid skills, such as communication skills, that are especially necessary for National Society staff and the members of organizations who are responsible for forming relationships with external resources. The course is addressed to relief workers, intervention groups, staff, organizations, and workplaces that are in need of psychological first aid (e.g., firefighters, high-risk industries, rescue workers, civil defense, social welfare agencies, and the education sector).

Two-Hour Unit

This community mobilization component is addressed to local people who normally might not have time to sit down in a classroom for a long course. Community mobilization implies a process of facilitating individuals, families, and communities to take action to address the problems of emergency situations. Active involvement, acceptance of responsibility, and community mobilization counteract the potential for being cast in a victim role. The quicker that individuals become involved and active after experiencing a traumatic event, the less that event will affect them, and the quicker those individuals, their families, and their community will adapt and become resilient once again. This two-hour unit presents practical steps to facilitate self-help and community mobilization.

Conclusions

Psychological support—a process aimed at facilitating resilience through empathy, understanding, and sensitivity—has become more and more needed today in a world beset by wars, crises, and epidemics. Each situation is unique, however, and requires both an assessment of community and individual needs and a prioritization of how to meet those needs. Emergencies and disaster situations affect each individual and community differently, and for some people the stress and trauma experienced can result in substantial dysfunction. Proper assessment of the situation can help us to identify who is in need and what resources are available to help them. Much of what is taught in PSP training is purely common sense, in that these are skills and abilities already used by many of us in our daily lives. But the systematic dissemination of this information and a plan for who will respond to what, and in what fashion, helps to ensure that these skills will be available when needed.

The cooperative enterprise to promote PSP, involving the Reference Centre for Psychological Support—located in Denmark—and the national Red Cross society in Cuba, stands as a model of international collaboration. The Reference Centre provided a trainer who was able to train Cuban nationals in just two weeks, providing them with skills that could then be disseminated to every corner of their country. One year later, a representative of the Reference Center conducted a visit as part of a national conference on PSP held in Havana. That representative reported that the CRC had successfully developed a durable nationwide capacity to respond to the psychological needs of disaster survivors.

These accomplishments are not inherently limited to the Red Cross movement or to any particular nation or region of the world. Rather, the model described here could be adopted by any nation, either through the auspices of its Red Cross or Red Crescent society or by some other means. Humanitarian organizations other than the IFRC and its national society members are also involved in the development of psychosocial support programs, training materials, and models of training and development. The Red Cross movement has a unique capacity for such activities because of its 142-year longevity and its 181 member societies, but other humanitarian agencies also have the strengths and resources necessary to promote mental health in the face of disasters and other humanitarian emergencies. The model presented in this chapter can perhaps inform others and inspire them to undertake similar activities.

CHAPTER 7

Psychosocial Responses to the Bombing of the American Embassy in Nairobi: Challenges, Lessons, and Opportunities

David M. Ndetei, Rose Kasina, and Dammas M. Kathuku

Introduction

The Kenyan summer of 1998 was much like any other. The weather was hot and dry, the Moi government was firmly in control of the country, and refugees from the wars raging in nearby countries fled to the relative peace and stability of Kenya. Although internal strife flared up on occasion, the nation was at peace with its neighbors and had no known enemies. That doesn't mean that Kenyans were living in a paradise or were unaware of the political battles being waged to the north in Israel and Palestine. Nor were they oblivious to the violent acts carried out by terrorists in many parts of the world. Still, it is fair to say that the bombing of the American embassy in Nairobi on August 7 came as a shocking surprise.

Although the apparent targets were Americans, the vast majority of casualties were Kenyans occupying the immediate vicinity of the explosion. The scenes of carnage, broadcast on television and other news media, horrified the entire nation. As in any emergency, civil authorities and volunteers rushed to the aid of survivors and removed both dead and living victims from the rubble. The most severe physical injuries were treated in hospitals, while those that were not life-threatening were often treated at the scene. Families frantically searched to locate loved ones who may have been killed or injured, as public officials worked to identify the dead and notify next of kin.

As the immediate shock was wearing off and the human toll was being assessed, it became clear that not all of the wounds were of a physical nature that could be treated with medical resources. Those with some experience or expertise in working with victims of traumatic events warned that the profound emotional and psychological consequences of the terrorist attack were likely to require a mental health response comparable to that already being mobilized by the medical establishment.

The present chapter describes how local volunteers, mental health providers, international humanitarian agencies, and the American government competed, collaborated, and cooperated to provide mental health services to thousands of Kenyans who were psychosocially affected by the bombing of 1998. The activities of those involved in these efforts are described, as well as the obstacles they encountered and the solutions they implemented. The effectiveness of these measures is critically evaluated, with examples given of both successes and failures that are instructive for those engaged in international projects designed to serve the psychosocial needs of disaster survivors. The authors conclude with a series of lessons learned from this experience and recommendations for how the parties involved in similar projects might operate more effectively.

Awareness of Psychotrauma in Kenya Prior to the Embassy Bombing

Kenya has had its own share of disaster and psychotrauma, both natural and man-made, even before the American Embassy bomb-blast. Disasters involving many people have been reported locally and internationally, both in the distant and recent past. These include a terrorist bombing of one of the leading hotels in Nairobi in the late 1970s, because of an alleged Kenyan bias in the Middle East political conflict. Scores of Kenyans, as well as foreigners, were killed, and property was damaged. Natural disasters involving the deaths of many people and the destruction of property have included floods, mudslides (particularly in 1997), and frequent famines.

Arson incidents in Kenya are man-made disasters that have involved many people, with much loss of lives and property at the same time. Among those that have been particularly conspicuous were a series of arson episodes in school dormitories in which tens of students were sleeping, causing sudden and unexpected death or injury to many students. Other mass disasters had political connotations. They included tribal clashes in several parts of Kenya in which thousands of people were violently displaced and hundreds killed, with extensive damage to property. In any given instance of a transportation disaster, tens of people have been killed by train wrecks, air crashes, ferry sinkings, and motor vehicle accidents on the roads.

On a smaller scale—at the individual level—incidents in Kenya of rape, domestic violence, armed robbery, personal violence, and the like have always been reported in the Kenyan press, as well as in the international press. But until the American Embassy bombing, nothing happened beyond the initial condemnation, expressions of anger and helplessness, and the initial rescue operation. The country literally sat and waited for the next incident to happen. The American Embassy bombing changed all that.

The Nairobi Bomb-Blast

On Friday, August 7, 1998, at around 10:37 A.M. Kenyan time, a truck driven by terrorists forced its way into the parking lot of the United States Embassy building in Nairobi, and detonated a grenade that was followed by a loud blast estimated to be the result of a two-ton bomb. The site of the Nairobi Bomb-Blast (NBB) was a busy cosmopolitan area with high-density human activity and rail and motor transport connecting all areas of Kenya. Thus, there were arrivals from and departures to various parts of the city and the country, including a nearby fresh-produce market, the biggest in the country. Buildings in the vicinity were multistory structures that were heavily populated. On that day, a National Schools Musical Festival was being held in a nearby conference center, and a large number of students and their teachers from all over the country were traveling to and from the festival. Friday mid-mornings are usually very congested in Nairobi's central business district. In this setting, all of these factors presented the perfect conditions and timing for maximum destructive impact from a bomb.

The bomb-blast had an extensive destructive effect over a radius of a mile in the central district where the embassy building was located. Also damaged were other significant business and government multistory buildings. One seven-story building adjacent to the American Embassy was reduced to rubble, trapping and killing most of the occupants in and around it. People were thrown from one corner of their workrooms to the other, and those on the streets were also tossed around. Others were struck by flying objects and broken glass as a result of the blast, and cars were damaged extensively. Fumes billowed from falling and burning buildings and other structures. Blood flowed freely as the injured fled in all directions, oblivious to their precarious state. Hence, the death toll rose to 213 on site, and about 5,000 survivors sustained various types of injuries.

The subsequent governmental, nongovernmental, private, and general population reaction and response were spontaneous and overwhelming in addressing rescue operations and the medical and psychosocial needs of those affected. This response can be divided and discussed in several phases: (1) the initial rescue phase (including medical); (2) the immediate psychosocial response; (3) an intermediate phase of the psychosocial response; (4) and termination (or phase-out) of the psychosocial response. Some people will continue to need long-term response into the foreseeable future.

The Initial Rescue
The Local Effort

Almost immediately following the blast, the initial search for and rescue of the injured involved furious and desperate efforts. Everybody took care of anybody else who was worse off. The walking-injured assisted the immobile-injured. The general population pitched in and helped those bleeding or injured in any way. Any vehicle available was used to ferry the injured to a hospital. Kenyatta National Hospital (KNH) was the linchpin of the emergency response. However, a total of 22 hospitals and clinics were confirmed as having received the injured for treatment. Hospital staff were overwhelmed by emergency work. The survivors helped one another in any way possible to ease pressure on the staff, so that they could attend to the neediest victims. The Nairobi City Mortuary Services assumed custody of many of the dead, and private arrangements were also put in place, mainly by the American Embassy. The embassy also made arrangements for medical care for the majority of their staff.

This initial local rescue operation generated some conflicts between the locals and embassy security. Immediately after the blast, the general population moved to assist the injured at the disaster site. American Embassy security personnel also moved into battle mode to protect the embassy and its contents. An exchange between the swelling crowd and the embassy security personnel ensued, with the latter threatening to shoot the former. The media disseminated pictures of this fracas, and thereafter the American Embassy was depicted quite negatively as being insensitive to human suffering and preferring embassy property to human life. This perception was to last for quite some time, although the American ambassador did her best to correct it.

International Effort

The U.S. response was immediate, with initial daily rescue flights into the country starting the next day, with the first evacuation during the next two days. Apart from the United States, Israel, France, Egypt, Canada, Germany, and the United Kingdom responded by sending rescue personnel and equipment. Other supplies were sent by France, the UK, Saudi Arabia, Kuwait, and Iran. Humanitarian organizations included the World Food Programme (WFP) and the International Federation of Red Cross and Red Crescent Societies (IFRC), by way of the Kenya Red Cross (KRC).

The Initial Psychosocial Response

Given the extreme impact of the bombing, which resulted in so many deaths and even more people severely injured, the first priority was to save lives and treat the physical wounds of the survivors. It quickly became apparent, however, that the psychosocial effects of the bombing, such as psychotrauma and intense grief, also deserved attention. This attention took several forms.

1. Counseling services were initiated at Kenyatta National Hospital (KNH) by hospital and volunteer staff. On the third day, they were joined by a medical combat stress control team from a U.S. base in Germany. Their services consisted mainly of explaining to those concerned what was happening and suggesting ways of handling the situation. These efforts involved hospital staff helping the survivors of the blast, the surviving relatives of those who were killed, and the general Nairobi population at large. Cooperatively, they trained 150 professionals and debriefed 360 people.

2. Training in psychotrauma was also put in place. Kenyatta National Hospital and the Department of Psychiatry at the University of Nairobi established a two-day structured crisis training program dealing with stress and trauma management, which went on to train 500 generic counselors. These counselors were intended to go into the general population and work with community-based organizations (CBOs) to address the effects of the Nairobi Bomb-Blast.

3. There was a significant religious response as well. Most religious organizations responded with counseling and prayers in order to mitigate the effects of the disaster. Most of this activity took place in institutions allied with houses of worship. Staff members were generally not trained in critical incident stress management, so most counseling was unstructured and consisted of methods that were not easy to quantify. However, this ad-hoc mode of counseling culminated in the formation of Operation Recovery.

4. The Operation Recovery (OpRec) project, created by the Kenya Medical Association, consisted of counselors and psychologists with little or no training in counseling psychology, plus a few Kenyan psychologists and psychiatrists. Their efforts focused on supporting the survivors and the bereaved. The service element of OpRec suffered greatly as a result of constraints on personnel and finances. The quality of the counselors was under scrutiny by service consumers, who often found the counselors to be too young to share intimate matters with. This situation arose from a cultural aspect of transgenerational relationships in Kenya, and it complicated the OpRec efforts.

As OpRec services progressed, it became evident that the economic well-being of the clients was the single most important concern for both the counselors and the counselees. Many questioned the benefit of the counseling services in light of the dire economic conditions they were facing. Most had no money for food, clothing, rent, school fees and other necessities, and OpRec lacked sufficient funds to address these pressing and stressful financial hardships. The counselors' allowances became difficult to obtain, which soon led to a high dropout rate among the volunteer counseling staff. The funding problem for OpRec had less to do with the unwillingness of donors to respond than with the actual operation of OpRec itself. OpRec operations ceased when the program was handed over to the Kenya Red Cross about one year after the bombing.

Challenges and Opportunities

Even at this stage of initial psychosocial response, difficult challenges began to emerge. They were mainly due to lack of previous experience in psychosocial response beyond that required for rescue operations. Hence, the organization of services was on ad-hoc basis, with an element of competition for limited resources instead of pooling resources together. Economic factors were another major challenge, creating the dilemma of how to provide counseling to economically deprived people who were more concerned with the basic needs required for physical survival than with processing their emotional reactions.

A third challenge was a cultural one. Kenya has more than 40 ethnic groupings with as many different cultural practices. In the face of atrocities and disasters, each group has specific and general responses, and expected interventions. In some ethnic groups of Kenya, bereavement is met with emotional displays of catastrophic proportions, whereas others are more reserved and discreet about showing emotions. This diversity posed a challenge for inexperienced counselors, and the need for a more organized and perceptive disaster response—with better professional skills developed through training—began to be recognized at this early stage.

Transition from Initial to Intermediate Response

The United States Agency for International Development (USAID) requested $37 million from the U.S. Congress for the bomb-blast response operations in Kenya. Subsequently, a USAID request for proposals to implement a $1 million mental health program was advertised in the local media in Kenya. This contract was won by the International Federation of Red Cross and Red Crescent Societies (IFRC), with the Kenya Red Cross (KRC) as the local implementer.

Opportunities and Challenges for KRC

The Kenya Red Cross was in an advantageous position because its volunteers had responded almost immediately after the explosion. This was accomplished by the volunteer service of three of its branches in and around Nairobi. It also had branches spread across Kenya, and therefore had the potential to achieve wide coverage across the entire country. When KRC won the USAID contract, these volunteers became the seed personnel for long-term service provision.

But KRC had some teething problems. OpRec was unable to transfer its operations to KRC because of sponsorship and administrative problems, so KRC had to start its program from scratch. Thus, the Crisis Mental Health Assistance Programme (CMHAP) was launched in June 1999, specifically for this project. It was based at the KRC's Nairobi offices in the central business district, which is about 10 kilometers from their administrative headquarters. The new program had to completely renovate these offices, put in utilities, purchase equipment (e.g., transport vehicles, furniture, office supplies, and communication equipment), and hire adequate personnel before it could effectively deliver the services. These logistical problems—as well as the country's unpreparedness for such an effort—caused delays in delivering much-needed services.

Goals of the Kenya Red Cross

The CMHAP program consisted of set goals in various activity areas, including:

- Outreach to serve as many survivors as possible
- Training for counselors and community opinion leaders on how to recognize trauma, and where and how to get help
- Providing both counseling and psychiatric services, and collaborating with other services

Outreach was performed by extension workers and the mass media. Training, counseling, and psychiatric services were provided by KRC in-house staff and were also contracted out to agencies. Documentation was the sole responsibility of KRC in-house staff. Collaborating with other services was handled administratively by the KRC program administration.

The First and Last Evaluation of the Program by KRC

One year after the operation was transferred to the Kenya Red Cross, an evaluation workshop was held at a retreat outside Nairobi in order to assess the effectiveness and efficiency of the Crisis Mental Health Assistance Programme in meeting the desired goals. The objectives of the evaluation workshop were to provide a forum for examining the extent to which the program's activities were implemented on time, at what costs, and under what specifications, as well as to provide necessary recommendations to enhance future management of the program. It was an opportunity to re-examine the goals themselves, the challenges faced, the lessons learned, and strategies for future development.

The Participants

A total of 28 representatives from the Kenya Red Cross Society, the International Federation of Red Cross and Red Crescent Societies, USAID, and the various collaborating and implementing partners attended the workshop. These partners included counselors, psychiatrists, social workers, and volunteers.

The Methodology

The deliberations began with a series of reports by KRC staff and by implementing agencies involved in delivering psychosocial services. There were also group brainstorming sessions on the future course and conduct of the Crisis Mental Health Assistance Program. The groups discussed the following issues concerning the program:

1. Structure and function
2. Implementation and constraints
3. Achievements versus set goals
4. The way forward

Finally, a plenary session deliberated the group reports and final conclusions, and recommendations were made.

Presentations by KRC

The keynote presentation was made by the CMHAP technical advisor, who was operationally the technical and administrative head of the program. He gave a brief background of CMHAP, highlighting the elements of the program, the structure under which it had been operating since December 1999, and how the program elements were interacting with each other and with the sociopolitical environment. He also gave an overview of the process, the instruments used to evaluate and do research on the beneficiaries' information, and the flow charts for both adults and children. Other KRC staff made presentations on outreach and counseling activities. The KRC documentation section had been involved in the generation of the data presented. Data were being collected from all around the country and would be used to evaluate the performance of the program.

Challenges Raised by the KRC Presentation

Deliberations ensuing from the KRC presentations raised the following issues:

1. Persons not involved in the bomb-blast were taking advantage of the program.
2. The participants felt that the screening process used to recruit beneficiaries into the program should be reliable enough to disqualify clients unrelated to the bomb-blast.
3. It was observed that outreach activity, based on home visits, was the most effective way of reaching the beneficiaries. This activity was prone to logistical problems because of the vast distances and limited resources.
4. Adhering to pre-agreed quality assurance guidelines was important.

5. The need for professionalism was stressed.
6. Training was also classified as an outreach activity.
7. Documentation of all the data, for purposes of program evaluation and research, was emphasized and should be improved.

Presentations by Implementing Agencies: Challenges and Opportunities

Eleven implementing agencies made presentations based on their experiences and expectations. They emphasized the need to address various issues and problems related to or arising from the disaster, including medical, psychiatric, psychological, socioeconomic, and occupational needs. Counseling and support were necessary in helping people to progress from denial and bitterness to acceptance and forgiveness. In all of these areas, people were to be helped toward independence and carrying on with life as normally as possible.

Recommendations from the KRC Evaluation Workshop

The final plenary made the following recommendations:

1. The status quo of the operational structure and function of the Crisis Mental Health Assistance Program should be maintained
2. Additional administrative structure should be introduced in CMHAP
3. The policy structure of the program should be well understood
4. There should be less bureaucracy and red tape

Other recommendations for future activities emerged from the final plenary session:

1. Networking with other nongovernmental organizations (NGOs) and faith-based or religious organizations should be implemented in order to sensitize and educate the beneficiaries on the sustainability of the programs
2. Capacity-building for the beneficiaries should be put in place
3. Beneficiaries of the programs should occasionally be invited for a focus group discussion so that they can give their own suggestions on how best to address their program needs and the way forward.
4. Vehicles and other program facilitating tools should be put in place
5. There should be program review meetings among the program officers
6. Monitoring and evaluation procedures should be put in place

It is worth noting that this workshop was also intended to ease the transition occasioned by the IFRC. As administrator of the grant, IFRC chose to surrender the funding back to USAID because of various technical and administrative issues. This deprived the KRC of financial support as local administrator of the fund. Thus KRC, like OpRec before it, administered the program for only one year.

Administrative Transition from KRC to Amani

If the CMHPS were to continue following the withdrawal of the IFRC, a new administrative agency had to be designated. Amani Counselling Centre and Training Institute (ACCTI), one of several implementing partners for the CMHAP when it was under the KRC, was chosen by USAID to take over the administration of the program, while still functioning as one of the main service providers.

Opportunities and Challenges for Amani:
The Amani Takeover Proposal

Amani had some clear advantages as a suitable host for the program, given its long history in the areas of providing direct counseling services and training counselors. Further, Amani was willing to take on the already-existing collaborating partners, with additional provision for a technical manager for the program. However, Amani had to take over the project as an ongoing program, with little if any room for modification. This meant that time was required to study and understand the program in its already structured format. The results of that study included a restatement of the program's goals:

1. Continue a needs-driven counseling program informed by outreach activities. This would be coordinated through the assessment instruments that were used by the Kenya Red Cross.
2. People affected by the bombing will continue to have access to mental health services during the transition. Coordination of existing outreach activities are to be improved, and services to specific populations added.
3. Increase public awareness of disaster preparedness. Amani would achieve this result through continued training, outreach, and information programs.
4. Counseled people will demonstrate increased positive coping mechanisms as a result of accessing quality professional counseling services. This result would be documented.
5. Mental health professionals will provide services that measure up to professional standards. That achievement will be assessed through a quality assurance program.
6. A mental health response strategy for future disasters (disaster preparedness) will be developed through the documentation program.

In their initial takeover proposal, Amani identified several critical indicators for monitoring the extent to which the results listed above were being achieved. These indicators took the form of projected outcomes to be achieved through outreach, educational, and service provision activities. These included reaching out to as many people as possible who were affected and needed services, provision of services, supplemental education in psychotrauma for mental health workers, and improved documentation.

A major flaw in both the goals and the indicators is that there were no specifications on how these outcomes would be measured.

The ACCTI steering committee took over the management of CMHAP from the Kenya Red Cross in September, 2000 after a successful bid to implement the program as an ongoing venture. However, CMHAP was to be managed as a parallel program to keep it separate from ACCTI's mainstream activities. It continued to be housed on the same premises as when it was under the KRC.

The Program under Amani: Mid-Term Evaluation

As Amani began to understand what was required in program implementation, it became necessary to revisit the proposal. The targets were adjusted so as to make them more realistic and achievable within the allotted timeframe for the program and with the financial resources that were available. One such revision was undertaken from April to June, 2001, and the figures proposed then have been used to assess the achievement of program objectives over the two years. Measurable objectives for each service department (i.e., Outreach, Counseling, Training, and Documentation) were developed, and detailed activities to be undertaken to achieve those objectives were identified. The four main objectives, and the detailed activities proposed for achieving each of them, are summarized in Table 7.1.

Table 7.1
Amani Program Objectives and Activities

OBJECTIVE 1: To ensure that people affected by the bomb have access to mental health services

Activity 1	Provide counseling treatment, through implementing partners, to 900 adult survivors (bereaved, injured, and rescue workers) within two years
Activity 2	Provide psychiatric treatment, through implementing partners, to 142 affected adult survivors with severe psychological disorders within two years
Activity 3	Provide counseling treatment, through implementing partners, to 300 affected children survivors within two years
Activity 4	Provide psychiatric treatment, through implementing partners, to 100 affected children with severe psychological disorders for two years
Activity 5	Provide 48 clinical supervision meetings for implementing partners within two years

---

(continued)

Table 7.1   (*continued*)

OBJECTIVE 2: To provide knowledge, skills, and attitude change regarding the psychological management of disaster trauma

Activity 1	Train 360 counselors from implementing agencies in areas of trauma mental health within two years
Activity 2	Train 560 teachers in areas of trauma mental health within two years
Activity 3	Train 90 mental health providers and key decision makers in areas of trauma mental health within two years
Activity 4	Train 180 community-based mental health providers at the district level in areas of trauma mental health, and conduct a follow-up workshop within two years

OBJECTIVE 3: To reach out to survivors and their families and create awareness and sensitivity about the Crisis Mental Health Assistance Program

Activity 1	Reach out to and assess 1,500 affected children within two years
Activity 2	Reach out to 1,260 affected families living up-country, through 10 volunteers, within two years
Activity 3	Reach out to 300 affected families living up-country, through 10 volunteers, within two years
Activity 4	Reach out to 300 permanently or seriously injured survivors, through six peer counselors, within two years
Activity 5	Offer eight children and family days or events within two years
Activity 6	Conduct 12 community meetings (Barazas) within two years
Activity 7	Develop 70 media dissemination activities within two years

OBJECTIVE 4: To develop a comprehensive research and documentation program for all internal and external documents with a statistical reporting

Activity 1	Develop a comprehensive database system, with timely information for program monitoring and evaluation, within two years
Activity 2	Process and analyze data from 1,038 adult assessments and 936 child assessments and publish the information five times within two years

These objectives and activities result from a revision halfway through the program period, when it became evident that some aspects of the program, especially counseling, were generating a lot of sessions. If this trend had continued, then it would not have been possible to contain the program within the budget. These new targets have been used to measure the level of achievement or success of the program. Perhaps more importantly and positively, several recommendations in this mid-term evaluation demonstrated growing interest in trauma-related mental health activities beyond the response to the bombing. These recommendations included:

1. Establish liaison with universities involved in trauma-related clinical services and research
2. Establish a directory of qualified mental health workers
3. A trauma response unit is needed to coordinate logistics, funds, and human resources so as to be ready when disaster strikes
4. Training of teachers in disaster management and crisis intervention should continue, with follow-up evaluations conducted to monitor progress
5. Continued private and public sector mental health activities are needed beyond the bomb-blast program to achieve capacity-building

The Program under Amani: Challenges and Opportunities

Challenges and Opportunities Related to Operations of the Program

Within the context of its operations, Amani was faced with some challenges that it had to address to ensure the program's effectiveness and success.

1. Legal: Two organizations that were discontinued for fraudulent activity threatened Amani with legal action.
2. Political: The unstable political environment and the uncertainty occasioned by the rapidly approaching general elections were problematic.
3. Transition: Changing the administrator of the program from KRC to Amani created confusion and loss of clients. In the meantime the targets had been lowered and the budget reduced, which implied a reduction in the number of clients to be counseled.
4. Outreach to children: For Kenyans, support services made available through counseling was a new concept in disaster response. There was stigma to be broken in terms of the social acceptance of psychiatrists. Further, the timing of the Bomb-Blast coincided with a period when there were widespread incidences of child abductions, and this constrained outreach to children. Schools did not want school programs interrupted, and this was another constraining factor.
5. Funding: There were high expectations that the funding period for recovery programs would correspond to that of the Oklahoma City

bombing (i.e., six years). These expectations persisted, despite the fact that targets and budgets had already been reduced.

6. Program timing: The timing of the project was also a big challenge, because it coincided with Amani (ACCTI) undergoing one of its worst administrative crises.

7. Turnover of counselors: High turnover of counselors threatened continuity and subsequent improvement in the mental health of survivors. The high turnover was attributed to low payments by the implementing partners. Amani addressed the problem in its role of an implementing partner by taking some counselors on to continue counseling survivors and others who were affected.

Challenges and Opportunities Related to the Program Design

The program design and implementation created further challenges to Amani:

1. Assumptions: One of the main assumptions was based on experience in Oklahoma. The process and structure of the program had to be adapted to the local context. A case in point was the use of complex and lengthy instruments for assessment and data gathering in a predominantly oral culture. This may have led to unreliable and invalid results. Counseling as a profession is very young in Kenya, yet there was an assumption that counseling organizations would be regulated and would operate professionally. The Kenya Association of Counselors' set of professional regulations has not yet been enacted by an act of Parliament and cannot be effective in playing a regulatory role in regard to the counselors. Thus, there is need to develop local models for mental health intervention, rather than using Western models.

2. Financial inflexibility: The program design limited Amani's use of financial resources. There was zero flexibility regarding payments, which were rigidly pegged to the numbers of counseling sessions provided. This created the temptation among some partners to provide unnecessary counseling sessions in order to log the numbers that generated money for their agencies. The program could have functioned better and with greater flexibility if, for instance, a fee was paid for counseling, along with other objectives built in by Amani.

3. Executive powers: Control was greatly decentralized, to the extent that the program administrator felt impotent to act in some challenging situations, including instances of unprofessional staff conduct.

4. Restrictions prohibiting Amani from providing counseling: The design did not allow Amani to provide counseling services and had to be revised to accommodate such services. This opportunity was critical in order for Amani to provide exposure and capacity building for its personnel, to help ensure the long-term sustainability of trauma counseling within the organization.

5. Regulatory role: There was a need to strengthen monitoring for greater program effectiveness by allowing Amani more regulatory control over the implementing partners.

Challenges and Opportunities Related to the Time Plan for the Program

The program duration of two years provided double-edged challenges. Two years was not adequate to comprehensively address the problems. On the other hand, serving Bomb-Blast survivors too long could create dependency and prolong suffering. To paraphrase the recommendation within in the executive summary of *Up from the Ashes* (Driscoll, 2001), it is important to make it clear to USAID/Washington and to Congress that infrastructure reconstruction and rehabilitation programs need approval for time enough to complete all activities. Some of the most important recovery programs—mental health counseling, scholarship, construction—are lengthy. Amani was on the program for two years, and just as they started to have a real feel of things, it was time to start phasing out. If Amani had been on board from the beginning, it would have given them additional years of core funding which would have made phase-out easier, as structures for sustainability would be better understood and established (pp. 30–33).

Challenges and Opportunities Related to Research

This is one area where opportunities with profound impact on science were, most unfortunately and most regrettably, lost! This loss was particularly bad for Kenya, as well as for the international community. This lost opportunity can partly be attributed to failing to involve the local universities and research institutions, right from the inception of the program. This contrasts sharply with events following the Oklahoma City bombing, where the need for scientific examination was acknowledged and supported. Kenya's universities were rich in human resources and experience with psychotrauma, even prior to the Bomb-Blast, but this went unrecognized and unutilized. Perhaps most importantly, involving local research institutions would have exposed students to these types of exploratory activities, thus enhancing the multiplier effect and resulting in superior capacity building.

Research was not adequately done, because there was no full-time professional charged with the responsibility. The KRCS technical coordinator had devised and implemented a research-based program operations process that was elaborate and self-checking. This process was continued, though reluctantly, during the Amani phase. Had it been fully implemented, it would have led to a comprehensive documentation of the whole process over time, and would have laid a firm baseline foundation for follow-up.

There were other difficulties. Implementing partners were not cooperative because they were not familiar with research methods. But even after training them there was high counselor turnover. There was also a lot of urban–rural migration, and consequently a high turnover of clients. Research assistants (post-graduate students in education psychology) were recruited from a nearby public university to assist. Those working in the Documentation Department established the database, and an expert from another nearby public university was brought in later (a year before phase-out, and as an afterthought) to do the analysis. These delaying factors decreased the usefulness of the research for the project because the feedback was belated.

Delay in keying in research data also affected the research process up to the time of the program evaluation. It was a case of missed opportunity. Publishing research on the program during its lifetime might have demonstrated change, thus enhancing Amani's effort to obtain further funding for keeping the program going. Of course, the use of culturally relevant tools for assessment and research is necessary. There is a need to create local psychometric instruments relevant to Kenya. Better still, there is a need to validate for local use some of the many instruments that are well established and widely used in the West, for purposes of transcultural comparisons. This poses a challenge to the local universities to work in consultation with consumers and validate existing instruments, or else come up with new ones.

There is a need to consider more qualitative, rather than just quantitative, information from clients, with a smaller number of questions posed to each respondent. In the absence of such tools, the Western ones were adopted without going through a rigorous process of adoption and validation. Later, a locally derived psychiatric instrument, named the NOK after its authors (Ndetei, Othieno, and Kathuku), was incorporated, although it was unpublished and still in development. Nevertheless, there is still potential for scientifically reliable and valid data to be gathered and analyzed on the psychosocial impact of the bomb-blast.

Challenges and Opportunities Related to Sustainability

There were no adequate structures in existence to continue the program beyond the funding period. Most implementing partners will probably revert back to previous program activities from before the bombing, with minimal or no attention to disaster response—largely because they lack the institutional capacity to do more. The counseling employment market in Kenya cannot adequately absorb the surplus numbers of individuals who were trained to work as counselors. Counseling is a relatively new field in Kenya, and counseling services are usually subsidized in this country.

The decentralization of executive powers and control for the purpose of strengthening collaboration and networking was not negotiated with the program administrator. It created insecurity in regard to ownership of the program when the funding partner is removed from the scene. This would also have implications for the roles played by other partners when the program was discontinued. Nevertheless, the role played by USAID (as the funding partner and "owner" of the program) in ensuring decentralization and strengthening collaboration cannot be underestimated.

The Program under Amani: Facilitation, Management, and Implementation Strengths

Despite all the difficulties, there were mechanisms mitigating the challenges, and there were strengths to fall back on:

1. There was effective and prompt conflict resolution among the implementers—by the USAID program director.
2. Bureaucracy and red tape in management were minimized.
3. A relatively well-established database provided useful and timely information for planning, implementation, monitoring, and reporting on the program.
4. The relative availability of funds and resources for adequately rising to the challenges as they arose greatly enhanced program implementation.
5. Weekly staff and coordinators' meetings were very helpful in keeping everyone on board and in touch with what was going on in a new, challenging, and highly dynamic situation. Most of these personnel were inherited from the KRCS mental health program.
6. There was a lot of collaboration between highly reputable partners at the local level and government agencies, nongovernmental organizations, and religious bodies. The government agencies included the Ministry of Education; the office of the President, Ministry of Social Services; and the Ministry of Health. The NGOs were the Adventist Development and Relief Agency (ADRA), the Kenya Society for the Blind, AMREF, Ernst and Young, and the United Disabled People of Kenya (UDPK).
7. There was international collaboration with the World Health Organization and various U.S. agencies and institutions such as the University of Oklahoma, as well as attendance at international and national conferences on trauma.

The Program under Amani: Direct Opportunities from the Program

This program provided great opportunities for Amani in institutional capacity building.

The whole process of program management was a good learning experience for ACCTI, which had not handled such a project before. The very supportive working relationship with USAID enhanced the steering committee's confidence to handle other projects in the future.

1. Empowerment at the individual level enhanced staff employment opportunities. This empowerment translated into the professional

training of staff and enhanced awareness of disaster management among staff and other caregivers.

2. An exchange of survivors from the Nairobi and Oklahoma City bombings helped give bomb-blast victims and service providers a new perspective.

3. The program revealed that there was not just one agent, but several collaborators in multidisciplinary disaster response.

4. The design created a potential for capacity building in the long term. In other words, partners at both the organizational and personal level got enough exposure and can pursue a variety of socioeconomic activities related to disaster response at various levels: grassroots, national, and international.

5. The design has a multiplier effect that will serve the Kenyan population and beyond.

6. Short-term gains, such as client recovery and rehabilitation, were inspiring and provided tremendous impetus for partners, staff, and caregivers throughout the implementation process.

7. In addition to human resource development, the program provided Amani with vital financial and material resources that were invested in capacity building.

The Program under Amani: The Multiplier Effect

1. In addition to Amani, this program involved not just one agent, but several collaborators, in multidisciplinary disaster response.

2. This program brought together various disciplines for the first time, all working together for a common course.

3. The design created a potential for capacity building in the long term. In other words, partners at both the organizational and personal level got enough exposure and can pursue a variety of socioeconomic activities related to disaster response at various levels: grassroots, national, and international.

4. The design had a multiplier effect that will serve the Kenyan population and beyond.

The Program under Amani:
The End-Program Evaluation and Phaseout

An end-program assessment was executed in August 2002, two years after Amani took over—unlike the one-year assessments for both OpRec and KRC. In the two years under Amani, the program had assorted impacts, some reaching or even exceeding their targets and others not achieving their targets. These effects were felt in three areas: counseling and psychiatric services, outreach, and training services.

Targets for the counseling of adults and children and also for the provision of psychiatric services to adult survivors were exceeded, for more or less the same reasons: effective outreach, but also the possibility that others who were not affected by the bombing were also being included. However, there was underachievement in regard to the targets for providing psychiatric treatment to child survivors and for clinical supervision meetings. Reasons for underachievement in the area of psychiatric treatment for children included few referrals to the psychiatrists, a shortage of trained child therapists, and the stigma that parents associated with seeing a psychiatrist. The tools for assessment of the children were poorly understood, and the fact that clinical supervision is a new concept in Kenya could be an explanation for the underachievement.

On the outreach side, only the target on the upcountry families was achieved. This was because of the large, extended families in Kenya, and also because many people migrated from Nairobi after the bombing. The rest of the outreach targets were underachieved: affected children, adults, families who were seriously injured, community meetings, and media presentations. The reasons for this underachievement varied from transport and communication problems to administrative constraints.

Similar patterns were noted in regard to the set targets for training services, with overachievement in the training of mental health providers and key decision makers, and also in the training of community-based mental health providers. The target for staff development was also achieved. The main reason for these achievements was the enthusiasm shown by the trainees. However, there was underachievement in the set target for training counselors from implementing partners and in the training of teachers in trauma mental health. The reasons for underachievement in these areas included a lack of qualified counselors to do the training, and administrative constraints. The key goal of the program still remained: to provide mental health assistance to people affected by the bomb on August 7, 1998, that would enable them to cope with effects of the disaster. The purpose was to provide people with mental health services that would assist them in developing adaptive coping mechanisms.

The target population was classified into five groups:

1. Primary victims—those who were directly hit by the blast and needed psychiatric treatment, intensive counseling, and psychological and educational awareness.
2. The bereaved—those whose next of kin had died and who mostly were the breadwinners in their families. They needed direct material support and grief and loss counseling.
3. Rescue workers—those who rescued the injured and recovered bodies. They needed direct psychiatric treatment (for some), individual and group counseling, and psychoeducational awareness.
4. Community members—those who lived and worked in the vicinity of the bombing. They needed basic psychoeducational awareness,

group counseling and information on trauma management, and potential referral to metal health services.

5. Outside community—the larger public, which through their communities and involvement had been psychologically affected by the disaster. They needed information about symptoms of trauma-related stress and where resources were available for help.

Beyond the Crisis Mental Health Support Program

The following have been direct results of the impact of the American Embassy bombing:

1. There is increased awareness in Kenya about the impact of terrorism and the need to contain it.
2. There is increased awareness of disasters and the need for disaster preparedness and management. Indeed, a disaster response unit has been put in place in the office of the president.
3. There is increased awareness of psychotrauma among the general public.
4. Some of the implementing partners and agencies associated with the response have continued to pursue trauma- and disaster-related activities in such areas as advocacy, service provision, research, and teaching.
5. Several research activities concerned with disaster and psychotrauma in Kenya have been undertaken, and others are in the process of being undertaken mainly by the United States International University (USIU), as well as by the University of Nairobi's Department of Psychiatry and the Africa Mental Health Foundation. These have been published as university Master's degree dissertations, monographs, and articles in peer-referred journals.
6. The University of Nairobi's Department of Psychiatry now has an operational postgraduate program on psychotrauma, with student enrolment from outside Kenya.
7. Psychological counseling and clinical psychology are being taught as professional degree programs in the local universities, with the University of Nairobi's Departments of Psychiatry and Psychology playing the leading roles in the country and in the region.
8. Disaster preparedness is being taught as both separate units and full courses, with the University of Nairobi playing the leading role in the country and the region.
9. Many seminars on disaster and psychotrauma are being organized, both locally and regionally.
10. In summary, the achievements described in this chapter indicate that something good came out of the August 7, 1998, terrorist bombing at the American Embassy building in Nairobi.

Acknowledgments

To the Amani Counseling Center and Training Institute (ACCTI) for providing records (listed below) from which the factual details were extracted.

To members of the Steering Committee, led by Dr. Margaret Meck, for agreeing to be interviewed. Also interviewed were other people associated with the program in various capacities.

To all implementing partners, the Kenya Red Cross, Operation Recovery, all crisis mental health staff and survivors, and Dr. Gordon R. Dodge, PhD, L.P., for overall support and guidance on this Mental Health Response Program.

To the Africa Mental Health Foundation (AMHF) for supporting a three-day, out-of-town residential writing workshop to put the report together and edit it. Grace Mutevu of the AMHF typed and retyped the many drafts of the report.

Reference

Driscoll, G. S. (2001). *Up from the ashes: Lessons learned from the bombing of the United States embassy Nairobi, Kenya* [USAID Project 615-0269.00]. Washington, DC: U.S. Department of State. Retrieved October 5, 2005, from http://pdf.dec.org/pdf_docs/PNACN621.pdf

CHAPTER 8

Psychosocial Research and Interventions after the Rwanda Genocide

Richard Neugebauer

Introduction

Low-intensity internecine warfare is endemic in many regions of sub-Saharan Africa. These wars, nourished by recruitment of child soldiers and characterized by the indiscriminate killing of civilians and the attendant forced migrations, has marked and enduring consequences for the mental health burden of these societies. In the last decade and a half, international agencies, local governmental, and nongovernmental organizations (NGOs) have turned their attention to the mental health problems produced by complex humanitarian crises (Neugebauer, 1997, 1999a, 1999b). Operating in resource poor settings, confronted with enormous affected populations living under highly disorganized, often harrowing circumstances, the staff of these agencies unavoidably draw heavily on the expertise of Western mental health consultants when designing research and interventions. The work of these organizations deserves respect, given the extraordinarily difficult, hastily assembled resources and dire circumstances under which their programs were established. Insofar as this chapter is critical of the mental health initiatives in Rwanda, such criticism should not detract from the courage and powerful humanitarian drive motivating the creators of these programs. However, we are obliged to evaluate the guiding theory, evidence, implementation, and evaluation of these research and intervention programs to harvest appropriate lessons.

Rwandan Program for Trauma Recovery

Following the 1994 genocide, UNICEF Rwanda, together with the ministries of the new Rwandan government, initiated an ambitious, nationwide programmatic response to address the mental health consequences of the conflict. These efforts, intended primarily for children, were directed and implemented with the assistance of several Western, predominantly Scandinavian, clinical consultants. We focus on three key elements of these initiatives implemented in the period 1994–1997: descriptive epidemiological research, psychosocial interventions, and evaluation of effectiveness of these interventions.

The interventions pursued a public health agenda insofar as the "treatment" was intended for all children, whether or not they evidenced signs of psychological distress, and care was delivered through existing social institutions, namely, primary schools. Efforts started as early as the summer of 1994 to establish what became the National Trauma Centre (NTC), a facility located near the capital, Kigali, that was staffed by Rwandan mental health professionals and foreign consultants. The center's aims were to conduct a nationwide child mental health survey—the National Trauma Survey—to estimate the prevalence of children's exposure to wartime violence and symptoms of post-traumatic stress disorder (PTSD); to establish a centralized program for educating Rwandan paraprofessionals—known as trauma advisers—about the recognition and treatment of psychological responses to trauma; to create a decentralized, community-based program in which the trauma advisers disseminated an abbreviated elementary version of their own training to community leaders, who were then expected to implement trauma recovery programs in their localities; and to form a specialized trauma clinic, housed in the NTC and staffed by psychologists and psychiatric nurses, to serve both as a walk-in outpatient service and a tertiary care center for more severely affected children and adults.

In 1997, at the request of UNICEF Rwanda, acting in concert with the Ministry of Health, the author assembled a team of mental health experts to evaluate the NTC programs. The group consisted of three American and European mental health professionals joined by two members of the Ministry of Health. Generous assistance was also provided by UNICEF staff members and by the director and staff of the NTC (Jensen et al., 1997). This chapter is based on materials examined during this evaluation, together with subsequent reports issued by UNICEF and published in journals by some of the foreign consultants. The views expressed here are solely those of the current author and are not necessarily shared by all members of the 1997 evaluation team.

National Trauma Survey: Estimating Exposure to Violence and Symptoms of Post-Traumatic Stress Disorder among Rwandan Children

A National Trauma Survey was conducted in 1995, constituting the first cross-sectional study (Wave 1) of what was to be a multiwave investigation. Approximately 3,000 children age 8–19 years, drawn from 11 of Rwanda's 12 prefectures were interviewed. By design, half of the sample were boys; half of the sample was also selected from orphanages (Unaccompanied Children Centres [UCCs]), and the rest from primary and secondary schools. On average, the children had five years of schooling (range, 0–12 years; Dyregrov, Gupta, Gjestad, & Mukanoheli, 2000; Gupta, 1996, 1997).

The interviews obtained demographic data on each child and inquired about wartime exposures to violence. It also included a 22-item revised version of the Impact of Events Scale (Horowitz, Wilner, & Alvarez, 1979), an inventory of post-traumatic stress symptoms. Children indicated whether they had experienced a particular symptom "not at all," "rarely," "sometimes," or "often" in the last two weeks. The published report of this study only counted as present symptoms occurring "often," a practice we adopt here as well (Dyregrov et al., 2000.)

Children's levels of exposure to wartime violence were extraordinarily high. Nearly all children (87 percent) reported having seen dead bodies or parts of bodies, 80 percent had experienced the death of a family member during the war, one-third had specifically witnessed the killing of a family member, and 50 percent had been present during massacres (see Table 8.1).

As expected, post-traumatic stress symptoms in this group were extremely common: 35 percent reported intrusive thoughts or images, 67 percent avoided reminders of the war, 15 percent had difficulty concentrating, and 20 percent experienced exaggerated startle reactions (see Table 8.2).

Surveys of this type are invaluable assets in efforts to recruit the attention and increase the likelihood of humanitarian assistance from the international community. Thus, the descriptive findings from this survey—most notably, the near universality of children's exposure to atrocious acts of violence—received media attention at the time and probably helped to convey to the wider public through these child witnesses something of the scale and psychological lethality of the genocide. In this regard, the survey was well conceived and executed and the findings widely and appropriately disseminated. However, in epidemiological research, cross-sectional surveys are typically used to assess the burden of disease, distress, or disability in the community and to thereby guide rational allocation of health care resources.

Despite the initial plans of the investigators (Dyregrov et al., 2000; Jensen et al. 1997), the epidemiological as contrasted with the advocacy yield from the National Trauma Survey has proved comparatively meager. Several reasons for the limited programmatic and epidemiological value of the survey

Table 8.1
National Trauma Center/UNICEF 1995 Survey of Rwandan
Children's Exposure to War Scenes in the 1994 Genocide (N = 3,030)

Traumatic Exposure	Percentage Answering Affirmatively
Bereavement	
Have you experienced death in your family due to war?	78.3
If yes, were both parents killed?	36.5
Sister(s)	21.9
Brother(s)	30.9
Witnessed violence	
Have you witnessed with your own eyes someone being injured or killed?	69.8
Did you hear people screaming for help?	79.1
Someone being shot	43.3
Killings/injuries with pangas (machetes)	58.3
Rape or sexual assault	30.8
Dead bodies/parts of bodies	87.4
Many people killed at one time (massacres)	52.5
Children participating in killing(s) or injuring	35.7
Family members being killed	35.6
Contact with cadavers	
Hid under dead bodies?	16.0
Length of time you hid (four to eight weeks or longer)?	52.7

results may be noted. First, the post-traumatic stress symptom data were reported and later analyzed by symptom, not by child. The proportion of comparatively asymptomatic children, of symptomatic children reporting only reexperiencing and avoidant behaviors, and of children reporting the full panoply of symptomatology characteristic of post-traumatic stress disorder— reexperiencing, avoidance, hyperarousal—have not been reported. Second, as readily recognized by the investigators, information on the clinical signifi- cance of the symptoms, for example, on the degree of associated social impairment, was not obtained. As a consequence, no estimates are available as to the proportion of children who might have met full criteria for post- traumatic stress disorder and who were severely impaired in day-to-day activities and relationships. Although the social meaning and utility of a diagnostic approach to distress on such a massive scale may be legitimately questioned (Summerfield, 2000), nonetheless, if we aim to assess whether the psychosocial devastation of the genocide attenuates over time or is

Table 8.2
Rwandan Children's Symptoms of Post-Traumatic Stress National Trauma Survey
1995 (N = 1,830)

Post-Traumatic Stress Symptom	Percentage Reporting Symptom "Often"
Reexperiencing	
Think about events when you do not want to	34.9
Pictures of the event suddenly pop into your head	17.2
Reminders of event make you tremble, heart beat fast	31.6
Avoidance/affective blunting	
Avoid reminders of the event	67.1
Trouble experiencing feelings like love, happiness, sadness	19.0
Less interested in activities you used to enjoy	9.9
Increased arousal	
Difficulty paying attention/concentrating	14.1
Startle more easily because of loud noises	20.2
More irritable than before	14.2

responsive to community-based or individual-focused interventions, these diagnostic categories are one convenient metric for addressing these questions. Third, focusing almost exclusively on trauma symptoms precluded any opportunity to learn about other psychiatric consequences of the genocide. Fourth, for the children living in the community, no information was obtained on their current residential circumstances; for example, whether they lived in child-headed households or with adult relatives or with nonrelations. Thus, an opportunity to identify environmental, familial, economic, or cultural factors that might exacerbate or inoculate against the development and persistence of traumatic and other classes of symptoms was apparently overlooked.

Wave 2 of the survey was fielded the following year. In part because of security considerations, only 327 children were interviewed. Among these children, 44 percent were living in UCCs; half were male; mean age, 14.6 years. The level of traumatic exposure during the genocide among the children in the Wave 2 subsample was similar to that in the original Wave 1 sample. However, post-traumatic symptoms were notably higher in the Wave 2 sample. For example, 18 percent of the Wave 2 children reported difficulty sleeping; in Wave 1 it was 10 percent. The corresponding numbers for loss of interest in activities once enjoyed were 26 percent versus 10 percent; for intrusive images, 34 percent versus 17 percent; for heightened irritability, 14 percent versus 30 percent, respectively.

At first glance, these findings give the impression that children's traumatic symptom levels had increased, not declined, over time. However, Wave 2 children were not a random sample of children drawn from Wave 1, and furthermore, symptoms of the children in the Wave 2 sample have not yet been compared with their own Wave 1 symptom levels. In addition, a more rigorous analysis would need to take account of traumatic exposures occurring between Wave 1 and Wave 2. As a consequence, these data at present do not elucidate the direction of symptom change in the years following the genocide—a matter of urgent public health concern as well as of scientific interest.

Epidemiological surveys conducted in the aftermath of a loss or a trauma may confer unintended therapeutic benefits (Neugebauer et al., 1992). By the same token, they may produce unintended harm, for example, through retraumatization. Accordingly, researchers are obligated to undertake some type of monitoring activity to assess such untoward effects. Equally compelling is their obligation to provide or at least to offer care or referral for care to severely disturbed individuals. Determined and systematic efforts to provide these protections for the children participating in the survey were not undertaken.

Trauma Alleviation Programs

Training of Trauma Advisers and "Social Agents"

The trauma adviser training at the NTC was approximately three months in duration. It consisted of didactic instruction, a "practicum" in a locality, monthly supervisory sessions and additional training two days per month. Training sessions were run by UNICEF's senior mental health consultants. The didactic instruction aimed to give trainees a basic understanding of child development, attachment theory, bereavement, and the nature and characteristics of symptom formation following traumatic experiences. The trainees also learned the cardinal elements of trauma alleviation methods that emphasized ventilation and emotional processing through reworking of the traumatic events (e.g., by means of artwork, dance, and storytelling). These methods also entailed normalization of emotional reactions to the trauma, seeking thereby to assist the child in shaping and reshaping these otherwise deeply troubling, inchoate experiences (Nambaje, 1997; Raundalen, 1995; UNICEF, 1995b).

Typically, two trauma advisers were assigned to each prefecture. They were responsible for disseminating knowledge about trauma and its treatment to local "social agents" (i.e., primary and secondary school teachers, community leaders, UCC staff, and health workers). Trauma advisers organized two- to four-day training sessions with groups of approximately 20 social agents each. These sessions were intended to teach social agents to recognize traumatic reactions and to train them in simple counseling techniques to be implemented in schools and in other group settings. A typical program plan for primary school teachers recommended these counseling sessions for two hours per week for four or more weeks in succession. During the first two-hour session, the children, guided by the teacher, discussed their lives before the conflict. At the following meeting, they were urged to recount their experiences during the war, both the violence they had witnessed or been subjected to and the feelings triggered by these experiences. The third group session afforded the teacher an opportunity to offer the children some explanation of the social and political origins of the war. In the concluding meeting, the children described their hopes and expectations for the future.

Theory Underlying Trauma Intervention

Although not so identified, this approach resembles a more extended version of psychological debriefing developed for the alleviation or prevention of post-traumatic stress disorder. It takes as its premise the inability of post-traumatic stress reactions to resolve naturally, without assistance even from the passage of time. It assumes, as well, that recollection and expression of the feelings associated with the trauma are safe and effective means for achieving symptom relief. As a consequence, participation in this therapy is seen as requisite for the restoration of mental health.)

An Uncontrolled Trial of Trauma Alleviation Methods

According to UNICEF estimates, several thousand school teachers were trained in these methods, making it altogether possible that well over 100,000 children were offered some type of trauma intervention in their classroom (Jensen et al., 1997). Despite the impressive scope and goals of this undertaking, apparently only one treatment trial was conducted to evaluate the effectiveness of these school-based trauma recovery programs.

In 1995, 22 teachers were given the two-day trauma training program and then proceeded to implement the program in classrooms in one Kigali primary school. Roughly 400 students, from 6 to 16 years of age, participated in these sessions over a three- to five-week period (UNICEF, 1995a). A month after the intervention, the students completed questionnaires, sometimes assisted by their teachers, asking them to compare their current symptom levels (e.g., nightmares, intrusive thoughts and images, ability to concentrate) with levels before the intervention. Most of the students reported improvement in each of these areas (see Figure 8.1). However, 30 percent of the children indicated an increase rather than a decrease in nightmares, 25 percent reported increased problems with intrusive thoughts and images, and 16 percent mentioned increased difficulty concentrating.

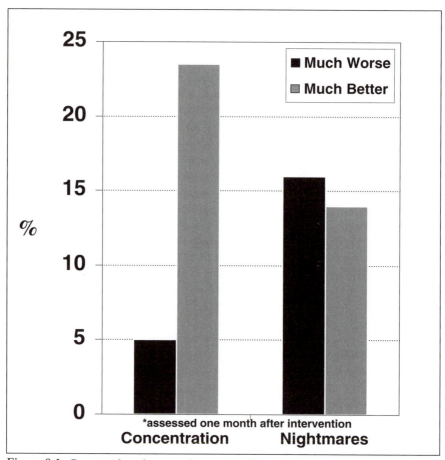

Figure 8.1 Open trial evaluation of a trauma alleviation program in Kigali primary and secondary schools, UNICEF Rwanda, 1995. Percentage of children reporting marked improvement or marked deterioration in concentration and nightmares.

These findings appear to indicate that the intervention benefited the plurality of children while, at the same time, a substantial proportion were harmed. However, without a control group, these results are uninformative. It is important to note that a finding of universal improvement for all children among those treated is entirely compatible with a beneficial, harmful, or null effect of the intervention. If the natural course of post-traumatic stress symptoms in untreated individuals is dramatic improvement over 12 months, then moderate improvement in symptoms among treated children affords evidence that the intervention retards recovery and therefore is potentially harmful. If the natural course of symptoms in untreated individuals is moderate improvement, then moderate improvement in the treated group indicates that treatment itself confers no advantage over normal recovery. Only if the natural course of symptoms in untreated individuals is for symptom levels to remain unchanged or to increase does a finding of symptom decline in treated individuals provide clear support for treatment efficacy. Recent meta-analyses indicate that debriefing after psychological trauma confers no advantage whatsoever over natural recovery. In fact, some individual studies found increased risk for development of post-traumatic stress disorder (Rose, Brewin, Andrews, & Kirk, 1999; Van Emmerik, Kamphuis, Hulsbosch, & Emmelkamp, 2002) in the months following treatment. As a consequence, we are not entitled to assume either that mental health interventions after a major trauma are beneficial, or even that they are safe. Whether the UNICEF Rwandan trauma alleviation program increased, decreased, or did not influence the persistent post-traumatic stress symptoms among participating children is not known.

Wave 1 data from the National Trauma Survey also afforded a valuable opportunity to examine possible intervention effectiveness within the framework of an observational study design. As expected, that survey found that children's levels of traumatic symptoms were directly correlated with degree of exposure to wartime violence: children with higher levels of exposure to violence reported greater numbers of symptoms. However, whereas the UCC children had experienced more wartime violence compared with the community-based children, the UCC children had lower levels of traumatic symptoms compared with the community children. The UCCs had been the sites of systematic implementation of trauma alleviation programs. These findings prompted the investigators to raise the possibility that the genocide so damaged traditional social systems—at least in the early years following the war—as to render placement in families less beneficial for children's mental health than retention in orphanages with staff able to offer psychosocial treatment for traumatization. Accordingly, the authors questioned the established preference within UNICEF of emphasizing rapid return to children to families living in the community.

Interpretation of study findings as indicating a preference for orphanage with trauma alleviation programs over home warrants critical examination and must be reviewed critically, especially because its translation into policy would reverse currently accepted practices. The absence of evidence of program effectiveness or efficacy from any randomized controlled trials is sufficient grounds to remain skeptical of such interpretations. Reasonable alternative explanations for these findings abound. For example, although the children living in the community reported lower levels of exposure to wartime violence, they may have experienced substantially more exposure to post—emergency-phase violence than the UCC children, thereby reigniting or maintaining their earlier post-traumatic stress symptoms. Thus, reduced opportunity for additional exposures, rather than the effectiveness of psychosocial treatments, may explain the lower symptom levels among UCC children. Another explanatory scenario pertains to the criterion used by center directors or by school teachers in selecting students for evaluation. UCC directors may have put forward less-symptomatic children in an effort

to advertise the psychological benefits of their centers. The teachers, in contrast, may have selected more symptomatic children, thinking to advocate
for UNICEF programming in the schools.

Post-Traumatic Stress Symptoms as the Litmus Test for the Best Interests of the Child

Apart from methodological caveats, drawing programmatic inferences
from National Trauma Survey findings is problematic on more fundamental
grounds. The survey takes as its unstated premise that the level of post-traumatic stress symptoms can serve as an adequate litmus test and guide in
selecting programs and placements in the best interests of the child. Psychiatric research sometimes overlooks the fact that illness exists within a specific social and cultural framework; public health solutions that are at odds
with this framework may be hazardous to health in the longer term for
afflicted individual and the community alike. Whatever the possible benefits
derived from sequestering children in UCCs, with regard to post-traumatic
stress symptoms, needs to be weighed against the effect of such institutional-
ization on child development. Further, outside the scope of this public
health calculus is the inestimable value for children (and for the larger society) of being nested within, rather than at a distance from, their own community and culture.

Conclusion

In 1998, UNICEF Rwanda substantially reduced funding for the trauma
recovery program. Thus, the 1997 evaluation was the last to be conducted
before the trauma recovery program, installed in the months immediately following the genocide, was dramatically scaled back. As such, the evaluation
assessed the UNICEF Rwanda program at a major juncture in its history.

What lessons can be learned from this ambitious post–emergency mental
health program? First, of note is that the qualitative evidence accumulated
during the 1997 evaluation—a detailed presentation of which is beyond the
scope of this chapter—was highly supportive of the program's goals and
accomplishments (Jensen et al., 1997). Staff from the National Trauma Center, trauma advisers, school teachers, and nongovernmental organization
staff were strongly convinced that these mental health initiatives were
acceptable and suitable for the Rwandan population at large. In a geograph-
ically broad-based survey, teachers indicated that they had readily adopted
these elementary methods of trauma alleviation in their classrooms and
judged them to be effective. Accordingly, the most commonly expressed dis-
satisfaction was not with any possible irrelevance of the brief course they
had been offered but, rather, with the absence of further training to enable
them to help more severely affected children (Nambaje, 1997). However, it
should be remembered that the information provided in the in-person inter-

views and in the written questionnaires was likely influenced by respondents' knowledge that the evaluators were affiliated with UNICEF, a principal humanitarian funding agency in Rwanda.

Despite its farsighted and arduous efforts to implement mental health interventions in Rwanda, the quantitative data collected by UNICEF pertaining to these initiatives were insufficiently informative to guide future projects. It is unclear, for example, what effects—if any—were achieved by the community-based psychosocial interventions. Nor is it possible to use the quantitative data to elucidate, to confirm, or to discredit the qualitative findings. Interpretable findings would have required the introduction of rigorous evaluation mechanisms or proper study designs implemented at the outset or in the course of program development. Such efforts were not undertaken.

The UNICEF Rwanda trauma recovery program suffered from at least two major shortcomings: First, a decontextualized approach to psychiatric symptoms was taken; second, the conviction, borne of clinical experience not clinical trials, that "talking cures" are safe and efficacious was assumed. By and large, the UNICEF programs focused single-mindedly on the symptomatic sequelae of trauma—specifically, the classic symptoms of posttraumatic stress disorder—without weighing their clinical significance or effect on social functioning. Although relief from the subjective suffering associated with these symptoms is a crucial concern for mental health clinicians, equally important is the restoration of social functioning, because it is such functioning that is key to engagement in family and community life, the resumption of participation in the reassuring routines of everyday existence in civil society, and the recovery of culture. Social functioning was not investigated in the National Trauma Survey.

Talking cures were seen as the sole mechanisms capable of alleviating traumatic stress symptoms. Neither nature nor nurture was judged sufficient to restore mental health and well-being. Current evidence indicates that the exact reverse may be more correct. In sum, the mental health research undertaken by UNICEF in Rwanda provides little guidance for developing mental health services or training of mental health professionals. At the same time, to date, the safety and effectiveness of the mental health interventions introduced into Rwanda is unknown, and with the significant passage of time since its inception, it will probably remain so.

References

Dyregrov, A., Gupta, L., Gjestad, R., & Mukanoheli, E. (2000). Trauma exposure and psychological reactions to genocide among Rwandan children. *Journal of Traumatic Stress, 13*, 3–19.

Gupta, L. (1996). *Exposure to war-related violence among Rwandan children and adolescents: A brief report of the national baseline trauma survey* [internal report]. Kigali, Rwanda: UNICEF, Trauma Recovery Programme.

————. (1997). Follow-up survey of Rwandan children's reactions to war related violence from the genocide in 1994. Rwanda: UNICEF. Retrieved March 7, 2005, from http://www.unicef.org/evaldatabase/index_14242.html

Horowitz, M., Wilner, N., & Alvarez, W. (1979). Impact of Events Scale: A measure of subjective distress. *Psychosomatic Medicine, 41,* 209–218.

Jensen, S. B., Neugebauer, R., Marner, T., George. S., Ndahiro, L., & Rurangwa, E. (1997). The Rwandan children and their families: Understanding, prevention and health of traumatization [RWA 1997/002]. Rwanda: UNICEF. Retrieved March 7, 2005, from http://www.unicef.org/evaldatabase/index_15409.html

Nambaje, A. (1997). Final consultancy report of activities at the National Trauma Center (May, 1996–June, 1997). Kigali: UNICEF.

Neugebauer, R. (1997). The uses of psychological epidemiology in promoting refugee health. *American Journal of Public Health, 87,* 726–728.

————. (1999a). Mind matters: The importance of mental disorders in public health's 21st century mission. *American Journal of Public Health, 89,* 1309–1311.

————. (1999b). Research on violence in developing countries: Benefits and perils. *American Journal of Public Health, 89,* 1473–1474.

————, Kline, J., O'Connor, P., Shrout, P., Johnson, J., Skodol, A., et al. (1992). Depressive symptoms in the six months after miscarriage. *American Journal of Obstetrics and Gynecology, 166,* 104–109.

Raundalen, M. (1995). War traumatized children: Guidelines for trauma advisors. Kigali: Child Recovery Centre.

Rose, S., Brewin, C. R., Andrews, B., & Kirk, M. (1999). A randomized controlled trial of individual psychological debriefing for victims of violent crime. *Psychological Medicine, 29,* 793–799.

Summerfield, D. (2000). Childhood, war, refugeedom and "trauma": Three core questions for mental health professionals. *Transcultural Psychiatry, 37,* 417-433.

United Nations Children's Fund. (1995a). Alleviating trauma in school: Report after teacher training, and evaluation on trauma alleviation in schools in Kigali. Kigali: Author.

————. (1995b). Guidelines for teachers helping war traumatized children in schools. Trauma Recovery Programme. Kigali, Rwanda: Author.

Van Emmerik, A., Kamphuis, J., Hulsbosch, A., & Emmelkamp, P. (2002). Single session debriefing after psychological trauma: A meta-analysis. *The Lancet, 360,* 766–771.

CHAPTER 9

APPROACHES TO PSYCHOSOCIAL HEALING: CASE EXAMPLES FROM LUSOPHONE AFRICA

Inger Agger

This chapter is based on a study that was part of a multidisciplinary research program: "Conflict and its aftermath: Health and social consequences of a complex emergency in Guinea-Bissau; preconditions and long-term consequences." The research program, which started in June 1999, ran over a three-year period and was funded by the Danish Council for Development Research/Danish International Development Agency.

The objective of the study was to contribute to the understanding of complex emergencies in Africa by analyzing psychosocial aspects of armed conflict and humanitarian interventions exemplified by case studies from Lusophone Africa (Angola, Mozambique, and Guinea-Bissau). The material for the study was collected and elaborated during a one-year period (from June 1, 1999, to June 2000) that included language studies and fieldwork among nongovernmental organizations (NGOs) in Lisbon in June 1999, fieldwork in Guinea-Bissau in October 1999, and work in Angola in June 2000.

Introduction

Although there is little doubt about the need for assisting the ever-increasing numbers of civilians who are exposed to armed conflict (even de Waal [1997], who is strongly critical of humanitarian aid, says that "it is morally unacceptable to allow people to suffer and die on the grounds that relieving their suffering will support an obnoxious government or army," p. 220), the ways and means of providing this humanitarian assistance are diverse and subject to much dispute. This chapter primarily concerns a specific type of assistance, namely, psychosocial interventions for war-affected people. An intervention is here understood as an organized action carried out by an international or local humanitarian organization with a specific purpose—in this case, with the stated purpose of promoting the psychological or social well-being of a designated group of people.

Through case examples, various discourses of healing are examined—with special emphasis on two main approaches that are currently widely disputed in the aid community: the protection-oriented rights approach, associated with interventions that respect and protect the "rights" of local culture and traditions, versus the more treatment-oriented trauma approach, associated with the application of Western, "medical" intervention modes in developing countries. The dichotomy between these two approaches is mirrored in present-day discussions about Denmark's new strategy in development aid, in which an approach of "advocacy" is opposed to "service delivery," with Denmark now emphasizing the advocacy approach (Danish International Development Agency, 2000).

The chapter presents material about psychosocial healing from three African countries that have recently been involved in armed conflict: Angola, Mozambique, and Guinea-Bissau. These countries are all Lusophone, that is, former Portuguese colonies in Africa, in which Portuguese is still the official language. In Angola and Mozambique traditional, local modes of healing war trauma have been revived and systematically investigated in an exceptional manner during the 1990s, and it is the author's hypothesis that this development is related to the history of these two countries as Portuguese colonies and to the Portuguese ideology from colonial times, lusotropicalism, and its successor, Afro-Marxism.

The official revival of traditional modes of healing in these countries by local professionals and authorities could be related to a revolt against the "exotic interest" of colonial days when Portuguese anthropologists studied the "strange" tribal habits, a better survival of traditional modes in relation to other African countries because of the disinterest of the Portuguese in "developing" their colonies, or an expression of people's rights to their own ethnic identity after having passed through an Afro-Marxist period that adored modernity. It is the hypothesis that the discourse of lusotropicalism is still an element in the social identity of Portuguese NGO staff and African "cadres" during times of crisis. This was seen in the recent armed conflict in Guinea-Bissau and manifested in a sense of having a unique, although ambivalent, relationship with each other. A section about Guinea-Bissau describes the first crisis interventions by international organizations. It shows examples of how the planning of psychosocial interventions was not informed by the knowledge already developed in Angola and Mozambique, a knowledge that was widely recognized by international organizations working in these countries. In Guinea-Bissau, where traditional modes of healing are very much alive, people find their own ways of alleviating suffering, as

I demonstrate with two case examples. It is an open question whether interventions were needed in that context. The last section suggests transcultural
factors active in healing processes, especially the similarities between Western psychosomatic approaches and traditional African healing rituals, in
which participants enter into altered states of consciousness.

Armed Conflict in Africa

During the decolonization processes and revolutions following the end of
World War II, issues of national and ethnic identity gained major significance across much of Africa. All of the former Portuguese colonies fought
very long liberation wars, and after gaining independence, several
attempted to follow the Soviet political model. The collapse of the Soviet
Union and the end of the Cold War brought a new era of instability, chaos,
and civil wars that upset the balance of the political systems throughout
much of Africa and the developing world. Wars were more frequently
fought within states than between states and were often ignited by ethnopolitical ideologies. As experienced by the author in the civil wars of the Caucasus and the Balkans in the 1990s, questions of ethnic, national, and gender
identity became core issues among people whose social fabric had been torn
apart when the old political structures were disrupted (Agger, 2001a, 2001b).

Across decades of crisis, traditional African extended family and cultural
patterns in Angola and Mozambique came under severe stress accompanied
by new needs for defining group identity. In situations that, on both the family and the societal levels, threatened personal safety, ethnicity became a
major means of defining group identity. The rupture of family and community coherence can also be presumed to have challenged the capacity to
manage war trauma in traditional ways, and local healing patterns probably
underwent changes along with the population movements. Moreover, some
Afro-Marxist leaders did not encourage traditional healing modes, finding
that they were not compatible with modernity and development. However,
as demonstrated in this chapter, traditional healing modes eventually underwent a revival in Angola and Mozambique.

The wars in Lusophone Africa were bitter and extremely protracted. In
Angola the war started in 1961 as an anticolonialist war and continued as a
civil war for more 40 years. A whole generation has grown up there without knowing any condition other than war. Angola is the only Lusophone
country with rich natural resources of oil and diamonds—a fact that has
contributed to the protracted conflict there. The anticolonialist war in
Mozambique lasted from 1964 to 1975 and led to independence, which
was then followed by 16 years of civil war. Similarly, Guinea-Bissau's revo-
lutionary war began in 1963 and led to independence in September 1973.
However, unlike Mozambique, peace endured in Guinea-Bissau until
1998, when armed conflict again broke out, spurred by a rebellion within
the armed forces.

Lusotropicalism

The word "lusotropicalism" describes the idea that a new and better civilization was created in the Portuguese colonies as a result of conversion to Christianity and interracial procreation between colonists and the indigenous peoples. One of the doctrines of lusotropicalism was that Portuguese colonialists were different from other colonialists because they felt class solidarity with the Africans. This was attributed to the fact that most of the Portuguese colonialists were poor, many of them were "degradados" who had been released from prisons in Portugal, and they therefore felt closer to the local population with whom they intermarried and worked on an equal footing. Today, many Portuguese who view themselves as anticolonialist continue to employ the discourse of lusotropicalism, which has been "used to explain and justify the Portuguese presence in Africa" (Bender, 1978, p. 3). Although the Lusophone countries have now been independent for more than 25 years, there are still remnants of the colonial discourse in the relationship between Portugal and its former colonies.

There are five main ingredients in the lusotropicalist discourse: the Portuguese had a special ability to adapt to the tropics; the poor Portuguese colonialist felt much closer to the African people than to colonialists from richer, industrialized European countries; Brazil is the proof of this, with its large mestizo population; there were no racist laws in Portuguese Africa; any discrimination in the PALOP (Países africanos de lingual portuguesa—African countries whose official language is Portuguese: Angola, Cape Verde, Guinea-Bissau, Mozambique, Sao Tomé e Príncipe) countries were the result of class, not racial prejudice.

The discourse of "lusotropicalism" is examined in this chapter to understand the background for the official revival of traditional modes of healing in Angola and Mozambique. In the 1990s, the value of local traditions were recaptured and given new significance. In Angola and Mozambique, traditional healing modes were made the object of systematic research and were "officially" sanctioned by local authorities and leading local and international professionals. This revival was related to the managing of war trauma on both the individual and the community levels after disruptive civil wars had raged for many years.

Angola

The concern of both local and international organizations has been much needed in Angola. Many Angolans do not have any recollection of life in peaceful circumstances. A peace accord negotiated in 1991 established a cease-fire, but national elections led to renewed fighting when the losing faction refused to acknowledge their electoral defeat. Between 1992 and 1994, the fighting was particularly violent, with a great number of civilian casualties, indiscriminate bombings, executions, and tortures, as well as recruitment of child soldiers (Wessells & Monteiro, 2000). By 1994, there were more than a million internally displaced people (IDPs) in the country, and Angola was ranked as one of the most heavily mined countries in the world. After a series of cease-fires and the establishment of a new "unity" government, governmental and civil institutions are still weak and tensions remain high (Danish International Development Agency, 1999).

In some areas, the IDPs lived under extreme circumstances of deprivation characterized by malnutrition, lack of medical services, and inadequate water and sanitation. This has, in conjunction with inhumane shelter conditions with overcrowding, led to serious health problems and high risks of abuse, particularly for women and children. There were many international and national actors on the humanitarian aid scene, and some international and local organizations, such as United Nations Children's Fund (UNICEF), Save the Children, and Christian Children's Fund (CCF), were also providing psychosocial assistance for the war-affected children.

The Effect of War on Children

The psychological effect of the war on children has, according to investigations, been severe (UNICEF, 1996). Large percentages of children have experienced attacks and starvation, seen dead and wounded people, or suffered loss of relatives and belongings. Data show that many children experience fears, nightmares, concentration difficulties, heightened aggression, and chronic isolation. These problems are also evident in children's spontaneous drawings often depicting war-related scenes. However, as no pre-war data on children's psychological problems exist, these findings must be interpreted with care. The problems may not only be attributed to children's direct war experiences, but also to the indirect effects of war manifested in a general increase in family and community violence (Green & Wessells, 1997).

The war is estimated to have killed 500.000 children, and countless children who are mine victims suffer serious psychological problems in addition to their physical handicap. Many youth have become involved in banditry, having been socialized for fighting as child soldiers or through the general violent environment. Thus, "socialization for fighting is both a psychosocial impact of war and a source of continued violence" (Wessells & Monteiro, 2001, p. 7). For those with access to primary schools, the quality of education is constrained by teachers who are poorly motivated, trained, and paid, in addition to the lack of essential training materials. Moreover, there are large numbers of unaccompanied children all over Angola who have voluntarily or involuntarily separated from their families. They live either in institutions, with relatives, or on the streets (UNICEF, 2000). Recently, a new problem has arisen—that of children being accused by their families of being "witches" and thereafter abandoned. According to Monteiro (personal communication, 2000), this has never been a problem before in Angola, and this belief may have developed among returnees who have been influenced by the culture of neighboring countries.

Traditional Healing Rituals in Psychosocial Assistance to Child Soldiers

Some of the children needing attention had been involved in the conflicts as "child soldiers." Most of these children had been recruited by force and were taken from schools, taken from their homes, or kidnapped during military attacks. Those who joined the army out of their own will did it from political or ethnic motivations, from peer pressure, or in a search for protection, food, or the power that comes from owning a gun. Having a gun enabled the children to loot and to challenge the authority of the elders. The children were exposed to harsh military training that often included a process of "psychological pressure [that] made them lose their previous identity and assume a new one: that of a merciless killer" (Monteiro, personal communication, 2000). Girls were mostly used for domestic work, and many were also sexually exploited.

Many families received no news of their children for more than two or three years, and many presumed that they had died. Families were helped to find and reunite with their returning children, some of whom had fought on the opposing side. On arriving back in their communities, most of the former child soldiers were received with traditional ceremonies and purification rites, which in themselves helped in the reintegration process and gave the minors spiritual tranquillity. These ceremonies varied from region to region and involved the minor's family and the community itself. The role of traditional healers, who were also consulted at a later date if a youngster manifested some illness or some sort of psychosocial disturbance, was concerned mainly with purification and expulsion of evil spirits (Monteiro, personal communication, 2000).

Angolan professionals working with an American NGO, the CCF, took the lead in the revival and integration of traditional methods of healing for war-affected children. During the 1990s, CCF staff turned their attention to the healing of war trauma with projects like the one for reintegration of demobilized child soldiers. The general objective of that project was to contribute to the psychological and social reintegration of child soldiers. Critical of the Western "trauma" approach, the CCF staff criticized the widespread use of the clinical diagnosis of post-traumatic stress disorder in work with war-affected children. A number of articles were published advocating an integration of traditional African and Western methods. Local healing methods may involve the services of different Christian churches, traditional village chiefs, and traditional healers.

Evil Spirits

Psychological distress and trauma have social and cultural dimensions, and there is a body of knowledge in local traditions that can be useful in understanding how they operate. However, according to Honwana (1998), some traditional healing practices are considered to be dangerous and damaging, and it is therefore important to identify safe and helpful practices for the healing of the social wounds of war. For instance, in the widely exercised cult of the ancestors, spirits of the dead are responsible for promoting the well-being of individuals and entire communities, but can also do harm if they want to punish people. The spirits of the dead must be placated through rituals of veneration, but—very important in this context—the dead must also be given a proper burial ritual for the living to be able to establish a positive relationship with them.

In wars it becomes extremely difficult to bury the dead properly, and their spirits are believed to be unhappy and unsettled, with an enormous potential for harming the community. Mostly, during wars, the relatives have to perform the burial ritual without the dead body, and it is believed that the spirit of the dead would come with the wind to join the relatives when they organize a ritual. In times of war, when the breakdown of normal life does not allow the usual burial rituals to take place, it would therefore be important to perform collective ceremonies in honor of the dead. In a postwar reconstruction of the social fabric, such rituals for the dead would be essential in addressing the social pollution caused by the anger of the spirits of the dead.

In some communities, it was believed that the spirits of those whom the child soldiers had killed could haunt the youngsters and their families for the rest of their lives, and so it became extremely important to perform a symbolic cleansing before they resumed normal social life. A more complex healing process performed by specialist healers is needed when the spirits of the killed or tortured people take revenge on the ex-soldiers and cause conditions such as insanity, mental disturbance, sleeplessness, or panic attacks. In this ritual, the healer also talks with the youngster about what happened in the war—in this way having a cathartic function that could remind one of Western psychotherapeutic methods. However, as repeatedly emphasized by Honwana (1999), recounting and remembering the traumatic experiences is not necessarily seen as a condition for healing. On the contrary, "it is often believed to open the space for the malevolent forces to intervene" (p. 115). Healing primarily happens through nonverbal symbolic forces.

However, the Angolan professionals also found it useful to have access to Western approaches: "Without sensitization and training, local people typically do not connect their children's problematic behaviors—social isolation, heightened aggression, sleep and concentration problems, and so on—with the children's experiences of war and violence" (Wessells & Monteiro, 2000, p. 198). What the CCF has found to be most effective has been a pluralistic approach that combines several healing strategies such as traditional, Western, and religious healing. As noted by Honwana (1999), people at the local level often find their own ways of creating spaces in which they can heal the social wounds of war. They do not wait for humanitarian interventions.

Mozambique

Mozambique has had peace since 1992. However, although the war has ceased, daily life is still dominated by violence, poverty, hunger, displacement, and lack of dignity for many people (Honwana, 1999). Traditional modes of healing have been much more widespread in Mozambique than in Angola.

The Effect of War on Children

A survey of war-affected children in Mozambique carried out in 1989 by Save the Children (Boothby, 1992) showed that the vast majority of children had witnessed murder (77 percent), and even more had witnessed physical abuse or torture (88 percent). Comparable proportions had witnessed rape or sexual abuse (63 percent), and half of all children had themselves been physically abused or tortured. A majority had also been abducted from their families and forced to serve as porters or in combat roles (64 percent). Boothby also describes how Mozambican child survivors could "be seen staggering into government-run refugee centers, physically malnourished and psychologically numbed—sometimes speechless, seemingly incapable of showing any emotion other than a kind of unnerving wait-and-see stoicism" (1992, pp. 169-170).

According to Gibbs (1994), Mozambican families and teachers mostly see children "as strong and as survivors" (p. 11) and not as a special and vulnerable group. They have suffered during the war just as everybody else—they will also recover in the same way as adults. The Mozambican perception of "normal" child development is therefore very different from Western notions. Gibbs promotes the importance of learning from this local analytical framework that emphasizes resilience as opposed to trauma and sees children as the active creators of their own worlds. Ironically, this is the same framework that sanctions the use of children as soldiers, and many ideas in this local belief system about childhood would clash with Western ideas about child protection as expressed in the U.N. Convention on the Rights of the Child.

Community Healing and Reconciliation

Nordstom (1997) describes how a "culture of war and peace" emerged in Mozambique as local healers (*curandeiros*) set up new ways of treating people in public gatherings, taking "this violence out of people" and teaching them "healthy ways of thinking and acting" (pp. 142–143). Myths, stories, poetry, theater, and many other creative tools were also used to circulate knowledge about surviving and resistance. Nordstrom (1997) also went to Angola to find out whether there were similar types of movement there. In Angola, however, the resistance did not have the same nationwide character, although many of the ritual practices were similar. She found the Angolan society to be more divided, a place where "everything has been politicized" (p. 230)—there was not the same type of "third space" in which creative resistance to the war could develop.

Honwana (1997) notes that these local processes are undermined in a country where the social fabric has been severely disrupted, "the effectiveness of customary remedies has come into question" (p. 7). In addition, traditional leaders had also been compromised during colonialism because they often had a role in the system of "indirect rule" exercised by the Portuguese colonial administration. Nevertheless, Honwana still finds a strong argument for supporting traditional modes of healing and reconciliation.

Chicuecue (1997) discusses whether healing and reconciliation would have been facilitated more in Mozambique with a formal truth commission resembling the commission in South Africa. The South African Truth Commission worked on the basis of a Western and religiously inspired "trauma" approach that tried to achieve social and individual healing through witnessing and talking about the evil (Buur, 2000). The Mozambicans used another approach, working at the grassroots level, rebuilding "a culture of peace" through "alternative" ways of healing—especially traditional purification rituals. These were traditional methods of healing and reconciliation in which healers and chiefs played a vital role involving rituals wherein offenders acknowledged their wrongdoing: "To be healed, or freed from bad spirits, an offender must go to a traditional healer, and confess and acknowledge his wrongful deeds in order to be forgiven or freed from punishment" (p. 486). Chicuecue, who represents UNESCO, gives strong support to the use of traditional methods and also notes that "UNICEF and the Red Cross have encouraged those working with traumatised children and child-soldiers to respect traditional culture and collaborate with communities in their reintegration" (p. 485).

A Danish Project for War-Traumatized Children

The emphasis on understanding the cultural dimension of war trauma is underlined by an investigation by Igreja, Schreuder, and Kleijn (1999) of adults from two rural villages in a former war zone in central Mozambique. They found that "traumatic experiences" for a Mozambican could include disruptions in the relationship between the living and the dead, as well as war-related disruptions of the ceremonies and rituals surrounding birth, marriage, and death.

The necessity for understanding this cultural dimension became apparent in a project that was started in 1992 by Ibis, a Danish NGO, to assist war-traumatized children (Jakobsen, Cassamo, & Revel, 1996). In 1988, the Ministry of Education adopted a methodology called STOP (structure, talking, organizing, parental support) for its program for special education in 1988. This psychosocial method was developed in the 1980s by international humanitarian organizations working in refugee camps in different parts of the world. The objective of the Ibis project was to help war-traumatized children recover from their trauma by training social workers, teachers, and health staff in how to employ the STOP method.

In 1995, Ibis created Centres for Psychosocial Rehabilitation to strengthen its work for traumatized children, but a consulting team that visited the project in 1996 found that "it has not been easy to make the objectives of the centers understood by the population, their major preoccupation being to have schools and health services" (Jakobsen et al., 1996). Parents conceived of the centers as schools without fees and that, counter to the Western framework, the children did not exhibit symptoms of being traumatized. The team also noted that these spiritual and cultural aspects of rural Mozambican society were much more significant for the approach to children than the Danish training courses. The project soon changed its objectives, moving away from direct "treatment" toward more capacity building and support of local organizations.

Guinea-Bissau

When civil war broke out in Guinea-Bissau in 1998, there had been peace since independence in 1974. During the fighting, most of the people living in the capital city of Bissau fled to outside areas. There were no camps for them, and they stayed with host families and friends under very crowded and difficult circumstances. In 1999, after the president fled the country and sought political asylum in Portugal, a national coalition government assumed leadership of the country until democratic elections in 1999. Following these elections, a coalition of two parties took office in February 2000. Since then, a major challenge has been to provide young people (including demobilized soldiers), who constitute almost two-thirds of the population, with education. Other problems include the precarious stability and security situation within the country, as well as tensions along the border with Senegal. One of the arguments for international aid has been based on how "deeply traumatized" the people of Guinea-Bissau are, which illustrates how the "trauma" discourse is being employed at the highest political levels.

Assistance to War-Affected Children

In the early crisis period, psychosocial assistance seemed to have been planned by international organizations with little regard for the results that had been achieved in Angola and Mozambique. The American NGO IRC (International Rescue Committee, 1999) proposed establishing a project for war-affected youth in Bissau. According to the proposal, the 11 months of war had a profound effect on the well-being of children and adolescents in Bissau:

- Psychological trauma: The stress of being under artillery fire; witnessing deaths of friends, family, or soldiers; and living in unfamiliar and extremely poor areas of refuge had caused psychological trauma.

- Education: Schools were closed during the war, and the children had lost this space for normal social exchange, learning, and recreation.
- Recreation: Children were separated from their close friends.
- Income: Adolescents lost their part-time jobs.
- Child soldiers: An unknown number of male and female adolescents were believed to have joined the military. They were either recruited officially or served informally as civilians. Many were given guns and enjoyed a degree of power that could give psychological aftereffects.
- Crime: Some adolescents resorted to theft to survive.
- Prostitution: Young girls had become prostitutes to survive, mostly with the foreign troops as customers.
- Substance abuse: Many adolescents had begun drinking—some also used drugs.

The IRC project planned to provide vocational training and tutoring services to assist youth in catching up with school. The program also wanted to increase the self-esteem of young girls who had been sexually exploited, through education, recreational activities, and courses in reproductive health (sexuality, women's role in Guinean society, child bearing, and use of birth control/condoms). Special efforts were made to locate child soldiers and provide them with special services, such as courses, job placement, and counseling on violence. However, the few children who had fought for the ousted president did not show signs of great distress, and there did not seem to be many cases of rejection by society as a whole (McCauley, personal communication, 1999).

Psychological Trauma

Tensions between the "rights" and the "trauma" discourses came up in the preparation of the IRC project for war-affected youth. One main tension concerned the issue of psychological trauma: The IRC project proposal was framed in the trauma discourse, whereas the coordinator of the project was unofficially advised by the organization to follow the rights approach in practice. The coordinator of the project wondered whether the children in the capital Bissau would accept the old healing methods that attribute psychological suffering to spirits. She found that people mix several healing methods: the Christian church, the ancestors, and the djambakos, who are traditional healers. IRC never received enough funding for the project to be realized—donors did not give priority to Guinea-Bissau—and only a vocational training project was implemented, which resulted in the building of a small number of latrines.

According to the Swedish Save the Children Fund, there were few indications of widespread psychological war trauma in a Western sense of the concept (McCauley, personal communication, 1999). The Save the Children Fund organization is a firm adherent to the "rights approach" and believes that it is more important that people restore their dignity through family and community economic and social empowerment than through a "medical-ized" trauma approach, which is not viewed as sustainable.

UNICEF, which was one of the few international organizations that stayed in Guinea-Bissau during the war, seems to have been in a dilemma regarding the approach to war-affected children. In the beginning of the emergency, the organization expected to find many war-affected children and seemed to be quite focused on a trauma approach. UNICEF recommended a project for psychological counseling and war trauma resolution in which 60 Guinean psychological counselors should be trained in trauma detection and psychological counseling, as well as recommending that workshops should be held for 3,000 teachers and social and health workers on trauma detection. It was then the plan that these trainees should give orientation and information to 100,000 Guinean people (families, communities), "on the existence of war psychological trauma, its symptoms and consequences" (United Nations, 1998, p. 59). However, after a survey carried out by Save the Children Fund found that only 500 children were in need for treatment, the UNICEF project was considerably reduced (United Nations, 1999).

In mid-1999, UNICEF held a six-week training program on post-traumatic stress disorder for 15 social-health workers, who would in turn train teachers and other health workers to assist families with war-traumatized children. In relation to this training, the UNICEF program coordinator remarked in a memorandum (UNICEF, 1999, p. 3, my translation):

> The notion of psychological trauma is almost unknown in Guinea-Bissau, and violent reactions can be registered when faced with something that they perceive as insanity. One mother said that she would kill her child if she knew that it was suffering from psychological troubles. The cultural traditions foresee the elimination of a deficient child who belongs to the spirits and is not fed, or is abandoned on the riverbank, from where the spirits will take it back.

The UNICEF coordinator notes that Guinean health and educational staff have not been educated in child development or (Western) pedagogical methods and that a major objective of the training program is to prevent families or teachers from using harsh disciplinary methods toward disturbed children. In the following three months, a national consultant continued training monitors and teachers in the detection of psychological trauma (U.N. Office for the Coordination of Humanitarian Affairs, 1999b).

General Approach to Mental Health

The Guinean people are not used to bringing mental problems to the hospital, and they have a very rich tradition of treating these problems themselves, including those relating to the anticolonial liberation war. The official mental health system, such as it is, has neither the capacity nor any recognized need for treating war trauma. Those practitioners who are trained according to Western principles of diagnosis and treatment seldom feel any positive regard for traditional healing practices. Most people, even in urban areas, still feel related to their place of origin and, especially in times of distress, may choose to consult traditional healers from back home. Thus, seeking the services of traditional Guinean healers who represent spiritual powers might actually prove more acceptable and effective for treating war-related stress than going to the very poorly equipped mental health services, which are mainly prepared for treating psychotic conditions.

The War Veteran

This section is based on an interview with a Dutch anthropologist in Bissau, October 1999. Every ethnic group has a place of origin (*Chao*; Creole for "homeland/earth/floor"), where their main ancestors are buried. A former major from the Liberation War traveled to his *Chao* and was ritually treated for his psychosocial problems, which included excessive drinking and unpredictable and explosive behavior. The ceremony started at 5 A.M. with the rebuilding of the ancestor shrines and asking the ancestors for permission to start the ritual. Thereafter, the ex-soldier and his family went to a small place nearby in the forest where an ancestor spirit was located. The ex-soldier sat down next to the tree representing the ancestor spirit and started an intimate conversation with the spirit about his experiences in the *luta* (the struggle against the Portuguese).

Some of these experiences had been very painful, as, for example, when almost all the men in the group he was commander of had been killed— something that he felt guilty about. He was rocking back and forth with his head bowed while he explained all the dangers he had gone through, and he showed his scars to the ancestor-tree, thanking the ancestors for his survival. During all this, one or two family members were listening in a concentrated manner, while others were more relaxed. However, the fact that the family was present would help the war-affected veteran gain social recognition of his suffering and spread "belief in the possibility of improvement" (Whyte, 1997, p. 232) to his surroundings as well at to himself. Rituals "treat" both the individual and the community, thus supporting individual healing by mobilizing social support to the suffering individual.

The CIFAP Bombing Incident

This section is based on an interview with a Guinean informant and an Italian priest who were present during the incident. Communal healing can also be carried out in different ways, as illustrated by the CIFAP bombing incident and its aftereffects. CIFAP is a center for education and training run by the St. Joseph Fathers (Italian priests) of the Catholic mission in Guinea-Bissau. During the last days of the war, when the uneasy truce broke into unexpected fighting, resulting in the flight of the president, more than 10,000 people had sought refuge in the CIFAP center. The center became completely overcrowded. In fact, it did not offer any type of physical protection, and the refugees came in spite of the priests' warnings because they thought that "God would be there, when the priests were there," and that they would therefore be protected.

On what proved to be the last day of the war, 73 people were killed, and many more were injured. The fathers were praying when the rockets came, probably from "their own side"—that is, the side of the military junta—and hit the center by a fatal error. A week later, the priests held a mass commemoration that was mainly for families of the people who had been killed in the bombing. A crucifix had been constructed with residues of the rockets and the roof. During this ceremony that was held in front of the crucifix, family members gave testimony about their religious feelings. A mother confessed that she had come to the center to join her three children that were already there, and she was sitting with her children around her when the rockets came. All three children were killed while she was saved. She was bewildered and did not understand how that was possible. Now she was all by herself without any children to help her. However, she still had confidence in God and believed that it was God's will to take her children.

A few days later, a traditional mourning ritual, *Chur*, was started involving the whole community of Bandim, from where the killed people came. These ceremonies, which are very important in Guinean society, generally last for a week, and which relatives, neighbors, and friends visit the home of the deceased person, offering their condolences to the family. They give hands to the family, show their sorrow, and sit and eat with them.

This *Chur* ceremony also helped the families cope with the CIFAP tragedy. Moreover, there was a general feeling of relief that the war was over, and that even if some of their relatives had been killed, this communal relief was more important than the private, individual suffering. The informants explained that they were suffering a lot, but that they were also thinking that now the war was over. In addition, they expressed their suffering so forcefully that it "goes out"—they do not keep it inside, "they will cry until they are tired of crying." It was a strange feeling that "the rest of Bissau was celebrating victory while they were crying in Bandim."

Obviously, people were not used to making demands—they did not demand individual justice or punishment of the guilty for the bombing. The cultural and spiritual ceremonies enabled them to live with the harsh conditions, just as the faith of the mother enabled her to accept the loss of her three children. The whole community was able to work with the trauma of the bombing. Rituals (both Western and non-Western) were employed to help people manage their suffering by ordering their emotions and creating structures in which they could mourn and integrate the loss.

Transcultural Healing Processes

Although transcultural healing processes have been frequently studied from a cultural and social perspective, fewer studies have compared different healing approaches from a biological perspective. Recent research in the psychobiology of traumatic stress (van der Kolk, McFarlane, & Weisaeth, 1996, p. 220) has shown that extreme stress seems to affect people on multiple levels of functioning. There are psychophysiological, neurohormonal, neuroanatomical, and immunological effects of exposure to overwhelming experiences. The living, feeling, knowing, awakened body/self keeps track of what happens to it (Levine, 1997). These findings have had implications for Western psychosomatic approaches, with a new emphasis on the whole body/self to facilitate contact with the biological layers of traumatic stress. In this connection, it is striking how many non-Western healing rituals also have an emphasis on the body in trance states, where healers and patients go through altered states of consciousness, involving the body in a variety of activities described in detail by many anthropologists (e.g., Desjarlais, 1992; Kapferer, 1983, 1997; Strathern, 1996).

The discussion about "the right" method for the healing of psychic wounds is at least as old as the history of psychotherapy, and it is well documented that there does not exist a universal "right" or "wrong" method of healing. Empirical studies of the relative effectiveness of different forms of Western psychotherapy show that virtually all psychotherapies do the patients some good, and all are potentially effective when embedded within social and cultural specifics. To this could be added that "belief" is an important ingredient in the therapeutic process. The healer/therapist needs to believe in his or her own method, and the patient needs to be motivated and believe in the powers of the healer/therapist (Frank, 1973).

Since 1983, the World Health Organization has recommended that Western health professionals learn to work with non-Western healers. Kleinman's studies of cross-cultural healing processes identify a "shared symbolic order" as the necessary ingredient in therapeutic transactions (Kleinman, 1988). Rather than specific healing effects belonging to specific techniques, healing seems to originate in nonspecific factors that are believed "to work through the activation of physiological processes owing to the patient's faith in the treatment or the healer" (1988, p. 112). This resembles a phenomenon that has been observed in many medical experiments with drugs and is referred to by the pejorative label "placebo effect." Kleinman proposes that the placebo effect has given us very important insight into the powerful relationships between of social interactions and human physiology (Kleinman, 1988, p. 112). That is, the activation of this healing system results more from the relationship between healer and patient than from the content of the treatment itself.

The anthropologist Katz (Katz, Biesele, & St. Denis, 1997) notes from his fieldwork among a group of bushmen, the Ju'hoansi, living in the Kalahari

Desert in Botswana and Namibia, that their healing rituals involve physical, psychological, social, and spiritual levels, and that healing "affects the individual, the group, the surrounding environment, and the cosmos . . . touching far more levels and forces than simply curing an individual's illness" (p. 1). However, the bushmen also seek the Western health care system if their own treatment does not work. Although Katz thinks that the two systems must collaborate and make referrals to each other, he warns against "integrating" the two approaches because he fears that the traditional system will be "subsumed under the Western system and eventually being stripped of its unique contributions, particularly its spiritual healing power" (p. 92).

Concluding Remarks

Automatically concluding that everyone in a war zone is traumatized may also promote the development of a passive, dependent victim identity. Therefore, it is important that interventions addressing the identity of war-affected people also recognize their resilience and coping abilities. People in the midst of complex emergencies sometimes feel betrayed or lose their trust in other people and may develop demonized images of others as their "enemies." Interventions that focus on rebuilding family and community networks are fundamental to rebuilding trust and a sense of belonging. In this complex context of destruction and human survival, believing in and acknowledging the remarkable resilience of human beings becomes a creative force that in itself may be healing.

Wessells (1999) points out that in times of social disintegration, "psychological" wounds are collective in nature and thus emphasize the importance of placing culture at the center of any type of psychosocial assistance. This, the author points out, helps to avoid further disempowering local voices and traditions, which could provide unique sources of strength. From an ethical viewpoint, he questions the virtues of interventions oriented solely toward relieving "trauma," arguing that these efforts should also champion human rights and promote constructive political change. However, advocating human rights and political change during civil wars or complex emergencies is a complicated endeavor and might endanger the possibilities for implementing the project as a result of hostile reactions from powerful groups. This problem is not specific to psychosocial activities but, rather, is central to all humanitarian assistance.

In psychosocial work, it is important to connect to local cultural resources (e.g., traditions) and human resources (e.g., traditional healers, elders, women groups, teachers, and key people within the religious communities). Community processes and resources, both traditional and official, should be brought into the work. Unfortunately, an all too common remnant of colonialism is that local people tend to view their own approaches as inferior, and this "deeply ingrained sense of inferiority is and is itself a major form of psychological damage" (Wessells, 1999, p. 276). Therefore, part of any psychosocial intervention should consist of supporting the recognition of traditional practices and collaborating with community structures to plan the project while seeking to integrate Western and traditional modes of healing.

Angolan and Mozambican professionals rebelled against the residues of colonialism and Afro-Marxist dogma that were still part of their discourse. They started investigating and valuing their own approaches to healing and contributed with important insights into how combinations of Western medical techniques and traditional approaches could help protect dignity and heal insanity in their war-torn countries. Often, however, as noted by Whyte (1997), interventions fail, and the problem of suffering continues unabated.

Humanitarian aid, when seen as international social welfare, suffers from the same dilemma as other types of social assistance: When a person is "helped" by someone, an unequal power relationship is often established, and the beneficiary may become further victimized, helpless, and dependent. Regaining dignity and sanity is the major challenge in situations of civil war and social disruptions, and it is a problematic venture to try to assist anyone in that effort.

References

Agger, I. (2001a). Reducing trauma during ethno-political conflict: A personal account of psycho-social work under war conditions in Bosnia. In D. J. Christie, R. Wagner, & D. Winther (Eds.), *Peace, conflict, & violence: Peace psychology for the 21st century.* Englewood Cliffs, NJ: Prentice Hall.

———. (2001b). Psychosocial assistance during ethnopolitical warfare in the former Yugoslavia. In D. Chirot & M. Seligman (Eds.), *Ethnopolitical warfare: Causes, consequences, and possible solutions.* Washington, DC: American Psychological Association.

Bender, G. J. (1978). *Angola under the Portuguese: The myth and the reality.* London: Heinemann.

Boothby, N. (1992). Children of war: Survival as a collective act. In M. McCallin (Ed.), *The psychological well-being of refugee children: Research, practice and policy issues* (pp. 169–184). Geneva: International Catholic Child Bureau.

Buur, L. (2000). *Institutionalising truth: Victims, perpetrators and professionals in the everyday work of the South African Truth and Reconciliation Commission.* Submitted doctoral dissertation, Aarhus University, Denmark.

Chicuecue, N. M. (1997). Reconciliation: The role of truth commissions and alternative ways of healing. *Development in Practice, 7,* 483–486.

Danish International Development Agency. (1999). *Evaluation of Danish humanitarian assistance to Angola 1992–98.* Copenhagen, Denmark: T&B Consult.

———. (2000). *Strategi for dansk støtte til civilsamfundet i udviklingslandene—herunder samarbejdet med de danske NGO'er.* Copenhagen: Ministry of Foreign Affairs.

Desjarlais, R. R. (1992). *Body and emotion: The aesthetics of illness and healing in the Nepal Himalayas.* Philadelphia: University of Philadelphia Press.

De Waal, A. (1997). *Famine crimes: Politics & the disaster relief industry in Africa.* London: African Rights and The International African Institute.

Frank, J. D. (1973). *Persuasion and healing* (2nd ed.). Baltimore, MD: Johns Hopkins University Press.

Gibbs, S. (1994). *Post war social reconstruction in Mozambique: Preliminary findings, with special reference to children, from the district of Milange, Zambesia.* London: Save the Children.

Green, E. G., & Wessells, M. G. (1997). *Mid-term evaluation of the province-based war trauma team project: Meeting the psychological needs of children in Angola.* Arlington, VA: USAID Displaced Children and Orphans Fund and War Victims Fund.

Honwana, A. (1997). Sealing the past, facing the future: Trauma healing in rural Mozambique. *Accord: An international review of peace initiatives.* Retrieved February 24, 2005, from http://www.c-r.org/accord/moz/accord3/ honwana.shtml.

———. (1998). *'Okusiakala ondalo yokalye': Let us light a fire. Local knowledge in the post-war healing and reintegration of war-affected children in Angola.* Christian Children's psychosocial/inventory/pwg001/title.htm.

———. (1999). Non-western concepts of mental health. In M. Loughry & A. Ager (Eds.), *The refugee experience: Psychosocial training module.* Oxford: Refugee Studies Programme, University of Oxford.

Igreja, V., Schreuder, B., & Kleijn, W. (1999). The cultural dimension of war traumas in central Mozambique: The case of Gorongosa. *Transcultural Mental Health On-line* (pp. 1–13). Retrieved February 24, 2005, from http://www.priory.com/psych/traumacult.htm.

International Rescue Committee. (1999, June). *IRC Youth Center: Reintegrating youth in response to armed conflict* [Project proposal]. Guinea-Bissau.

Jakobsen, K., Cassamo, J., & Revel, N. (1996). *Evaluation review of the project for rehabilitation of children traumatized by war "Recrina" working in the province of Nampula Mozambique 1992–1997 within an agreement made between the Ministry of Coordination of Social Welfare and the Danish NGO, IBIS in 1991* [report]. Copenhagen: Ibis.

Kapferer, B. (1983). *A celebration of demons: exorcism and the aesthetics of healing in Sri Lanka.* Providence, RI: Berg and Smithsonian Institution Press.

———. (1997). *The feast of the sorcerer: practices of consciousness and power.* Chicago: The University of Chicago Press.

Katz, R., Biesele, M., & St. Denis, V. (1997). *Healing makes our hearts happy. Spirituality & cultural transformation among the Kalahari Ju|'hoansi.* Rochester, VT: Inner Traditions International.

Kleinman, A. (1988). *Rethinking psychiatry: from cultural category to personal experience.* New York: The Free Press.

Levine, P. (1997). *Waking the tiger: healing trauma.* Berkeley, CA: North Atlantic Books.

Nordstrom, C. (1997). *A different kind of war story.* Philadelphia: University of Pennsylvania Press.

Ribeiro, M. (1995). *O potencial das organizações não-governamentais portuguesas de desenvolvimento [ONGD].* Lisbon: CIDAC.

Strathern, A. J. (1996). *Body thoughts.* Ann Arbor: University of Michigan Press.

U.N. Children's Fund. (1996). *The state of the world's children 1996.* New York: Author.

———. (1999, July). *Note sur le programme d'appui psychologique aux enfants et la formation de travailleurs sociaux* [report]. Guinea-Bissau: UNICEF Bissau.

———. (2000). *UNICEF emergency programmes, Angola donor update 18 May 2000.* New York: Author.

United Nations. (1998, December). *United Nations consolidated inter-agency appeal for Guinea-Bissau, January–December 1999.* New York: United Nations.

––––––. (1999, July). *Mid-term review and revision of United Nations consolidated inter-agency appeal for Guinea-Bissau, 1999.* New York: United Nations.

U.N. Office for the Coordination of Humanitarian Affairs (1999b, August 16–31). *Humanitarian situation report Guinea-Bissau.* United Nations.

van der Kolk, B. A., McFarlane, A. C., & Weisaeth, L. (Eds.). (1996). *Traumatic stress: The effects of overwhelming experience on mind, body and society.* New York: Guilford Press.

Wessells, M. G. (1999). Culture, power, and community: intercultural approaches to psychosocial assistance and healing. In K. Nader, N. Dubrow, & B. H. Stamm (Eds.), *Honouring differences: cultural issues in the treatment of trauma and loss* (pp. 267-282). Philadelphia: Brunner/Mazel.

––––––, & Monteiro, C. (2000). Healing wounds of war in Angola: A community-based approach. In D. Donald, A. Dawes, & J. Louw (Eds.), *Addressing childhood adversity.* Cape Town: David Philip.

––––––. (2001). Psychological intervention and post-war reconstruction in Angola: Interweaving western and traditional approaches. In D. Christie, R. V. Wagner, & D. Winter (Eds.), *Peace, conflict, and violence: Peace psychology for the 21st century.* Englewood Cliffs, NJ: Prentice Hall.

Whyte, S.R. (1997). *Questioning misfortune: the pragmatics of uncertainty in Eastern Uganda.* Cambridge: Cambridge University Press.

CHAPTER 10

Participatory Tools for Monitoring and Evaluating Psychosocial Work with Children: Reflections on a Pilot Study in Eastern Sri Lanka

*Miranda Armstrong, Jo Boyden, Ananda Galappatti,
and Jason Hart*

Introduction and Background

This chapter is based on a study conducted in eastern Sri Lanka between April 2003 and January 2004. The purpose of the study was to pilot a range of participatory tools and methods with children affected by conflict and displacement, with the aim of establishing their utility for monitoring and evaluating psychosocial programs. Although the research took place in a particular locality, it was intended to address a general need for the enhancement of monitoring and evaluation of psychosocial interventions with children. The particular objective was to explore the potential of child participatory methods for achieving three main aims. The first of these was to increase accountability and effectiveness in interventions. The second was to enable agencies to demonstrate the effect and outcome of programs and thereby empower them in their relationship with donors. Finally, we were concerned with enhancing the profile of psychosocial programming through the introduction of effective monitoring and evaluation mechanisms.

The pilot was undertaken in Batticaloa, a district in the east of Sri Lanka, within the project activities of Koinonia, a local nongovernmental organization (NGO), the work of which forms part of a program run by Terre des hommes (Tdh), Lausanne. Batticaloa is one of the regions of Sri Lanka that has been most profoundly affected by the ethnic conflict between Tamil separatists and the Sinhala-dominated state. The conflict in this part of the island, which dates back to 1983, was sparked by riots and intercommunity violence. It has led to the death and injury of countless civilians and to numerous human rights abuses, including disappearances, arbitrary arrests, rape, and torture. The population of the Batticaloa District is composed mostly of Tamils and Muslims. In tandem with the larger Tamil–Sinhala conflict, the last two decades have also witnessed episodes of violence between Tamils and Muslims. These incidents have occurred at regular intervals, most notably in the early 1990s, when a number of intercommunal attacks and massacres took place.

Over the course of the conflict, the Liberation Tigers of Tamil Elam (LTTE) became an increasingly powerful military force within Tamil communities. At the time of the study, Batticaloa was a patchwork of government and LTTE-controlled enclaves. Civilians residing in the LTTE areas had suffered particularly from the lack of infrastructure, paucity of economic opportunities, and difficulties of mobility. Furthermore, they had been put under pressure to support the military efforts of the LTTE. At times, this reportedly included the widespread recruitment of children, often by force. A ceasefire between the Sri Lankan government and the LTTE in February 2002 led to a significant reduction in military activity and in tension among the local population. Nevertheless, a secure peace settlement remained elusive. Reports of the continued conscription of children by the LTTE were commonplace, and intercommunal relations, particularly between the local Tamil and Muslim populations, were still fragile.

Koinonia, our local partner for this project, runs an extensive network of after-school play centers in which children's psychosocial well-being is addressed through games, sports, nutritional supplements, and informal education. Following the ceasefire agreement, the organization decided to take advantage of the increased access to areas in Batticaloa controlled by the LTTE to establish seven new play centers. These centers, run by animators (young women from the locality employed to run activities) from the villages in which they are located, were the site of the research.

Conceptual Framework

There has been a common tendency for agencies working with conflict-affected children to assume in advance that the greatest causes of suffering and risk relate to past experiences of extreme violence. We were determined to avoid making such assumptions. Instead, we sought to identify the biggest problems for children within their lives as a whole. In other words, we adopted a holistic approach, seeking to see children's lives broadly and not simply in relation to the conflict. Furthermore, we did not want to privilege the past by seeing it in discrete and static terms. Instead, we proceeded on the assumption that the past and present interact dynamically, in that past experiences, both negative and positive, are subject to constant reworking in light of ongoing experience of life in the present. This process takes place not only at the level of the individual child but also within his or her family and community, as well as the wider society. The meaning of particular events and experiences and their consequences for children cannot be ascertained in advance, based on standardized notions about "stressors" (i.e., things that invoke a stress reaction) and "sequelae" (i.e., things that follow from earlier things).

A broad notion of "psychosocial well-being" was chosen deliberately as an alternative to narrow conceptualizations related to psychopathology and trauma. It was not that we denied the possible existence of trauma; rather, we felt that the employment of this concept and the possible psychomedical approach that goes with it would raise conceptual, ethical, and practical challenges that were beyond our ability to address satisfactorily. In particular, we were concerned with avoiding cross-cultural application of the diagnostic category of post-traumatic stress disorder (PTSD), about which a growing number of psychologists, psychiatrists, and anthropologists have expressed serious reservations (e.g., Boyden & Gibbs, 1996; Bracken, 1998; Bracken, Giller, & Sommerfield, 1995; Dawes, 1992; Richman, 1993; Young, 1995). It was our intention to focus on the elements that constitute and determine well-being, as well as the factors that threaten and enhance it. The term *psychosocial* was useful because it brought into view the wider social influences on well-being, thereby taking us beyond the location of problems (and healing) solely within the mind or emotions of individual children. Furthermore, as explained below, our understanding of "social" also embraces the material realm of children's lives.

Our contention is that psychosocial well-being must be understood as far as possible within the social and cultural context where the intervention is taking place. This understanding implied drawing on children's views of what they considered to be positive and negative psychological and social states and which personal and environmental factors they regarded as contributing to these states. We did, however, bring with us a broad notion of psychosocial well-being that builds on a model developed for use in complex emergencies by the Psychosocial Working Group (PWG), a collaborative international partnership between five academic and five humanitarian institutions (Psychosocial Working Group, 2003; Strang & Ager, 2001).

The conceptual framework that we used comprises three distinct domains: human capacity, social ecology, and material environment. Human capacity refers to children's individual resources, their cognitive capacity, social competence, personal identity and valuation, emotional well-being, skills, and knowledge—as is necessary for good functioning and interaction within their social, cultural, and material environment. The circumstances of children's social worlds are the focus of social ecology. This includes their relationships (both the extent and quality) with peers, kin, neighbors, and others; the degree and nature of social support, care, mentoring, and services available to them; and the implications of social identity (gender, class, location, ethnicity, religion) for life experiences and events. Finally, material environment refers to the material conditions of children's lives, including those pertaining to physical environment and infrastructure, nutritional status, livelihood, and degree of physical safety and comfort.

Our typology represents a partial alteration of the framework suggested by the Psychosocial Working Group. In the original schema of the PWG, "culture and values" constitute a domain in their own right. Our view was that we could not consider culture and values as separable in this way, and we therefore replaced this category with "material environment." In our adaptation of the PWG model (see Figure 10.1), culture and values are considered to shape the content of the three domains: for example, the particular qualities and competencies that a child is expected to possess to be considered capable (human capacity).

Although "creativity" and "expressiveness," for instance, may be qualities that middle-class European or North American parents currently look for in their children, neither of these was alluded to in the location where we conducted our fieldwork. Instead, much mention was made of characteristics such as "obedience" and "cleanliness." Although the notion of human capacity seems to have relevance in these two very different settings, the manner in which it is perceived will be understood differently in accordance with local culture and values.

We confirmed the relevance of the three domains for the context of our fieldwork during an initial workshop held in Colombo with a number of Sri Lankan experts in the psychosocial field, and we repeated this exercise in Batticaloa. Each of these domains is a broad category within which we sought to identify specific factors that contribute to or detract from chil-

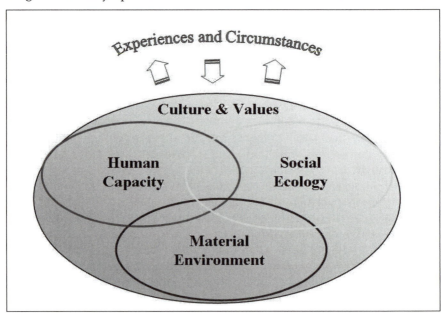

Figure 10.1 Pictorial Representation of Conceptual Framework

dren's psychosocial well-being. The pictorial representation of our conceptual framework in Figure 10.1 illustrates the necessarily overlapping nature of the three domains because factors that are important aspects of one domain may well have direct relevance for others as well, often through causal relationships. For example, the ability to get along well with others ("human capacity") has obvious bearing on the networks of friendship and support that an individual child may enjoy ("social ecology").

All of our activities were designed with a view of identifying not only factors that negatively affect children but also resources that might be drawn on for positive effect. Within the domain of human capacity, for example, this concern led us to consider personal resilience as well as suffering. The identification of resources alongside risks was not only important in terms of our understanding of psychosocial well-being but may also provide a basis from which to work with children and supporting agencies in the development of interventions.

The interest in resources and risks derives from our understanding of the relationship between experiences and circumstances on one hand, and psychosocial well-being on the other (see Figure 10.1). Experiences may be positive or negative, and this applies to both actual and anticipated incidents. Thus, for example, the fear of forced recruitment may be an extremely negative experience (and therefore a risk), as well as actual recruitment. Similarly, the anticipation of support or salvation by a deity may be an important resource helping to strengthen a child's resilience. From this perspective, it is clear that an outsider cannot predetermine what will constitute positive and negative experiences in the lives of any particular group of children. The purpose of participatory research is to learn from and with children about those experiences that are important for them and why.

We do not intend in any way to ignore or underplay the devastating effect of conflict upon children. At the same time, we maintain that children are and should be seen as not only victims but also social actors with important insights into their lives and an important role to play in the enhancement of their own well-being and that of their peers. This viewpoint necessitates a participatory approach to monitoring and evaluation.

In addition, aside from working with children, a consistent effort was made to gather data from a range of adults—Koinonia staff, parents, and other local residents. We sought information from them about recent events connected with the conflict; the local economic, social, and political situation; service provision; children's lives; and other related topics. The intention was to cross-check data gathered from the children with those collected from adults, compare adults' and children's perspectives, and generally enrich our understanding of the environment in which children live.

Methodology and Methods

Methodological Considerations

In this section, we describe the methodological rationale underlying the pilot project. First, our intention was to ensure that monitoring would aid the assessment of program progress and effect, as well as the planning of future measures. Data needs were also determined by the aims, objectives, scope, strategies, and activities of the program. Psychosocial initiatives should aim at the very least to positively influence children's well-being, coping, and resilience. There may be other, more specific objectives, such as the prevention of depression or enlistment in the military. Projects that are rooted in an ecological and interactive approach will also try to influence the environment in which children live, to both reduce the level of risk and increase the opportunities and systems of support and protection to which they have access. The program of Koinonia and Tdh fits into this latter category, in that it supports children within their own communities and families through collective play activities and home visits. Measures of this nature require a broad spectrum of monitoring data—beyond the psychological states of children—that also encompass family and community functioning, service provision, and other context-related issues. Accordingly, the choice of methods for participatory monitoring and evaluation in the pilot was determined by their effectiveness in capturing children's perspectives in three broad areas: functioning (emotional states, feelings, aspirations, actions, social and cognitive competencies, and the like), project role and effect, and environmental opportunities or constraints (especially risks and resources related to family, community, institutions, and material environment).

Second, our insistence on focusing on the psychosocial well-being of groups rather than on individual children fits with an emerging emphasis in the field of psychosocial programming on community-based healing and support. This represents a move away from efforts to treat individuals. The stress on groups was further motivated by three concerns. First, we questioned the ethics of an individualistic approach when the resources (both our own and those of the implementing agency) to offer a response to individual cases of need were extremely limited. Second, we were nervous about compromising the safety of individual children by encouraging them to share information that may be politically sensitive. By working as a group, instead, we believed that general trends would be identified without the potential risks of focusing on the particularities of any one case. Finally, experience taught us that there was a greater likelihood of local acceptability and sustainability when approaches do not single out specific individuals but instead contribute to the well-being of children in general.

In addition, it was vital that the methods should be amenable to use by children in as broad an age range as possible, and with limited or no literacy.

They should also yield data that (a) could be employed in monitoring and evaluation and (b) related to all three of the domains outlined in the conceptual framework.

Third, one critical assumption underlying the pilot was that the methods, if applied systematically at the outset of an intervention and at regular intervals subsequently, would reveal trends over time in children's well-being, resilience, and coping, as well as in local child protection and support systems. In other words, negative and positive factors in children's well-being and coping, and environmental constraints and opportunities highlighted during baseline assessment, can be noted for their presence or absence, increase or reduction, in follow-up monitoring exercises. If the methods are to be effective for monitoring, they must also reveal the extent and ways in which these trends are influenced by the program. Positive effects of projects can be measured through a shift in child functioning toward greater competence and resilience, the emergence of more effective risk-reduction strategies, and so on. Effects on children's environment may be recorded through the disappearance or more effective management of previously noted risks, greater social support, and increased service access. Clearly, it is important to be able to distinguish between changes that have occurred as a result of intervention and changes that are the result of extraneous factors, such as improvements in security or the economy. This requires detailed consideration of the program context and careful analysis.

Fourth, the methods piloted fall into several broad groups in terms of the way in which information is generated. One group is made up of mapping exercises and diagrams. These involve the production of visual images that depict actual objects and people as well as more abstract, metaphorical representation. Examples of such exercises include risk/resource maps, body maps, and problem trees. A second group of methods entails the listing of issues and categories, identifying the characteristics of these categories, and sorting and ranking them to arrive at distributions or priorities within a population. The well-being exercise (described below) exemplifies this type of tool. The third group involves exploration of fictional situations or events that can be taken to be a proxy for, or typical of, the real experiences and lives of children. Role plays, or in our case Image Theater exercises, achieve this aim.

There is a discernible connection between individual methods and the types of information they tend to provide, although few of the tools focus exclusively or exhaustively on a particular domain (human capacity, material environment, or social ecology). The two methods that focused most closely on human capacity were body maps and the well-being exercise. Information on social ecology was obtained largely through social maps, problem trees, spider diagrams, and others, whereas the material environment was addressed mainly through the risk/resource maps and timeline exercises. However, it was apparent that information generated in relation to one domain would often be linked to issues in another domain. For example, a cut on a foot drawn by mothers during a body map exercise was described by them as linked to being preoccupied with or "thinking too much" (human capacity) about their situation of financial insecurity (material environment) while clearing the forest as laborers—a form of work now necessary since the loss of the support from spouses (social ecology) who have been murdered or disappeared.

Practical Issues

Aside from appropriateness for research with children and efficacy in producing information covering all the domains, a number of other practical and ethical criteria were important in guiding the selection of methods. It was also vital that all methods employed should be productive of data that could be analyzed conceptually or statistically; child participatory; easy to implement, and therefore suitable for local agency staff with limited training in psychosocial work; and in accordance with ethical standards.

It was decided in advance that individual sessions with the children should be restricted in length to about two hours, so as not to tire them, with plenty of time for games. Drinks and biscuits were provided when possible. Extensive use was made of drawing and group discussion, these two media often being more attractive to children than interviews and writing. We sought to use methods that reduced power imbalances between adult monitors and child project participants, and encouraged children to feel comfortable with the process and as far as possible, to contribute their own views and perspectives. The employment of methods involving groups of children collaborating rather than working as individuals on their own entails both opportunities and constraints. Although children in groups may feel constrained in what they can discuss publicly, they may find solace in sharing their experiences and concerns with peers. Similarly, whereas collective methods enable wider coverage of respondents in a shorter period of time, individual methods can better facilitate the building of trust between the adult researcher and the child respondent. Possibly the greatest advantage of collective methods, however, is their potential as a vehicle for building interactive, problem-solving, planning, and other competencies in children—all critical processes in children's social development. Hence, collective participatory methods can, in themselves, contribute to psychosocial well-being, coping, and resilience.

It is also worth highlighting that information obtained from these methods can generally be enhanced through a semistructured focus group discussion held immediately afterward, while the subject of inquiry is still fresh in children's minds. This can be extremely helpful in cross-checking information and probing key issues. Above all, however, it provides an opportunity to work through issues children raise during the main session that may still be causing them concern.

With methods based on collective knowledge and experience, it is important to pay careful attention to gathering child respondents into appropriate groupings. In some cases, the methods involve an initial and a follow-up stage; often children can remain together in one large group for the first stage. However, it is seldom possible to work effectively with large groups of children during the more detailed information-gathering stage. To minimize possible unease among the children and consolidate knowledge built on common experience and understanding, it is normally desirable to group individuals with similar social and personal characteristics together. In other words, the aim should be to group the children as far as possible by those factors (e.g., gender, age, sociocultural or religious background) that are pertinent locally. Of course, care should be taken to ensure that such grouping does not emphasize or contribute to divisions between sections of the wider community. It is important to stress that familiarity among group members is not always an advantage, especially in areas of armed conflict, where neighbors can spy on or betray each other. It is essential that the recorder identifies and the facilitator works to address, reduce, or resolve, such tensions and disputes as far as possible.

The original aim was to work with children aged between approximately 5 and 16. However, it soon became apparent that younger children (those under age 10 or so) were not responding well to the exercises. There were several problems. Sometimes the younger children were unable to understand what the task entailed. Sometimes they were able to provide very little information that could be used or were simply too shy to engage in an activity. Often, they preferred to play independently. In the end, given the limited time available to us, rather than developing methods more suited to younger children, we were forced to abandon working with this age group. That said, we would not wish to imply that these methods are inherently unsuitable for young children. It may have been that the younger children in this particular area were unable to respond to these exercises as a result of years of impaired health and nutritional intake, limited opportunity to express their views, and extremely restricted access to and very poor quality of education. Given more time and the possibility of working in small groups, it is quite possible that at least some of our tools could have proved effective. In summary, it appears that cognitive capacity and prior experiences of participation and articulation of personal viewpoints may function as key factors in determining the efficacy of these methods in work with young children.

Use of collective methods implies careful facilitation and recording and hence requires a minimum of two people, each with a distinct and clearly defined role. Ideally, the facilitator should be someone known and trusted by the children. In this respect, the pilot team was seriously disadvantaged not only because we were strangers to the children but also because three of us were foreigners unfamiliar with the Tamil language. Although we were lucky enough to work with excellent interpreters, given the numbers of children involved and the fact that often several conversations were being conducted concurrently, we managed to capture only a fraction of the total information that was conveyed to us.

Ideally, the recorder should not be involved in the process but remain apart, observing and taking detailed notes on all that happens, how the children respond to the exercise, and what is said. Together with the actual products of the tools and methods (maps, drawings, etc.), these notes provide a vital record of the exercise and should be used in the analysis of findings. It is extremely important that these records be exact rather than summaries and that children's actual words be recorded, because using children's own terms and concepts while planning and reflecting on programmatic initiatives with them will maintain congruence with their perspectives and aid mutual understanding. The children need to agree both to being recorded and to the subsequent use of their materials.

In terms of facilitation, one of the main difficulties was the size of some of the groups of children and the fact that the age range was so broad that at times it was impossible to direct and control the process. Sometimes upward of 30 or 50 children aged between 5 and 15 would be present, all wanting to be involved. Another challenge was how to prevent different groups of children copying from each other, as this is particularly likely when using collective methods and given the informality of the process. Some methods were more prone to this problem than others.

Given that the Koinonia program focused on play activities, it was hardly surprising to find that children expected that the monitoring exercises would be fun and involve some kind of recreational element. We tried to select methods that the children would enjoy and to intersperse use of these with lively games. However, most of the methods do involve an element of concentration and, because of the use of pencils, paper, and so on, do resemble schoolwork to some extent. Therefore, it was often quite difficult to settle everyone down at the start. That said, we noticed a marked change in the children over time as they became more familiar with us and with the nature of the activities.

Specific Methods

It is not possible here to describe all the methods used in great detail. Readers interested to learn more should see the larger report on which this chapter is based (for detailed descriptions of the individual methods pilot tested, refer to Armstrong, Boyden, Galappatti, & Hart, 2004). However, to give some idea of the kinds of activity undertaken, the nature of data yielded, and the challenges involved, we offer description of two specific methods: the risk/resource map (RRM) and the Well-Being Exercise.

Risk/Resource Maps

This is an adaptation of one of the methods typically used in Participatory Rural Appraisals (Jones, 1997). Essentially, it involves children drawing a map of their immediate surroundings, their home, community, and other areas they frequently visit. Aside from depicting the natural and man-made environment as children view it, this method can be employed to identify what children find threatening and which things, people, and institutions they recognize as sources of support and protection in their daily lives or during a crisis. Importantly, children were able to use this method to highlight how some things (e.g., lakes or the sea) constitute both a hazard and a resource for them. The method is not intended to yield information solely with regard to a particular domain, but in practice it tends to provide more insight about children's material environment than the other two domains. It can be used very effectively in conjunction with a timeline exercise to explore change.

The RRM was the first tool to be piloted, and it generally makes a good starting point for any baseline inquiry. It was tested initially through role-play with adults and then administered with children in six villages. The method allowed the identification of both the crosscutting issues that affect all children in the region as well as those that are village specific. For example, snakebites featured as a major source of fear in all of the villages, whereas traffic accidents were mentioned in only one. In this way, the maps indicate the extent of an issue, problem, or resource, although not necessarily its severity. For information on the latter, other tools are needed in which children can rank their problems and concerns in order of priority.

This was a popular method that was easily understood by the great majority of the children, including the younger ones, and that generated a lot of very useful information and discussion. Most groups began drawing fairly quickly once the activity had been explained. Some were able to draw a map of their community or area, whereas others produced drawings that depicted the risks and resources randomly as items that had no particular spatial relation to each other or to a defined territory. Both forms of reproduction are appropriate because the main objective is to yield information about children's worlds and life experiences rather than produce "perfect" maps. Some groups worked cooperatively and generated a complete map through discussion and agreement, whereas in others, some of the children tended to work more individually.

The method provided information on a range of issues that the children are worried about, as well as on a series of resources that they value. Table 10-1 outlines the key risks and resources illustrated by children in one village and gives some of their explanations as to why these particular items were included.

In this village, a group of girls represented trees, chilies, flowers, and a tortoise as resources. They told us that the trees are useful because they provide coconuts and wood. The chilies can be eaten or sold, whereas flowers are used as temple offerings. They cited dogs, snakes, and *pey* (i.e., ghosts or spirits) as risks. Dogs, they explained, sometimes bite people, but were not a major worry. Snakes, in contrast, were a source of serious anxiety because they bite children quite frequently and are highly dangerous. They told us that a snake bite makes them faint and that they have to go to the local

Table 10.1
Risks and Resources Identified by Children in One Village

Risks	Resources
Tank [man-made irrigation lake] (drowning)	Coconut/mango trees (food and firewood)
Snakes (bites)	Flowers (to take to the temple/put in front of religious pictures)
Dogs [possibly rabid] (attacks)	School (for studying)
Liquor (drunken in excess by adults)	Post Office (to receive letters of support from far away)
Forest (may contain lions and elephants)	Road (to travel to get medicine and see relatives)
Ghosts/spirits (present near/in graveyards, cause fear especially when walking home from school)	Houses (for protection from the elements)
Bulls (attack people)	Sunlight
Rain (leading to flooding)	Preschool
Army (shooting/stopping people at checkpoints)	Well (for water, this also can sometimes be a risk, as children can fall inside the well)
Thieves (burglary and theft of livestock)	Cows (for milk)
Sea (drowning)	Buses and bikes (for mobility)
Traffic (accidents)	Kovil (Hindu temple)
Planes (dropping bombs)	Church (for hiding in during the war)
Policemen with guns (both the LTTE and the Sri Lankan army)	Paddy fields (staple)
	Market (for selling and buying goods)
	Korlum [white powder used for religious ceremonies]
	Karate classes

hospital for treatment. They are very scared of *pey,* which live in a nearby cemetery and come out in the afternoons. Even though few children had seen a ghost, they were still very frightened of them. Protection against ghosts, we were told, entails frying seeds and scattering them around the house. Other children suggested that traveling in a group could help.

Another group (boys and girls) in this village drew a fairly accurate map. A well was described as both useful and potentially dangerous. The school was considered useful as it enabled children to study. The church was an asset during the war particularly because people would seek refuge in it. The group commented, however, that no one went there anymore. There was also a picture of a bus stand and a bird. The local lake was cited as a risk because people might drown in it, but it was also regarded as a resource for bathing. Foxes were noted as a problem because they caught fowl and goats and ate them. Elephants were sometimes useful because they could carry heavy goods like logs, but they could also be very destructive. There were also pictures of several checkpoints that were located in the vicinity, one belonging to the LTTE and the rest to the Sri Lankan army. The children drew a soldier with a gun and explained that armed military personnel made people get down from their vehicles and check their papers. This was the first time that children in this village had identified both the LTTE and the army as a risk.

Although the method proved very effective in many ways, one limitation emerged of particular relevance from a planning point of view: The resources children identify tend not to have a particular bearing on the risks they highlight. This could be due to the fact that the children were not able to make an analytical connection between the particular risks and the resources they had at hand in their communities. Alternatively, it could be that the resources that they had access to are not really appropriate or sufficient for the particular risks and threats they confront. It may also be that they had no real practice in mobilizing resources to serve their needs because, as children, they had little authority within their families and communities and were generally ignored in planning and decision making. Clearly it is easier to reduce risks if the resources children use can be harnessed to address those specific risks. Although there was no opportunity to do this during the piloting, it might be helpful to hold a focus group discussion following this exercise in which the efficacy of particular resources is analyzed and possible links between risks and resources are explored with the children.

A second challenge relates to the fact that mapping can yield information about problems that are not amenable to change through intervention. This may be especially likely in situations of armed conflict where violations are commonplace, many normal civic processes are suspended, and local governance is dominated by military interests. For example, during the pilot children identified the checkpoints as a major source of concern. Obviously it may be possible to work with the children, local leaders, and the armed forces themselves to find ways of reducing contact between children and armed personnel or of putting a stop to violations by these forces. However, removal of a checkpoint (the ideal solution) is unlikely to be a feasible option within the scope of a humanitarian intervention.

A third consideration relates to how children may have to negotiate politically sensitive issues. Although the Sri Lanka army was often identified as a risk through images of a soldier with a gun, children were more circumspect about representing the LTTE on their maps. Although in discussion children mentioned the LTTE in relation to both risks (i.e., forced recruitment) and resources (i.e., resolving disputes in the village), they seemed reluctant to identify it in visual form. It is necessary to be attuned to children's judgment of the political climate and respect this while seeking to provide them with safe ways of articulating important but sensitive issues.

Well-Being Exercise

This exercise was adapted from one developed by Jon Hubbard, Director of Research at the Center for Victims of Torture in Minneapolis, Minnesota. Its aim is to identify the criteria by which well-being is understood in a particular culture or community. Participants are asked to think of a child they know who, in their view, is doing well in life. They should then think of the things about this child that indicate to them that he or she is doing well. The characteristics that emerge from this process can then be used as indicators of well-being. By combining the indicators provided by all the children and clustering together those that are the same or very similar, it becomes possible to obtain a view of normative ideas about well-being and ill-being for the community in question.

The exercise was implemented with relative ease among groups of both parents and children in five villages. The concept of well-being was found to resonate with the Tamil phrase *nallam irukka,* which is meaningful for both children and adults locally. It was important that the activity be implemented to elicit both written and verbal responses, to determine whether there were significant differences in the form or content of written and vernacular communication in that language/culture. In this case, none were found. For work with persons who are illiterate or uncomfortable with reading and writing, it may be necessary to have a scribe enter individuals' responses directly onto the group's sheet. The disadvantage with this method is that individuals in the same group may influence one another—an effect noticed during field testing.

The fact that the activity related directly to real children who are known to the participants meant that the characteristics/concepts of well-being accessed through the activity were attainable and realistic, rather than being abstract ideals.

This exercise always generated a good amount of detailed data that were thematically consistent throughout the many villages in which it was piloted. Criteria of well-being related to key themes, such as socially valued behavior (studying well, helping with housework, etc.), good interpersonal qualities (getting along well with others, being loving, etc.), cognitive competencies (getting good grades, doing well at school, etc.) and health, hygiene, and fitness (keeping clean, washing often, playing games, etc.). Overall, considerable attention was given to accomplishments in relation to school, sociability, and kindness toward others and paying attention to manners and personal care.

There was some contrast between children's and parents' responses. Whereas parents appeared to focus on sociability in terms of getting along with others, children themselves placed far greater emphasis on being loving or kind in relationships (*anbu*). Small group discussions with children revealed, for example, that a child who was *anbu* in school might share pencils with others who do not have them, or might share her or his lunch.

Interestingly, obedience was much more important to adults than to children, who tended to focus instead on "good habits."

Table 10.2 shows a selection of responses from children in four villages. The age and gender distinctions indicated refer to the ideals of well-being that the participants expressed about—for example, 5- to 10-year-old girls or 10- to 15-year-old boys. This table contains only those responses that were repeated more than 10 times. Many other responses were offered between one and nine times.

The data generated by this exercise proved useful in various respects. First, the data are very amenable to quantification. Second, they allow monitoring of groups or individual children against age- and gender-appropriate indicators of well-being (and by default indicators for ill-being also) that are highly responsive to cultural norms and values and hence have very direct and significant meaning for the population concerned. It should be highlighted that the pilot did not carry this exercise through to completion as originally intended and provided for by the Center for Victims of Torture. In other words, although we generated children's indicators for well-being and clustered these into broad areas of competence (cognitive, social, etc.), we did not attempt to assess the performance of the children we met in relation to these indicators and competencies. This was for ethical reasons, on the grounds that the project could not provide therapeutic support for individual children identified through the exercise as having problems and would need further capacity building to cater properly to groups of children highlighted as being in difficulty.

In general this was a very productive exercise that seemed to capture the interest of both adult and child participants. With one group of parents, however, it proved difficult to move discussion away from the consideration of causes for why some children appear to be doing better than others. A good deal of frustration was expressed by mothers in the group at the obstacles to providing the care and support necessary to ensure that children in the village would enjoy well-being. In any event, by seeking to draw out participants' ideas of a child who is doing well, the reality of their own lives or that of their children may seem highly inadequate. From this point of view, the exercise may prove discouraging to some people.

On the positive side, the method provides an immediate picture of ideals of behavior, attitude, and competency that has direct relevance for program development. For example, within the context of the play centers, information yielded by this method could be used by animators and participants to develop a code of behavior to guide all interactions aimed at promoting a more cooperative and harmonious atmosphere in activities.

Conclusion

Reflections on the Piloting Process

Our work was undertaken in a context in which very little data about children's lives had been accumulated. Thus, the findings provided a baseline against which the subsequent effect of the program might be monitored and evaluated. To explain how this would happen in practice, we offer two examples. First, through the repeated use of the risk/resource map, it may be possible to explore how phenomena identified previously as risks have been overcome in the children's view or even turned into resources. For instance, irrigation ponds, which were commonly considered by children as places of danger, might, through the activities of the project, become places that are safe and considered beneficial and pleasurable to visit. Second, through various of the methods exploring social ecology, it may be possible to monitor the development of children's social networks in terms of both quantity of different categories of people identified as resources and quality of relationships.

Many of the methods piloted offer opportunities for the quantification of data. The rich qualitative data generated through open-ended activities can form the basis for additional exercises to rank and rate specific factors by importance, severity, or frequency. The challenge with quantification using this approach is first and foremost an ethical one. Asking children to evaluate themselves or their peers might prove very disempowering or distressing, especially in the context of the fledgling psychosocial support services being provided locally. We would also be nervous of using large-scale data-gathering methods in a politically unstable setting, where the acquisition of information in this manner may appear authoritarian and trigger a negative reaction.

The participatory nature of these methods makes it possible for children to identify their own concerns, the things that they find troubling or frightening, and the people and things they turn to when they need help. This is very different from researcher-led approaches in which threats to children are predetermined by adult monitors.

The immediacy and relevance of information produced through these methods is apparent from some of the findings during the pilot testing. This is a tremendous advantage for programming because it encourages a response from program staff. For example, Koinonia staff acted immediately on some of the findings. In one village where drowning was identified as a major risk, the "animators" approached people who live nearby and fish in the lake to find out about the factors affecting level of risk. They discovered that the most dangerous time of year is just after the rains, when the lakes are full, and that the mud is also hazardous as children may become stuck in it and drown. The animators explained the risks to the children and talked about appropriate protection strategies. With this new knowledge, the children began to inform others.

Monitoring and evaluation is not a neutral process. It involves power differences between those monitored and those monitoring. It is not just about who gets to ask and who gets to speak but is also about who is monitoring whom and for what purpose and who makes decisions based on the outcomes of processes. In fact, effective monitoring and evaluation—with the potential to lead to changes in the program—are likely to draw into competition the various interest

Table 10.2
Responses of Children in Four Villages

| | Ages 5-10 Years | | Ages 10-15 Years | | |
	Girls	Boys	Girls	Boys	Total
Kind/loving (*anbu*)	18	14	17	19	68
Studies well	8	14	17	18	57
Plays well	7	11	11	10	39
Goes to school regularly	8	8	10	8	34
Healthy	10	4	7	11	32
Good habits	5	5	9	11	30
Clean	7	6	8	8	29
Affectionate	7	3	10	8	28
Moves well with others	6	1	5	6	18
Gets good nourishment	5	4	5	4	18
Clever in studies	8	3	4	1	16
Good friends/meets regularly	3	6	3	3	15
Is very good	4	3	2	6	15
Plays with me	2	3	5	1	11
Active/does exercises	2	3	2	3	10
Drinks boiled/clean water	4	2	1	3	10

groups that may exist in communities and agencies. We have advocated the use of participatory methods that are sensitive to children's views and perspectives and to local values in the belief that such an approach helps to reduce power imbalances and the associated abuses. However, this does not remove the obligation of monitors to manage the dynamics of monitoring processes so as to ensure that they do not detrimentally affect relations between colleagues and between children and program staff.

On the basis of the experience of the pilot, it seems that the process of coming together to discuss and reflect on everyday life in an ordered and focused manner can, in itself, be valuable for children. If such activities continue, as an embedded part of a project, they would likely lead to the enhancement of children's capacity to make a connection between the risks and problems they encounter in everyday life and the resources that may be available to them. This capacity is vital for the creation of children's own strategies to address issues of concern.

Limitations and Concerns

As with any other approach, the manner in which we worked had its own inherent limitations, of which the following seem particularly important to note. First, the collective nature of our methods made it extremely difficult to elicit detailed information about the suffering of individuals. Also, it was often harder to learn about the threats experienced by children within the private space of the home than in more public settings. As a consequence, these methods do not lend themselves particularly well to the identification of appropriate responses to individual children.

Second, our status as outsiders seems likely to have contributed to the difficulty of eliciting information of a more personal nature. In addition, as outsiders we were not in a position to take forward the focus and energy generated by our sessions with children. It should also be noted that, together with the translators, we were a mixed group in terms of age, gender, and social class. It was our impression that particular constraints may have existed for those of us who were male and for the older members of the team in terms of establishing an easy rapport with children, especially girls. With parents, conversely, the older members had a possible advantage.

Third, we focused broadly on the psychosocial status of children and the factors that affect this, rather than on program performance in relation to explicitly stated objectives. This was partly because the work in the centers was very new and it would therefore have been premature to try to assess effect and outcome. In this sense, as noted, the data yielded from the pilot served mostly as a baseline against which changes obtained through future monitoring can be highlighted. Such a baseline, naturally, is an important first step in the establishment of a monitoring and evaluation system. Having highlighted this limitation with the piloting process, these tools are clearly amenable to ongoing monitoring, since, in the case of programs with well-elaborated objectives, they will reveal the extent to which an intervention's objectives are being met.

Fourth, we encountered particular difficulties in attempting to pilot the methods with younger children. A good deal of further work specifically focused on the piloting of methods for this younger age group would appear to be necessary.

Fifth, we recognize that the methods piloted would not specifically identify children suffering trauma and mental health problems. We agree that it can be feasible and appropriate to attempt to assess the mental health of individuals who appear to be confronting particular difficulties, so long as the program has the capacity and intention to respond to these children. Such monitoring would require different methods but can be conducted alongside and as a complement to the methods discussed here. However, we recommend use of local concepts and understandings of mental health and distress as far as possible, rather than importing categories and notions from outside the cultural context.

Acknowledgments

We express our debt of gratitude to the following organizations: the Displaced Children and Orphans Fund of USAID and the Andrew W. Mellon Foundation, CARE International in Sri Lanka, Terre des hommes (Lausanne), Koinonia, the Eastern Self-Reliant Community Awakening Organisation (ESCO), and YMCA Batticaloa, the Psychosocial Support Programme. We are grateful to Jon Hubbard and Martin Woodhead for generously allowing us to implement methods developed by them, and most especially, to the children who attend the play activity centers and the many parents and grandparents who took time to speak with us and share important and difficult details about their lives.

References

Armstrong, M., Boyden, J., Galappatti, A., & Hart, J. (2004, March). *Piloting methods for the evaluation of psychosocial programme impact in eastern Sri Lanka.* Refugee Studies Centre final report for USAID. Oxford: University of Oxford, International Development Centre. Retrieved January 11, 2005 from http://www.rsc.ox.ac.uk/PDFs/rrpilotingmethods04.pdf

Boyden, J., & Gibbs, S. (1996). *Children of war: Responses to psycho-social distress in Cambodia.* Geneva: The United Nations Research Institute for Social Development.

Bracken, P. J. (1998). Hidden agendas: Deconstructing post traumatic stress disorder. In P. J. Bracken & C. Petty (Eds.), *Rethinking the trauma of war* (pp. 38–59). London: Free Association Books.

———, Giller, J. E., & Sommerfield, D. (1995). Psychological responses to war and atrocities: The limitations of current concepts. *Social Science and Medicine, 40*(8), 1073–1082.

Dawes, A. (1992). *Psychological discourse about political violence and its effects on children.* Paper presented at the meeting of the Mental Health of Refugee Children Exposed to Violent Environments, Refugee Studies Programme, University of Oxford, Oxford, United Kingdom.

Jones, C. (1997). *PRA in Central Asia: Coping with change.* Oxford: INTRAC.

Psychosocial Working Group. (2003, October). *Psychosocial intervention in complex emergencies: A conceptual framework.* Retrieved January 11, 2005 from http://www.forcedmigration.org/psychosocial/papers/PWGpapers.htm.

Richman, N. (1993). *Communicating with children: Helping children in distress.* Save the Children Development Manual number 2. London: Save the Children.

Strang, A., & Ager, A. (2001). *Building a conceptual framework for psychosocial intervention in complex emergencies.* (Centre for International Health Studies working paper). Queen Margaret University College, Edinburgh, United Kingdom. Retrieved January 11, 2005, from http://www.ishhr.org/conference/articles/strang.pdf

Young, A. (1995). *The harmony of illusions: Inventing posttraumatic stress disorder.* Princeton NJ: Princeton University Press.

CONCLUSIONS AND RECOMMENDATIONS FOR FURTHER PROGRESS

Gilbert Reyes

A frequently expressed concern in humanitarian circles is that we are chronically engaged in the inefficient process of "reinventing the wheel." Frustrations regarding this issue seem justified, given the tendency of humanitarian organizations to operate in a more territorial and insular manner than is either necessary or wise. Counterarguments point to frequent conferences among these NGOs, but such meetings seldom result in substantive changes in policies or operations, and cooperative agreements are the exception rather than the rule. A reasonable inference can be drawn that some humanitarian organizations would rather take a proprietary stance toward "wheel development," preferring the autonomy and distinctiveness of creating their own "wheel" to the efficiency and communality involved in working cooperatively with others of their kind. Similar observations can be made regarding mental health professionals, who are sometimes better rewarded for relabeling borrowed "wheels" than they would be for adopting existing wheels with minimal adaptations to suit the particular conditions of their situation. One might say that, rather than reinventing the wheel (i.e., the general model of psychological support), a more efficient procedure is to adapt elements of wheels successfully used by others to fit the characteristics of one's own particular terrain. The responsibility for ensuring that a modified "wheel" (i.e., a situation-specific model) will be culturally congruent rests with the people in the affected areas, who are free to select what to keep or discard and choose the placement and timing of its use. Thus, what gets adopted in any given situation will be generally useful principles, but the operational details and practices will vary in accordance with needs, cultures, and conditions.

A major intention of the *Handbook of International Disaster Psychology* has been to establish a sufficiently diversified base of information on when, where, why, and how disaster psychosocial services are implemented, as well as what is done and by whom. Accordingly, the contributing authors have articulated many of the most important ideas that have influenced the development of psychosocial humanitarian operations over the past decade. They have also shared their own activities and experiences in a transparent manner so that others might learn from their successes and failures. Their descriptions of the practices and principles that have been employed to help heal the psychological and social wounds among populations affected by potentially traumatic events offer a rich resource from which others with similar goals may borrow to formulate their own programs and practices.

Volume 1 provided an overview of the field and addressed the fundamentals issues and principles of concern to those who design and implement psychosocial programs for disaster survivors. Volume 2 described a variety of programs conducted around the world and the recommended practices for promoting effect healing at both individual and collective levels. Volume 3 focused specifically on mental health issues of refugees and the favored approaches to needs assessment and psychosocial care under a complex set of conditions and stages of migration. Volume 4 identified several populations whose special needs and circumstances tend to be overlooked and thus require conscientious consideration to ensure adequate care. The authors, all of whom are experienced members of the international humanitarian community, represent a broad spectrum of nationalities, cultures, and viewpoints. The stories told in these pages should prove instructive and inspiring to anyone concerned with promoting the psychosocial welfare of people who have endured the fear and loss that accompany widespread violence and social upheaval. Readers are encouraged to glean from these works the most useful and inspiring ideas from which they can develop their own skills, practices, and programs.

Politics, Cultures, and Controversies Cannot Be Ignored

International psychosocial support activities have not unfolded without controversy. Some have argued that the humanitarian psychosocial movement reflects Western ideology with a vision of life and its norms that is at odds with native cultures indigenous to those places where catastrophic events are most likely to occur. Critics invoke images of cultural imperialism perpetrated by the former colonial aggressors against the relatively innocent and primitive captives of their misguided ministrations. There is certainly some truth in these accusations, given the asymmetry of a humanitarian community dominated by lighter-skinned people of the Northern Hemisphere "serving" the darker-skinned peoples of the Southern Hemisphere in a present version of *White Man's Burden* (Kipling, 1899). But the comparisons employed by these critics are commonly as dramatic, overwrought, and anecdotal as the claims their adversaries use to compel the forces of "compassionate" action. In the absence of reliable evidence, what poses for truth may be unfounded but persuasive claims which better serve the political or religious agendas of their purveyors than they do the psychosocial needs of their targets.

Cultural differences are often invoked as obstacles to effective helping. Cultures do have expectations and values that set boundaries around actions and influence the effectiveness of our means and the appropriateness of our goals. But that does not mean that intercultural collaboration is all about obstacles (Marsella & Christopher, 2004; Szegedy-Maszak, 2005). Cultures are also resilient and malleable to conditions, and can be understood as resources rather than obstacles. Moreover, because the most prominent voices against disseminating "Western models" of psychological support are often Western intellectuals (Pupavac, 2001; Summerfield, 1999, 2005), the discourse is suspiciously devoid of non-Western voices. That is, it would appear to be an argument among "Western" factions, rather than between Western and non-Western voices. This invites a comparison with the colonial era, during which factions within the dominant powers argued over what was in the best interest of the cultures and people whom they held in subordination. The time for Western speakers to serve as proxies for non-Westerners should be passing, and the fact that non-Western speakers often call for more collaboration casts suspicion on the claims of the anti-Western Westerners.

This state of affairs is not specific to the debates over models or intervention strategies, but instead cuts across almost every issue and area of concern in humanitarian intervention. Representatives of developing nations are shamefully underrepresented in the discourse of assertions, arguments, and deliberations that converge to influence the development of humanitarian psychosocial policies affecting their regions. Moreover, even when governments and ministries from the developing world are somewhat represented, the same cannot be said for less affluent groups with little access to state power. This means that women, religious and ethnic minorities, indigenous tribes, and underclasses may have little say in the planning, implementation, and distribution of psychosocial services. Thus, a strong recommendation is presently expressed for greater inclusion of non-Western voices and perspectives in the discourse over which psychosocial beliefs and practices are appropriate, welcome, or desirable for use among disaster survivors in developing countries. Beyond this, it is also important to seek the insight and wisdom of groups at the margins of national and international power circles. Of particular concern is the muted influence of women from the least developed nations, whose lives (and those of their children) are among those most frequently and severely affected by war and other disasters.

Concerted International Efforts Are Needed

Humanitarian stakeholders share values and interests that should improve their prospects for collaborating toward commonly held aspirations.

Nevertheless, it is a widely held perception that they often function with a greater emphasis on autonomy than on cooperation. While it is understandable and predictable that the social psychology of these organizations would mirror those of governments and corporations, it is unfortunate that humanitarian organizations would rather tolerate waste and duplication than pursue cooperative partnerships that might allow a more efficient division of efforts and responsibilities. For example, psychosocial support for expatriate delegates has received considerable attention, and some, but not all, organizations have the requisite resources to provide mental health care for their field personnel. Cooperative agreements would allow psychosocial delegates from one NGO partner to share their services with personnel from another, resulting in better distribution of preventive care without the need for each NGO to develop its own psychosocial services.

As recently as 2001, the World Health Organization issued a declaration requesting that the international community agree to consensual guidelines for improving cooperation in the best interest of serving the psychosocial needs of refugees and other displaced populations (WHO, 2001). Such cooperation and collaboration would require division of roles and activities, a consequence of which would be to limit the autonomy of any given signatory organization. Unfortunately, the sovereignty of governments and NGOs alike tends to supersede such noble ideals as cooperative action or the placing of a beneficiary's interests above organizational politics. Nevertheless, leaders in the humanitarian community, faced with inadequate funding and an escalating spiral of mission objectives, should take a progressive route toward the forging of collaborative agreements that would improve efficiency and decrease unnecessary duplication of services.

International Standards of Care Are Needed

Psychosocial services have become a staple part of humanitarian relief operations around the world. Much of this progression has been driven by an increasing emphasis on the psychologically "traumatic" impact of war, disasters, and other tragic events. The fundamental propositions of international disaster psychology begin with the belief that extreme psychological distress and trauma predictably follow from events in which death, injury, and massive loss are involved. Specific claims are seldom made regarding the magnitude of the psychosocial consequences, but the impact is expected to include profound distress and substantial impairment of adaptive behavior among a large proportion of the population. A sense of extreme urgency is also evident in the alarming tone of news reports quoting claims by international mental health experts that major portions of populations affected by the 2004 Indian Ocean tsunami will develop trauma or other mental disorders (e.g., WHO, 2005). The responses to these alarms vary, with some ad hoc psychosocial emergency teams responding within the first few weeks (e.g., Kuriansky, 2005), while larger organizations take a more cautious, measured, and deliberative stance (Anderson, 2005).

Given the generally predictable occurrence of disasters, wars, and other catastrophic events, there would seem to be a third alternative in which planned action strategies are prepared well in advance. Once an activating event occurs, the strategy can quickly be reviewed and revised to fit any unanticipated conditions and the action plan can then be implemented without unnecessary delay. In fact, many governmental and nongovernmental organizations do exactly that with regard to material supplies such as food, water, medicines, munitions, and plastic sheeting. Indeed, this policy of preparedness for the unexpected is quite common for most goods that are considered essential to survival or social stability. Countless institutions, from police and fire departments to hospitals and insurance companies, exist to respond quickly when chronic problems arise, and many communities now have emergency mental health response capacities as well. Yet the global community, after more than a decade of experience with international disasters, remains relatively unprepared to respond to the psychosocial aspects of a major disaster in any systematic and concerted manner.

After nearly a decade of discussion regarding "best practices," no widely accepted standards of care have emerged. Contributing to this problem is the paucity of real research in this area. The present author recommends that humanitarian psychosocial organizations and experts (e.g., Psychosocial Working Group, 2004), convene not only to establish consensual endorsement of interventions, but also to develop action strategies for responding with all deliberate speed and coordination to address the psychosocial needs of disaster survivors. Organizations with an historical head start in developing psychosocial programs can help to inform others, and the sharing of lessons learned and approaches to delivering services can be exchanged in the service of all concerned. A more provocative suggestion would include establishing an international NGO dedicated specifically to providing psychosocial support in a manner analogous to that of Médecines Sans Frontières (Doctors Without Borders) in the arena of medical care.

Rapid Assessment of Psychosocial Needs Should Be a Standard Practice

Recent efforts directed toward the rapid assessment of psychosocial needs in disaster-affected populations have been helpful and instructive (e.g., Dodge, 2006; Jacobs et al., 2006), but episodic and limited in scope. The history of medical and psychosocial interventions demonstrates the importance of accurately assessing problems and resources before devising a plan to provide services. In the rush to relieve human suffering after catastrophic events, there is a danger in assuming the nature and magnitude of psychosocial needs while ignoring existing resource capacities in favor of imported experts. Although it is true that some presuppositions based on past experience are likely to prove true, important information may be missed or delayed unless needs assessment is granted a formal role in the overall service

plan. To ease the succession from needs assessment to intervention, it is possible to begin assessing very early and in tandem with the deploying and tailoring of services (i.e., listening to the beneficiaries and tailoring the service
model). It is also crucial to build an evaluation component into the service
model so that the lessons learned are less subject to global appraisals that
suit political rather than developmental aims.

Psychological Trauma versus Disaster Psychology

The international humanitarian community must operate on assumptions
that are either self-evident or adapted from analogous circumstances. Thus,
it is self-evident that supplies of clean water will be critically needed in
remote regions where refugees often assemble, and it stands to reason that
the emotional needs of people displaced by a wildfire will be analogous to
those of people displaced by an earthquake. Historical trends in the mental
health fields have elevated the concept of psychological trauma to a position
from which it eclipses any other explanatory framework or descriptive ter-
minology. This has led to a condition where psychological trauma is treated
as though its existence and importance are self-evident across every type of
human catastrophe, from war to flood and famine to disease. In turn, the
proper response to these events must center foremost on preventing or alleviating the formation of a traumatic disorder. Evidence to support the prop-
osition that refugees (Fazel, Wheeler, & Danesh, 2005), torture survivors
(Silove, 1999), and others who have suffered terribly in disasters often
develop trauma-related symptoms and clinical disorders is abundant and
convincing. But there are many psychosocial consequences other than
trauma that carry great importance and that are often more amenable to
change without intrusive interventions that may not be welcomed or valued
by disaster survivors. Thus, the emphasis on trauma may inadvertently
obscure the importance of less dramatic issues that are not as "sexy," compelling, and provocative in tone. Nevertheless, what is actually provided in
many instances is not "trauma-focused treatment," but instead consists of
more mundane-sounding approaches such as education, stress management,
and crisis intervention, which are often what is most useful for prevention
activities and immediate relief of acute stress.

Disaster psychology, while closely connected to traumatology, is also distinct
in several ways, including a decidedly normalizing stance toward short-term
responses to acute stress and a pronounced emphasis on community-based
interventions. In contrast to the clinical therapies typically applied in cases
of post-traumatic stress disorder, the techniques preferred by disaster psychologists are more akin to crisis intervention and stress management and
emphasize reduction of emotional arousal with brief support for problem
solving and other effective coping strategies. Disaster survivors are not
referred to as either clients or patients, and no "case" is ever formulated or
assigned to a particular provider. Privacy is almost impossible, confidentiality

is very limited, and no formal therapeutic relationship is either acknowledged or terminated. Rather, if the disaster psychologist detects the need for "clinical" services, a referral is made to an appropriately skilled provider who need not be experienced in disaster mental health. More often, the approach taken could best be described as a "public health" approach, with the purpose of taking steps to prevent the need for more targeted interventions by reducing the impact of known risk factors. This proactive model is superior in many ways to reactive models, but it requires very different skills and objectives from those needed for working with a more select group of survivors who display symptoms of clinical disorders. Thus, the qualifications for disaster psychologists are substantially different from those of traumatologists, and these areas of expertise are not interchangeable. Therefore, while skilled trauma-clinicians have much to offer in response to disaster survivors, they should also acknowledge the need to develop the pertinent skills for disaster field assignments.

Humanitarian Assistance and Military Aggression Are Incompatible

Interventions can take countless forms, and it is debatable whether the aims are indeed wholly altruistic and compassionate (i.e., humanitarian), or if there is another, more selfish agenda being disguised. The secular humanitarian movement has long been encumbered by the historical example of religious charities that blended compassionate deeds with missionary indoctrination. Selective governmental humanitarian efforts in the late twentieth century were often suspected of being part of a global propaganda struggle between the opposing powers of communism and capitalism during the Cold War. These examples illustrate the fragile credibility of altruistic acts across national and cultural boundaries and should inform true humanitarians of the dangers of blended agendas. In a spate of publications over the past decade, contributors have called the humanitarian community to task over its questionable behavior or suspect motives (Holzgrefe & Keohane, 2003; Moore, 1999; Smillie & Minear, 2004). Concurrently, the rates of intentional violence against humanitarian personnel have reached historically high levels (Sheik, Gutierrez, Bolton, Spiegel, Thieren, & Burnham, 2000), as illustrated by the 2003 bombings of the United Nations and Red Cross offices in Iraq during the American occupation. In such a climate of scrutiny, criticism, and profound security concerns, it is more important than ever that humanitarian motives be kept wholly distinct from partisan politics and military adventures.

Since its inception, the Red Cross/Red Crescent movement has wisely promoted and subscribed to principles of neutrality and impartiality in the pursuit of humanitarian goals. Only the strictest adherence to such principles can possibly serve to shield humanitarian workers and the people they seek to serve from becoming targets of terror, torture, and death. This is not to say that military means cannot be employed in the service of humanitarian ends. Indeed, the ostensible rationale behind many if not most wars is to serve the greater good of humanity while defeating some evil force. But in violence the ends are often believed to justify any means of achieving them, and this includes the resort to instrumental aggression in the service of geopolitical goals of domination, pacification, and exploitation. Conversely, in humanitarianism the means must conform to principles of compassion, dignity, and human rights if the ends are to maintain legitimacy. Anything less threatens to destroy the very foundation upon which the international humanitarian enterprise has been erected.

Psychosocial Issues Need Better Advocacy

In the competition for disaster relief resources, psychosocial concerns are given more lip service than action. Basic survival needs are so clear and compelling that humanitarian mental health advocates find themselves relegated to the margins while central planning concerns are pursued with fervor. This is to some extent a necessary and reasonable situation, since mental health is a relative luxury in the face of mass destruction and death. Nevertheless, if psychosocial interventions are ever to be both timely and effective, they must move from being marginal concerns toward being integral and influential in the overall scheme of disaster response planning.

At present the priorities are such that mental health and psychosocial support activities have more propaganda value than actual influence. This helps to keep the mental health sector in a reactive role, rather than supporting systematic, strategic development of responsive operational abilities and the undertaking of initiatives for building more resilient local capacity . Instead, the current state of affairs allows for a public voicing of compassion and vague claims of action for the anguish and trauma of the affected people, while the pace of response is more timid and tentative. This is to some extent due to legitimate doubts regarding the need for psychosocial interventions and an absence of evidence supporting the effectiveness of what is presently being offered. Thus, disaster mental health advocates will need to consider their steps carefully if they are to advance their cause while avoiding the temptation to overstate their importance at the risk of further undermining their precarious progress.

References

Anderson, N. B. (2005). The APA tsunami relief effort, part 2. *APA Monitor*, *36*(4), 9.
Dodge, G. R. (2006). Assessing the psychosocial needs of communities affected by disaster. In G. Reyes & G. A. Jacobs (Eds.), *Handbook of international disaster psychology, Vol. 1. Fundamentals and overview*. Westport, CT: Praeger Publishers.
Fazel, M., Wheeler, J., & Danesh, J. (2005). Prevalence of serious mental disorder in 7000 refugees resettled in Western countries: A systematic review. *Lancet*, *365*, 1309–1314.

Holzgrefe, J. L., & Keohane, R. O. (2003). *Humanitarian intervention: Ethical, legal, and political dilemmas.* New York: Cambridge University Press.

Jacobs, G. A., Revel, J. P., Reyes, G., & Quevillon, R. P. (2006). A tool for rapidly assessing the mental health needs of refugees and internally displaced populations. In G. Reyes & G. A. Jacobs (Eds.), *Handbook of international disaster psychology, Vol. 3. Refugee mental health.* Westport, CT: Praeger Publishers.

Kipling, R. (1899, February). The white man's burden: The United States and the Philippine Islands. *McClure's Magazine,* p. 12.

Kuriansky, J. (2005, February 21). Finding life in a living hell. Retrieved March 31, 2005, from http://www.nydailynews.com/front/story/283039p-242333c.html

Marsella, A. J., & Christopher, M. A. (2004). Ethnocultural considerations in disasters: An overview of research, issues, and directions. *Psychiatric Clinics of North America, 27,* 521–539.

Moore, J. (1999). *Hard choices: Moral dilemmas in humanitarian intervention.* New York: Rowman & Littlefield.

Psychosocial Working Group (2004). *Considerations in planning psychosocial programs.* Retrieved February 15, 2005, from http://www.forcedmigration.org/psychosocial/papers/PWGpapers.htm

Pupavac, V. (2001). Therapeutic governance: Psycho-social intervention and trauma risk management. *Disasters, 25,* 358–372.

Sheik, M., Gutierrez, M. I., Bolton, P., Spiegel, P., Thieren, M., & Burnham, G. (2000). Deaths among humanitarian workers. *British Medical Journal, 321,* 166–168.

Silove, D. (1999). The psychosocial effects of torture, mass human rights violations, and refugee trauma: Towards an integrated conceptual framework. *Journal of Nervous and Mental Disease, 187,* 200–207.

Smillie, I., & Minear, L. (2004). *The charity of nations: Humanitarian action in a calculating world.* Bloomfield, CT: Kumarian Press.

Summerfield, D. (1999). A critique of seven assumptions behind psychological trauma programmes in war-affected areas. *Social Science & Medicine, 48,* 1449–1462.

———. (2005). What exactly is emergency or disaster "mental health"? *Bulletin of the World Health Organization, 83,* 76.

Szegedy-Maszak, M. (2005, January 17). The borders of healing. *U.S. News & World Report, 138*(2), 36–37.

World Health Organization (WHO) (2001). Declaration of cooperation: Mental health of refugees, displaced and other populations affected by conflict and post-conflict situations. Author: Geneva.

———. (2005, January 19). Press release (SEA/PR/1384): WHO warns of widespread psychological trauma among Tsunami victims. Retrieved April 25, 2005, from http://w3.whosea.org/en/Section316/Section503/Section1861_8571.htm

EPILOGUE

Yael Danieli

This impressive, thoughtful *Handbook of International Disaster Psychology* succeeds in conveying and mapping many of the key issues and complex challenges that have confronted the field and influenced the development of psychosocial humanitarian operations over the past decade. The scope and depth of this superb compilation would not have been possible even a decade ago, demonstrating how far we have come as a field. But much of it is also a reminder of how far we have yet to go in a world that has unremittingly produced disasters that, despite growing awareness, are met at best by episodic and inconsistent response and a rather limited commitment to preventing them and their long-term—possibly multigenerational—effects.

Created on the ruins of the World War II, the United Nations (UN) was formed in a spirit of optimism. Never again would the world community permit such a devastating war to take place. The world organization was joined by numerous nongovernmental organizations (NGOs) in its efforts to create a new, intensified impetus to alleviate poverty, eradicate illness, and provide education to shape a better world. But despite 60 years of energetic action, problems abound, and are even increasing. Disasters and their consequences continue to torment individuals and societies, leaving trails of illness, suffering, poverty, and death. Life expectancy has increased in most countries, and the proportion of children in the world has risen dramatically as well, with a corresponding growth in the need for food, health care, and education.

Tragically, trauma is clearly as ubiquitous today as it was during and immediately following World War II, when the UN was created, in the words of the Charter, "to save succeeding generations from the scourge of war, which twice in our lifetime has brought untold sorrow to mankind, and to reaffirm faith in fundamental human rights, in the dignity and worth of the human person, in the equal rights of men and women and of nations large and small, and to establish conditions under which justice and respect for the obligations arising from treaties and other sources of international law can be maintained, and to promote social progress and better standards of life in larger freedom."

The end of the Cold War, and the vanishing of its ideological barriers, has given rise, not to a more peaceful world, but to a world in which nationalist and ethnic tensions have frequently exploded into conflict. International standards of human rights, although largely accepted by states, are discarded in the face of fanaticism and stored-up hatred. In addition, issues between states North and South—developed and underdeveloped—are growing more acute, and call for attention at the highest levels. The most recent recognition of this in the context of the UN is the Secretary-General's report, *In Larger Freedom: Towards Development, Security and Human Rights for All* (United Nations, 2005).

People today know more about what goes on in the world than ever before. Cameras transmit their revelations within minutes to living rooms around the globe. Modern mass communication has erased geographical distance and informs us of suffering immediately as it occurs. But increasing and intense coverage may lead to desensitization and apathy as efforts to cope with ever present, overwhelming news of disturbing events result in a psychological distancing from the suffering (Figley, 1995). With the parallel exposure to fictional film and video, the distinction between reality and fantasy becomes blurred. War and disasters may even become entertainment (note the proliferation of reality shows on television). The worst-case scenario occurs when the world is a helpless eye witness and its efforts merely symbolic, with the sole intention of giving the appearance that something is being done (among Sarajevo's 85,000 children, a symbolic group of 32 injured were evacuated). A contrasting scenario is the unprecedented, overwhelming generosity of pledges and outpouring of philanthropy, likely inspired by its proximity to gift-giving holidays, to the victims of the December 26, 2004, Asian tsunami. However, even if we accept that this response was due to the seemingly inherent political neutrality of natural disasters, how do we explain international neglect in the case of other natural disasters, as in El Salvador? The constant threat of terrorism and the aching persistence of war crimes, crimes against humanity, and genocide—previous, ongoing, and current—with the continued suffering of their victims, keep the international community ashamed.

Because the scars of traumatic stress can be both deep and long-lasting, their treatment is imperative. Such treatment, all too often neglected, is crucial in conflict resolution and in the building of peace—possibly the best preventer of further war and violence—among individuals and groups. Unless treated, the germ of hatred and holding on to the image of the enemy—both consequences of traumatic stress—may give rise to new conflicts and bloody clashes between ethnic or religious groups in an endless cycle of violence. Victims may become perpetrators as individuals, as members of families and communities, or as nations. Genuine peace cannot exist without the resolution of trauma. If traumatic stress constitutes one element in this terrible cycle, its interception could be one way to break the cycle. The cessation of wanton violence and abuse of power without full multidimensional integration of trauma (e.g., political, psychological, social, legal) will impair a nation's ability to maintain peace, to rebuild so that sustainable development is possible.

International Response

In addition to documenting the ubiquity of exposure to extreme events, history has recorded a wide variety of sociopolitical efforts to intervene in ways that address the needs of those who have been exposed and to prevent or minimize the impact of future exposures. Since the creation of the United Nations in 1945, the response by the organized international community and in particular by the UN system has been largely political. The main political imperatives have been from two opposite poles of conflict in finding political solutions: on the one hand, the continued existence of international concern about human suffering, stimulated by the modern media, and on the other hand, conceptions of state sovereignty that lead states to resist international interference in matters that they consider to be under their control and within their jurisdiction. By and large, the joint arrival of intergovernmental and nongovernmental organizations has been able to bring much relief to many victims of disasters, even though such relief tends to be temporary, may not alleviate all the hardships suffered by the victims, and will frequently not address the psychosocial damage. This book should help in keeping attention focused on remedying this unacceptable situation.

Trauma and the Continuity of Self: A Multidimensional, Multidisciplinary Integrative (TCMI) Framework

In my own attempt to describe the diverse and complex destruction caused by massive trauma such as is examined in this volume, I concluded that only a multidimensional, multidisciplinary integrative framework (Danieli, 1998) would be adequate. An individual's identity involves a complex interplay of multiple spheres or systems. Among these are (1) the physical and intrapsychic; (2) the interpersonal—familial, social, communal; (3) the ethnic, cultural, religious, spiritual, natural; (4) the educational/professional/occupational; and (5) the material/economic, legal, environmental, political, national, and international. These systems dynamically coexist along the time dimension to create a continuous conception of life from past through present to the future. Ideally, the individual should simultaneously have free psychological access to and movement within all these identity dimensions.

Trauma Exposure and "Fixity"

Trauma exposure can cause a rupture, a possible regression, and a state of being "stuck" in this free flow, which I (Danieli, 1998) have called *fixity*. The intent, place, time, frequency, duration, intensity, extent, and meaning of the trauma for the individual, and the survival strategies used to adapt to it (see, for example, Danieli, 1985) as well as post-victimization traumas, will determine the degree of rupture and the severity of the fixity. Fixity can be intensified in particular by the *conspiracy of silence* (Danieli, 1982, 1998), the survivors' reaction to the societal indifference (including that of health care and other professionals), avoidance, repression, and denial of the survivors' trauma experiences (see also Symonds, 1980). Society's initial emotional outburst, along with its simultaneous yet unspoken demand for rapid return to apparent normality, is an important example. This *conspiracy of silence* is detrimental to the survivors' familial and sociocultural (re)integration because it intensifies their already profound sense of isolation from and mistrust of society. It further impedes the possibility of the survivors' intrapsychic integration and healing, and makes the task of mourning their losses impossible. Fixity may increase vulnerability to further trauma. It also may render *chronic* the immediate reactions to trauma (e.g., acute stress disorder), and, in the extreme, become lifelong *post-trauma/victimization adaptational styles* (Danieli, 1985, 1997). This occurs when survival strategies generalize to a way of life and become an integral part of one's personality, repertoire of defense, or character armor.

Viewed from a family systems perspective, what happened in one generation will affect what happens in the next, though the actual behavior may take a variety of forms. Within an intergenerational context, the trauma and its impact may be passed down as the family legacy even to children born *after* the trauma. The awareness of the possibility of pathogenic intergenerational processes and the understanding of the mechanisms of transmission should contribute to finding effective means for preventing their transmission to succeeding generations (Danieli, 1985, 1993, 1998).

The possible long-term impact of trauma on one's personality and adaptation and the *intergenerational* transmission of victimization-related pathology still await explicit recognition and inclusion in future editions of the diagnostic nomenclature. Until they are included, the behavior of some survivors, and some children of survivors, may be misdiagnosed, its etiology misunderstood, and its treatment, at best, incomplete.

This framework allows evaluation of each system's degree of rupture or resilience, and thus informs the choice and development of optimal multi-level interventions. Repairing the rupture and thereby freeing the flow rarely means going back to "normal." Clinging to the possibility of "returning to normal" may indicate denial of the survivors' experiences and thereby fixity.

Exposure to trauma may also prompt review and reevaluation of one's self-perception, beliefs about the world, and values. Although changes in self-perception, beliefs, and values can be negative, varying percentages of trauma-exposed people report positive changes as a result of coping with the aftermath of trauma (called "post-traumatic growth," by Tedeschi & Calhoun, 1996). Survivors have described an increased appreciation for life, a reorganization of their priorities, and a realization that they are stronger than they thought. This is related to Danieli's (1994) recognition of competence vs. helplessness in coping with the aftermath of trauma. Competence (through one's own strength and/or the support of others), coupled with an awareness of options, can provide the basis of hope in recovery from traumatization.

Integration of the trauma must take place in *all* of life's relevant dimensions or systems and cannot be accomplished by the individual alone. Routes to integration may include reestablishing, relieving, and repairing the ruptured systems of the survivor and his or her community and nation, and restoring the surviving community's or nation's place in the international community. For example, in the context of examining the "Right to restitution, compensation and rehabilitation for victims of gross violations of human rights and fundamental freedoms" for the United Nations Centre for Human Rights (1992), some necessary components for integration and healing in the wake of massive trauma emerged from my interviews with victims/survivors of the Nazi Holocaust, interned Japanese-Americans, victims of political violence in Argentina and Chile, and professionals working with them, both in and outside their countries. Presented as goals and recommendations, these components are organized from the following perspectives: (A) individual, (B) societal, (C) national, and (D) international.

A. **Reestablishment of the victim's equality, power, and dignity—the basis of reparation.** This is accomplished by (a) compensation, both real and symbolic; (b) restitution; (c) rehabilitation; and (d) commemoration.
B. **Relieving the victim's stigmatization and separation from society.** This is accomplished by (a) commemoration; (b) memorials to heroism; (c) empowerment; (d) education.
C. **Repairing the nation's ability to provide and maintain equal value under law and the provisions of justice.** This is accomplished by (a) prosecution; (b) apology; (c) securing public records; (d) education; (e) creating national mechanisms for monitoring, conflict resolution, and preventive interventions.
D. **Asserting the commitment of the international community to combat impunity and provide and maintain equal value under law and the provisions of justice and redress.** This is accomplished by (a) creating ad hoc and permanent mechanisms for prosecution (e.g., ad hoc tribunals and ultimately an International Criminal Court); (b) securing

public records; (c) education; (d) creating international mechanisms for monitoring, conflict resolution, and preventive interventions.

It is important to emphasize that this comprehensive framework, rather than presenting *alternative* means of reparation, sets out necessary *complementary* elements, to be applied in different weights, in different situations and cultures, and at different points in time. It is also crucial that victims/survivors participate in the choice of the reparation measures adopted for them.

To fulfill the reparative and preventive goals of psychological recovery from trauma, perspective and integration through awareness and containment must be established so that one's sense of continuity, belongingness, and rootedness are restored. To be healing and even potentially self-actualizing, the integration of traumatic experiences must be examined from the perspective of the *totality* of the trauma survivors' and family members' lives.

With survivors it is especially hard to draw conclusions based on outward appearances. Survivors often display external markers of success (e.g., occupational achievement or established families) that in truth represent survival strategies. Clearly, such accomplishments may facilitate adaptation and produce feelings of fulfillment in many survivors. Thus, the external attainments do represent significant adaptive achievement in their lives. Nevertheless, even survivors in the "those who made it" category (Danieli, 1985) still experience difficulties related to their traumatic past, suggesting that overly optimistic views of adaptation may describe defense rather than effective coping. In fact, it is within this category that we observe the highest rates of suicide among survivors as well as their children. Furthermore, these optimistic views and accounts may cause survivors, who may have already felt isolated and alienated from those who did not undergo similar traumatic experiences, to see themselves as deficient, especially when compared to their "supercoper" counterparts, and deter them from seeking help.

The finding that survivors have areas of both vulnerability and resilience is not paradoxical when viewed within a multidimensional framework for multiple levels of post-traumatic adaptation. And tracing a history of multiple traumas along the time dimension at different stages of development reveals that, while time heals ills for many, for *traumatized* people time may not heal but may magnify their response to further trauma and may carry intergenerational implications.

Future Directions

In the context of prevention, an absolutely necessary precondition is the creation of a network of early warning systems, which necessitates thorough familiarity with, understanding of, and genuine respect for the local, national and regional culture(s) and history (Danieli, 1998). The United Nations and its related organizations have developed such systems concerning environmental threats, the risk of nuclear accident, natural disasters, mass movements of populations, the threat of famine, and the spread of disease. It is now time to include the potential effects of traumatic stress in preparing to confront these and other events.

Comparing this book's conclusions with our conclusions of "International Responses to Traumatic Stress: Humanitarian, Human Rights, Justice, Peace and Development Contributions, Collaborative Actions and Future Initiatives" (Danieli, Rodley, & Weisaeth, 1996), I felt delighted with the editor's assertion that psychosocial services have become "a staple part of humanitarian relief operations around the world" (Reyes, 2006, p. XX). But I must agree with him that, despite this progress, psychosocial issues still need further and greater advocacy. We have a long way to go toward ensuring that mental health concerns become integral and influential in the overall architecture of disaster response planning, in order to support systematic, strategic development of operational capabilities and initiatives to build more resilient local capacity.

I am saddened by the inefficient process of "reinventing the wheel" that persists among both national and international humanitarian organizations. It might be helpful for humanitarian psychosocial organizations and experts, without sacrificing their diversity and richness, to endorse core, evidence-based standards of care and interventions. It would also be useful to develop coordinated action strategies for flexibly available psychosocial preparedness to enable speedy, systematic responses that address the psychosocial needs of disaster survivors.

Although mostly Western, the authors are experienced members of the international humanitarian community, representing a broad spectrum of nationalities, cultures, and viewpoints. I agree with the editors that the time for Western speakers to serve as proxies for non-Westerners should be passing and that *all* voices and perspectives—not only those of the imported experts—must be included in the discourse over which psychosocial frameworks and practices are appropriate for use among disaster survivors in developing countries. The resources, insight, and wisdom of groups at the margins of national and international power circles must be included as well.

Concurring with the guidelines generated by the Task Force on International Trauma Training of the International Society for Traumatic Stress Studies (Weine, Danieli, Silove, van Ommeren, Fairbank, & Saul, 2002), the editor argues for rapid assessment of psychosocial needs to become standard practice, and for building an evaluation component into the service to assess its effectiveness. Such assessment and evaluation practices will guarantee that lessons learned are less subject to appraisals that suit political rather than developmental aims. The concern over the incompatibility of humanitarian assistance, partisan politics, and military aggression is repeated in this book as well, and reinforced by the recognition of the cost paid by humanitarian aid workers and others on the front line (Danieli, 2002).

The five Cs of disaster work—Communication, Cooperation, Collaboration, Coordination, and Complementarity—apply here, too. So does the need for leadership strategies, such as compassionate articulation (Spratt, 2002), that can reduce chaos and terror and thereby diminish the effectiveness of terrorism.

Nongovernmental organizations must improve their efforts at coordination. The greatest obstacle still seems to be competition for visibility and credit, which is essential if they are to compete effectively for increasingly scarce resources. At both the organizational level and in the field, the desire to have highly visible, quantitatively impressive programs can lead to competitiveness and jealousies that work against unified efforts.

There is a risk that the uncritical use of concepts such as coordination, which creates the impression of easy, quick solutions irrespective of the complexities of traumatic stress, may result in the loss of an operational meaning for these concepts. For example, the result may be too many coordinators and too few doing the work, or the actual work may be being reserved to nonprofessional and insufficiently trained volunteers. Such volunteers may serve for short periods of time, with traumatic detriment to themselves, and without contributing to the pool of accumulated knowledge that ought to move the field forward.

It is essential for UN agencies and programs, and for NGOs, to further define and develop complementary roles in their responses to traumatic stress. Complementarity involves the tolerance of, respect for, and capitalizing on the differing strengths of the various partners—UN bodies, governments, NGOs, and the communities they serve.

Some of the programs described in this work are inspiring in their excellence. But what comes through most of all is that, however superb some programs are, they are too few, and the challenges they must face are overwhelming. Each of the noble examples of programs is dwarfed by the needs with which our world is faced. In fact, the most striking theme that keeps emerging in the field is the enormous gulf between what needs to be done and the resources available to do it with. Although difficult in the short term, providing the international community with this needed expertise will lessen long-term costs, and possibly prevent intergenerational effects and the resulting much larger costs—both human and financial.

Another resource-related issue is that available funds tend to be used for emergency shipments of food, medicine, housing, and the like in reaction to situations that have been widely publicized by the media. Once the emergency is no longer new, and the dramatic pictures are no longer on the nightly news, funds usually dry up and are not available for sustaining the short-term gains or for long-term care.

The work in this area radiates good will, idealism, and commitment, despite cynicism and despair, and despite the realization—emerging from situations such as those in the former Yugoslavia, Rwanda, Kosovo, East Timor, Democratic Republic of Congo, and Darfur/Sudan—that humanity has failed to learn the lessons and honor the commitments made after World War II.

The same world that created the circumstances for the crime, the victimization, has also created the circumstances for good and kind and compassionate people to be there for each other, for the victims in time of need. Viewing our work through the prism of traumatic stress, within the multidimensional, multidisciplinary integrative (TCMI) framework, should thus have not only a healing, but also a humanizing, effect on the victims and on society as a whole.

We must pursue primary, secondary, and tertiary prevention. We must continue efforts to reduce the stigma that still exists against the field of mental health while broadening its reach to join hands with other disciplines. We must partner with others in fields at and beyond the boundaries of mental health and extend our investigations and preventive suggestions also to the root causes of disasters.

The danger of bioterrorism, with medically unexplained physical symptoms challenging patients, clinicians, scientists and policy makers, necessitates special training for all public health professionals. Its psychological casualties far outweigh the physical ones (Flynn, 2004), and its long-term social and psychological effects are likely to be as damaging as the acute ones, if not more so (Wessely, Hyams, & Bartholomew, 2001). The threat of bioterrorism also calls for revamping the health/mental health systems on all levels/dimensions—before, during, and after such attacks.

Despite growing awareness and the accumulated body of knowledge, there are still policy makers who either deny the existence of the invisible, psychological wounds, or feel that they have a lesser priority in an era of dwindling resources. At every level, government policy has yet to fully comprehend and embrace the centrality of psychosocial issues in understanding and responding to disasters, particularly to terrorism. For any nation to become optimally prepared to cope, homeland security must include, integrate, and adequately fund psychosocial security (Danieli, Brom, & Sills, 2005) and the full participation of the social sciences in all aspects of preparedness. This book should certainly advance this undertaking.

References

Danieli, Y. (1982). *Therapists' difficulties in treating survivors of the Nazi Holocaust and their children.* Dissertation Abstracts International, 42(12-B, Pt 1), 4927. (UMI No. 949-904).

———. (1985). The treatment and prevention of long-term effects and intergenerational transmission of victimization: A lesson from Holocaust survivors and their children. In C. R. Figley (Ed.), *Trauma and its Wake* (pp. 295–313). New York: Brunner/Mazel.

———. (1992). Preliminary reflections from a psychological perspective. In T.C. van Boven, C. Flinterman, F. Grunfeld & I. Westendorp (Eds.), *The Right to Restitution, Compensation and Rehabilitation for Victims of Gross Violations of Human Rights and Fundamental Freedoms.* Netherlands Institute of Human Rights [Studie-en Informatiecentrum Mensenrechten], Special issue No. 12.

————. (1993). The diagnostic and therapeutic use of the multi-generational family tree in working with survivors and children of survivors of the Nazi Holocaust. In J. P. Wilson & B. Raphael (Eds.) *International handbook of traumatic stress syndromes* [Stress and Coping Series, Donald Meichenbaum, Series Editor]. (pp. 889–898). New York: Plenum Publishing.

————. (1994). Resilience and hope. In G. Lejeune (Ed.), *Children Worldwide* (pp. 47–49). Geneva: International Catholic Child Bureau.

————. (1997). As survivors age: An overview. *Journal of Geriatric Psychiatry, 30* (1), 9–26.

————, Rodley, N.S., & Weisaeth, L. (Eds.) (1996). *International responses to traumatic stress: Humanitarian, human rights, justice, peace and development contributions, collaborative actions and future initiatives.* Amityville, NY: Baywood Publishing.

————. (Ed.). (1998). *International handbook of multigenerational legacies of trauma.* New York: Kluwer Academic/Plenum Publishing.

————. (Ed.). (2002). *Sharing the front line and the back hills: International protectors and providers, peacekeepers, humanitarian aid workers and the media in the midst of crisis.* Amityville, NY: Baywood Publishing.

————, Brom, D., & Sills, J. (Eds.). (2005). *The trauma of terrorism: Sharing knowledge and shared care. An international handbook.* Binghamton, NY: The Haworth Press.

Figley, C. R. (Ed.). (1995). *Compassion fatigue: Coping with secondary traumatic stress disorder in those who treat the traumatized.* New York: Brunner/Mazel.

Flynn, B. W., (2004) Letters to the Editor: Behavioral Health Aspects of Bioterrorism. *Biosecurity and Bioterrorism: Biodefense Strategy, Practice, and Science, 2,* 232.

Green, B. L., Friedman, M. J., de Jong, J., Solomon, S. D., Keane, T. M., Fairbank, J. A., Donelan, B., & Frey-Wouters, E. (Eds.) (2003). *Trauma interventions in war and peace: Prevention, practice, and policy.* New York: Kluwer Academic/Plenum Publishers.

Reyes, G. (2006). Conclusions and recommendations for further progress. In G. Reyes & G. A. Jacobs (Eds.), *Handbook of International Disaster Psychology.* Westport, CT: Praeger Publishers.

Spratt, M. (2002, August 28). 9/11 media may comfort, terrify. Retrieved on August 29, 2002, from http://www.dartcenter.org/articles/headlines/2002/2002_08_28.html

Symonds, M. (1980). The "second injury" to victims. *Evaluation and Change* [Special issue], 36–38.

Tedeschi, R. G., & Calhoun, L. G. (1996). The posttraumatic growth inventory: Measuring the positive legacy of trauma. *Journal of Traumatic Stress, 9,* 455–471.

United Nations (2005). *In larger freedom: Towards development, security and human rights for all. Report of the Secretary-General.* Retrieved May 31, 2005, from http://www.un.org/largerfreedom/contents.htm

Weine, S., Danieli, Y., Silove, D., Van Ommeren, M., Fairbank, J. A., & Saul, J. (2002). Guidelines for international training in mental health and psychosocial interventions for trauma exposed populations in clinical and community settings. *Psychiatry, 65*(2), 156–164.

Wessely, S., Hyams, K., & Bartholomew, R. (2001). Psychological implications of chemical and biological weapons. *British Medical Journal, 323,* 878–879.

INDEX

ABOUT THE VOLUME EDITORS

GILBERT REYES, PhD, is a licensed clinical psychologist and the Associate Dean for Clinical Training at Fielding Graduate University in Santa Barbara, California. He has responded to several major disasters in the United States, including the September 11, 2001, attack on the World Trade Center. Reyes has also consulted with the International Federation of Red Cross and Red Crescent Societies on various projects and in 2002 co-authored that organization's training manual for community-based psychological support. He recently co-authored a training course for the American Red Cross on children's disaster mental health needs and is now collaborating with the Terrorism and Disaster Center of the National Child Traumatic Stress Network on the development of interventions for children in disasters.

GERARD A. (JERRY) JACOBS, PhD, is Director of the Disaster Mental Health Institute (DMHI) and a Professor at the University of South Dakota. He is active in field work, training, program development, and consultation nationally and internationally for the Red Cross movement and the American Psychological Association. He is a co-author of the WHO *Tool for the Rapid Assessment of Mental Health* and served on the Institute of Medicine Committee on Responding to the Psychological Consequences of Terrorism. He also works with the Asian Disaster Preparedness Center in psychological support training and program development.

ABOUT THE CONTRIBUTORS

INGER AGGER is a social scientist and psychologist. She has a university research background and has worked extensively with child support, civil society development, and peace building in a number of crisis-affected regions with special focus on the support of children at risk, refugee and IDP women, ethnic minorities, and gender-related human rights violations. She is currently engaged as a Social Development Specialist in the "Governorate Capacity Building Project—Southern Iraq" for the British Department for International Development. She is the author of *The Blue Room* (1994) and *Trauma and Healing under State Terrorism* (1996, with Soren Buus Jensen).

MIRANDA ARMSTRONG is the Delegate for Terre des hommes in Benin and Togo, having previously held the same post in Sri Lanka. She has a degree in Development and Health for Disaster Management, and much of her work has focused on psychosocial programming and on the development of methods for assessing the well-being of children.

JOAN SWABY ATHERTON is the chief psychologist at the headquarters of the Cuban Red Cross. She organized the initial training workshops provided by the director of the Reference Centre for Psychological Support for the Cuban Red Cross in 2000, and the subsequent dissemination of the Psychological Support Programme throughout her country.

TAMARA BLANCO is a clinical psychologist and, at the time of the floods, was a student of Universidad Central de Venezuela's Clinical Psychology Specialization. She has been teaching applied psychology courses in several private Venezuelan universities and was the psychologist of one of the schools that provided psychosocial assistance to the victims of the Vargas's floods. In 2002, Blanco participated in the reactivation and efforts made by the PSN to provide relief for different groups affected by political confrontations. In 2003, she led the psychosocial support team that provided relief to children, teachers, and general population in Pueblo Llano (State Mérida), an Andinean village that survived floods.

JO BOYDEN is a social anthropologist who has specialized in policy and research on children, childhood, and child development. She has worked for many years as a consultant to a wide range of humanitarian and development agencies in South and Southeast Asia, parts of Africa, and the Andean Region. As Senior Research Officer at the University of Oxford, she is developing a research program on children affected by forced migration and armed conflict.

CLAUDIA CARRILLO participated in the response to the psychosocial needs of people affected by the floods and mudslides of December 1999. Since then, she has been working in Psychosocial Support in Disasters, and the Department of Planning and Preparation for Disasters, of the American Red Cross in Venezuela. She is currently conducting research at the Universidad Central de Venezuela on training teachers to provide psychological first aid in disasters.

RAQUEL E. COHEN, MD, is a graduate of and former Associate Professor at Harvard Medical School. She is a Professor Emeritus of Psychiatry at University of Miami Medical School. A world-renowned authority in psychological and social consequences from disasters, and intervention methods, she has worked with victim relief governmental and nongovernmental agencies around the world. Her recent book *Mental Health Services in Disasters: A Manual for Humanitarian Workers* was published by the Pan American Health Organization. She is now a consultant and trainer in the management of mental health needs of disaster and victims of terrorist events. She was Senior Consultant for the Office of Refugee Resettlement of the Cuban Youth Camp Program during the Mariel boatlift, responsible for developing programs for unaccompanied minors from Cuba. She has served as Associate Director of the Laboratory of Community Psychiatry at Harvard Medical School and as a Consultant to the National Institute of Mental Health, the Pan American Health Organization, and the American Psychiatric Association. Recently she was selected to the National Library of Medicine Exhibit, "Changing the Face of Medicine: Celebrating America's Women Physicians."

YAEL DANIELI, PhD, is a clinical psychologist in private practice in New York City, a traumatologist, and victimologist. She is also co-founder and Director, Group Project for Holocaust Survivors and Their Children; founding President, International Network for Holocaust and Genocide Survivors and Their Friends; and co-founder, past-President, Senior United Nations Representative, International Society for Traumatic Stress Studies (ISTSS). Dr. Danieli integrates treatment, worldwide study, teaching/training, publishing, expert advocacy, and consulting to numerous governments, news, international and national organizations, and institutions on victims rights and optimal care, including for their protectors and providers. Most recently she received the ISTSS Lifetime Achievement Award.

KIRSTEN FINNIS is a PhD candidate at the University of Otago. She gained her BSc (Hons) in Geology at the University of Queensland and moved to New Zealand to pursue research into the social impact of volcanic hazards and disaster prevention. Her thesis research focuses on aspects of social vulnerability and resilience to volcanic hazards from Mt. Taranaki. Research interests have grown to incorporate public education and disaster psychology, focusing especially on work with children. Kirsten has worked with the Institute of Geological & Nuclear Sciences and the Ministry of Civil Defence & Emergency Management on public education and hazard research projects.

ANANDA GALAPPATTI is a freelance consultant based in Sri Lanka, with an academic background in psychology and in medical anthropology. Since 1996, he has worked in training, research, and psychosocial program development in Sri Lanka. He is also a co-editor of *Intervention: The International Journal of Psychosocial Work, Mental Health and Counselling in Areas of Armed Conflict.* In the aftermath of the tsunami he has been working as advisor/coordinator to The Mangrove: Psychosocial Support and Coordination Unit, in Batticaloa, eastern Sri Lanka.

JASON HART is a research officer at the Refugee Studies Centre, University of Oxford, and, during 2004–2005, a research fellow in the Department of Anthropology, Johns Hopkins University. His work focuses principally on children and adolescents living amid political violence. A social anthropologist whose doctoral research was conducted with refugee children in Jordan, he has worked as a researcher and trainer for aid and development agencies in Africa, the Middle East, and South Asia.

DAVID M. JOHNSTON has been employed with the Institute of Geological and Nuclear Sciences since 1993, and his research is focused on reducing the vulnerability of society, economy, and infrastructure to hazards. He has been involved in developing integrated risk management strategies for many different hazard events, using techniques such as scenario development, mitigation planning, and community education programs. He is also interested in assessing social and economic impacts of natural and environmental hazard events. Johnston has had long-term relationships with a wide number of end-users through his research, consulting, and outreach activities. Currently he is Outreach Coordinator for New Zealand's EQC-funded GeoNet project, a member of the steering group of the Auckland Engineering Lifelines Group, and advisor to EQC on their education strategy. He holds adjunct positions at School of Psychology at Massey University (New Zealand) and the Geology Department at the University of Hawaii (USA).

NILA KAPOR-STANULOVIC, the first recipient of the APA International Humanitarian Award, is a professor of Human Development and Mental Health at the University of Novi Sad, Yugoslavia. As Psychosocial Rehabilitation Program Officer in UNICEF Belgrade (1993–1995), she was responsible for programs for psychosocial recovery of children affected by armed conflicts in Yugoslavia and Bosnia. Since 1995, she has been a consultant to the UNICEF offices in Armenia, Azerbaijan, and Georgia. Dr. Kapor has conceptualized country-specific programs for psychosocial assistance for children affected by armed conflicts and by the adverse consequences of socioeconomic transition in those countries. In addition to helping child victims of war, Dr. Kapor has participated in programs providing postwar rehabilitation to medical staff in Bosnia, in programs for psychosocial support to the victims of polio epidemics in Kosovo, for victims of the earthquake in Italy, and tsunami in Thailand.

ROSE KASINA is a social worker and counselling psychologist at the Amani Counselling Centre in Nairobi, Kenya. She worked with the Kenyan Red Cross to coordinate the psychological treatment for the survivors of 1998 terrorist bombing of the U.S. Embassy in Nairobi. She also worked with survivors of the 2002 terrorist bombing of a hotel in Mombasa, and the Kyanguli school fire of 2001. Recently she has helped to start centers in rural communities around Kenya with the aim of training teachers and religious leaders to expand local capacity in psychological counseling. Her work is increasingly dedicated to helping people affected by the HIV/AIDS pandemic.

DAMMAS M. KATHUKU is a senior lecturer at the University of Nairobi. He earned his Master's of medicine in psychiatry at the University of Nairobi and a Master's at Makereru University in Uganda, and he also trained with the United States Air Force at the Maxwell Air University in Alabama and the School of Aerospace Medicine in Texas, as well as at the Kenya Armed Forces Training College. He is a former director of the Kenyan Red Cross psychological support program for people affected by the 1998 U.S. embassy bombing in Nairobi.

DAVID M. NDETEI, MD, is a professor and Chair of Psychiatry at the University of Nairobi, and Director of the Africa Mental Health Foundation. He completed his medical training and qualification at the University of Nairobi, Kenya, his specialist training (residency) and qualifications in Psychiatry in the United Kingdom, and doctorate at the University of Nairobi. He joined the Department of Psychiatry at University of Nairobi in 1981 and has risen to the full Chair of Psychiatry, which he still holds. He has been involved in response activities in Rwanda, the American Embassy Bomb Blast, and the Kyanguli School fire tragedy. He has published widely. Besides academic activities (teaching and research), he enjoys the beautiful Kenyan landscape and wildlife.

RICHARD NEUGEBAUER, PhD, MPH, is a psychiatric and perinatal epidemiologist in the Faculty of Medicine of Columbia University; a Research Scientist in the Epidemiology of Developmental Brain Disorders Department at New York State Psychiatric Institute; and an Associate Professor, Department of International Health, School of Public Health and Tropical Medicine, Tulane University. Over the years his research has focused on the mental health effects of trauma and bereavement on children and adults, the contribution of prenatal and perinatal factors to offspring's risk for psychiatric disorder in adolescence and adulthood, and the design and implementation of randomized controlled trials of treatments for depressive disorders, both in the United States and in developing countries.

KEVIN R. RONAN, PhD, is the Chair in Clinical Psychology at Central Queensland University in Rockhampton, Queensland (Australia). In addition to an ongoing interest in hazards and disasters, he has published widely in areas of clinical psychology, including homework in therapy (including an edited book in press and a special series of the *Journal of Psychotherapy Integration*); treatment outcome with youth and families; schizophrenia; and other areas. He maintains an active clinical practice and advocates—both in his practice and in the training of clinical psychologists—for the clinician as "local scientist" (i.e., engaging in pragmatic evaluation of practice; using the evidence in day-to-day practice; increasing accountability for producing outcomes).

BENEDETTO SARACENO, MD, an internationally admired psychiatrist, is the Director of the Department of Mental Health in the World Health Organization (WHO). He has been a committed mental health reformer for over three decades, both in Italy and in the global arena. As a progressive voice for patients' rights and de-institutionalization, he has contributed to the reduction of the stigma associated with mental illnesses. Dr. Saraceno works closely with nongovernmental humanitarian organizations to promote greater awareness of the growing burden of mental illness around the world. He has recently worked tirelessly to ensure adequate and appropriate psychosocial support for victims of the Indian Ocean tsunamis.

METTE SONNIKS is a psychologist and the former director of the Reference Centre for Psychological Support at the Danish Red Cross in Copenhagen. She has trained and mentored hundreds of psychological support providers and trainers in dozens of countries, and helped to establish a remarkably successful model for the training-of-trainers throughout the Red Cross/Red Crescent movement.

CHARLES D. SPIELBERGER is Distinguished Research Professor of Psychology and Director of the Center for Research in Behavioral Medicine and Health Psychology at the University of South Florida. He previously directed the USF Doctoral Program in Clinical Psychology. An ABPP Diplomate in Clinical Psychology and Distinguished Practitioner of the National Academies of Practice, Spielberger focuses his current research on anxiety, curiosity, and the experience, expression, and control of anger; job stress and stress management; and the effects of stress, emotions, and lifestyle factors on hypertension, cardiovascular disorders, and cancer. During 1991–1992, Spielberger served as the 100th president of the American Psychological Association.

MARTIN VILLALOBOS is a clinical psychologist and one of four founders and coordinators of the Psychological Support Network that operated in Universidad Central de Venezuela in response to the Venezuelan Floods of 1999. He is Professor Aggregate and Coordinator of the Clinical Dynamic Psychology Department, as well as faculty member and Coordinator of Universidad Central de Venezuela's Clinical Psychology Specialization, postgraduate studies. He conducts triage in the Psychology Department of Student Well-Being Service and in the Clinical Neuropsychological Section in Neurology Service of the University Hospital. Villalobos participated in other efforts to provide psychological relief to different groups affected by political confrontations in 2002. In 2003, he coordinated with Consejo Estadal de Derechos del Niño y Adolescente (State Council of Child and Adolescent Rights) to provide the psychosocial support for Pueblo Llano (State Mérida, Venezuela), an Andinean village that survived floods.

ABOUT THE SERIES

As this new millennium dawns, humankind has evolved—some would argue has developed—exhibiting new and old behaviors that fascinate, infuriate, delight or fully perplex those of us seeking answers to the question, "Why?" In this series, experts from various disciplines peer through the lens of psychology telling us answers they see for questions of human behavior. Their topics may range from humanity's psychological ills—addictions, abuse, suicide, murder, and terrorism among them—to works focused on positive subjects including intelligence, creativity, athleticism, and resilience. Regardless of the topic, the goal of this series remains constant—to offer innovative ideas, provocative considerations, and useful beginnings to better understand human behavior.

Chris E. Stout
Series Editor

About the Series Editor and Advisory Board

CHRIS E. STOUT, PsyD, MBA, is a licensed clinical psychologist and is a Clinical Full Professor at the University of Illinois College of Medicine's Department of Psychiatry. He served as an NGO Special Representative to the United Nations, was appointed to the World Economic Forum's Global Leaders of Tomorrow, and has served as an Invited Faculty at the Annual Meeting in Davos. He is the Founding Director of the Center for Global Initiatives. Dr. Stout is a Fellow of the American Psychological Association, past-President of the Illinois Psychological Association, and a Distinguished Practitioner in the National Academies of Practice. Dr. Stout has published or presented over 300 papers and 30 books/manuals on various topics in psychology, and his works have been translated into six languages. He has lectured across the nation and internationally in 19 countries, visited 6 continents, and almost 70 countries. He was noted as being "one of the most frequently cited psychologists in the scientific literature" in a study by Hartwick College. He is the recipient of the American Psychological Association's International Humanitarian Award.

BRUCE BONECUTTER, PhD, is Director of Behavioral Services at the Elgin Community Mental Health Center, the Illinois Department of Human Services state hospital serving adults in greater Chicago. He is also a Clinical Assistant Professor of Psychology at the University of Illinois at Chicago. A clinical psychologist specializing in health, consulting, and forensic psychology, Mr. Bonecutter is also a longtime member of the American Psychological Association Taskforce on Children & the Family. He is a member of organizations including the Association for the Treatment of Sexual Abusers, International; the Alliance for the Mentally Ill; and the Mental Health Association of Illinois.

JOSEPH FLAHERTY, MD, is Chief of Psychiatry at the University of Illinois Hospital, a Professor of Psychiatry at the University of Illinois College of Medicine, and a Professor of Community Health Science at the UIC College of Public Health. He is a Founding Member of the Society for the Study of Culture and Psychiatry. Dr. Flaherty has been a consultant to the World Health Organization, the National Institutes of Mental Health, and also the Falk Institute in Jerusalem. He has been Director of Undergraduate Education and Graduate Education in the Department of Psychiatry at the University of Illinois. Dr. Flaherty has also been Staff Psychiatrist and Chief of Psychiatry at Veterans Administration West Side Hospital in Chicago.

MICHAEL HOROWITZ, PhD, is President and Professor of Clinical Psychology at the Chicago School of Professional Psychology, one of the nation's leading not-for-profit graduate schools of psychology. Earlier, he served as Dean and Professor of the Arizona School of Professional Psychology. A clinical psychologist practicing independently since 1987, he has focused his work on psychoanalysis, intensive individual therapy, and couples therapy. He has provided Disaster Mental Health Services to the American Red Cross. Mr. Horowitz's special interests include the study of fatherhood.

SHELDON I. MILLER, MD, is a Professor of Psychiatry at Northwestern University, and Director of the Stone Institute of Psychiatry at Northwestern Memorial Hospital. He is also Director of the American Board of Psychiatry and Neurology, Director of the American Board of Emergency Medicine, and Director of the Accreditation Council for Graduate Medical Education. Dr. Miller is also an Examiner for the American Board of Psychiatry and Neurology. He is Founding Editor of the American Journal of Addictions, and Founding Chairman of the American Psychiatric Association's Committee on Alcoholism. Dr. Miller has also been a Lieutenant Commander in the U.S. Public Health Service, serving as psychiatric consultant to the Navajo Area Indian Health Service at Window Rock, Arizona. He is a member and Past President of the Executive Committee for the American Academy of Psychiatrists in Alcoholism and Addictions.

DENNIS P. MORRISON, PhD, is Chief Executive Officer at the Center for Behavioral Health in Indiana, the first behavioral health company ever to win the JCAHO Codman Award for excellence in the use of outcomes management to achieve health care quality improvement. He is President of the Board of Directors for the Community Healthcare Foundation in Bloomington, and has been a member of the Board of Directors for the American College of Sports Psychology. He has served as a consultant to agencies including the Ohio Department of Mental Health, Tennessee Association of Mental Health Organizations, Oklahoma Psychological Association, the North Carolina Council of Community Mental Health Centers, and the National Center for Health Promotion in Michigan. Dr. Morrison served across 10 years as a Medical Service Corp Officer in the U.S. Navy.

WILLIAM H. REID, MD, is a clinical and forensic psychiatrist, and consultant to attorneys and courts throughout the United States. He is Clinical Professor of Psychiatry at the University of Texas Health Science Center. Dr. Miller is also an Adjunct Professor of Psychiatry at Texas A&M College of Medicine and Texas Tech University School of Medicine, as well as a Clinical Faculty member at the Austin Psychiatry Residency Program. He is Chairman of the Scientific Advisory Board and Medical Advisor to the Texas Depressive & Manic-Depressive Association, as well as an Examiner for the American Board of Psychiatry & Neurology. He has served as President of the American Academy of Psychiatry and the Law, as Chairman of the Research Section for an International Conference on the Psychiatric Aspects of Terrorism, and as Medical Director for the Texas Department of Mental Health and Mental Retardation. Dr. Reid earned an Exemplary Psychiatrist Award from the National Alliance for the Mentally Ill. He has been cited on the Best Doctors in America listing since 1998.